An
SCENES FOR AUDITION
Actor's
AND PERFORMANCE FROM
DICKENS
THE WORKS OF CHARLES DICKENS

Adapted & Edited by
BEATRICE MANLEY

An Applause Theatre & Cinema Books Original

AN ACTOR'S DICKENS: SCENES FOR AUDITION & PERFORMANCE FROM THE WORKS OF CHARLES DICKENS

Adapted and edited by Beatrice Manley

Copyright © 2001 by Beatrice Manley

Library of Congress Cataloguing-in-Publication Data

Library of Congress Card Number: 2001093676

British Library Cataloguing-in-Publication Data

A catalogue record for this book is available from the British Library

ISBN: 1-55783-469-5

**APPLAUSE THEATRE &
CINEMA BOOKS**
151 W 46th Street, 8th Floor
New York, NY 10036
Phone: (212) 575-9265
FAX: (646) 562-5852
email: info@applausepub.com
internet: www.applausepub.com

COMBINED BOOK SERVICES LTD.
Units I/K, Paddock Wood Distribution Centre
Paddock Wood, Tonbridge, Kent TN 12 6UU
Phone: (44) 01892 837171
Fax: (44) 01892 837272

SALES & DISTRIBUTION, HAL LEONARD CORP.
7777 West Bluemound Road, P.O. Box 13819
Milwaukee, WI 53213
Phone: (414) 774-3630 Fax: (414) 774-3259
email: halinfo@halleonard.com
internet: www.halleonard.com

Printed in Canada

To Dick & Jo

CONTENTS

CHAPTER ONE

WHY DICKENS?

Having learned about subtext, we actors now use it for everything. In fact, we can't act without it.

In Dickens, however, there are many scenes which need no explanation, which have no subtext. What is on the page is what is meant to be. In Samuel Beckett, in Chekov, in Strindberg, there is much to think about. You have to dig in and around the script to understand it. Not Dickens. When a con man is at work, you know it. When a spinster is hoping to entrap a man, you know it. The hypocrites, the bamboozled, the proud, the ill-begotten, all of Dickens' wonderful characters are in the full flush of their personalities and all we actors have to do is feel free to get into their skin.

This acting does not require analysis or labored and extensive work on a background; it does not require a past history. It does not need to be studied in advance; it needs nothing but the author's description of setting and character; it needs the actor only to read down the page to understand the character and play the scene. Simplicity.

In an interview on why he prefers to work in modern dance, Mikhail Baryshnikov says much the same thing on discovering certain qualities that belong to modern dance alone:

> "It's much more exposed. You have just this plain thing to do, and you have to decide how you will do it. So it teaches how to pace, how to suppress unnecessary impulses—just to do the steps, *but fully.*"

He wishes he had had more practice in modern dance while he was still dancing the nineteenth-century ballets:

"My timing would have been much more interesting. Young dancers in classical dance, they over-dance everything. That's what I did-over-jump, over-turn, over-act. When I see another wunderkind—which I was myself, for a few years, then I say, 'I already know what will happen…he will get worse and worse and worse. And so on through the next few years, and then he will disappear."

That Baryshnikov didn't disappear seems to him cause for gratitude and he feels he owes this in part to the chastening influence of modern dance. It took him a while to convert to modern dance – to its plainness.

Of course, if a script needs study, we study. If it doesn't require a Beckettian examination, we don't need to give it one.

BODY OVER MIND IN ACTING

When actors pick up a script, mostly I see a rush of fear, a sudden "Can I do this?' in the eyes. They make themselves play the scene and then feel they have failed. This is actor's suffering. It need not be. One of the reasons actors are inhibited is that there are too many rules going through the mind; too much silent talking, the actors giving themselves instructions. Walter Matthau, when interviewed, grumbled that he didn't analyze the roles he played; that too much thinking resulted in thinking but not acting.

The body where so many of our emotions are stored and where our physical senses respond to the imagination is being overlooked, and shallow thought is doing all the work of feeling, thinking, reacting – overburdening the human system.

Non-thinking. It's in that first flow of breath that we have the emotions of the scene. We need not put our thoughts into all those silent words that we speak to ourselves. Thoughts without words. That's where the acting starts.

You need not fear that you will not give enough to the character because you are not thinking or applying the rules of the techniques that you have been taught. Just as energy begets energy, so feelings beget feeling. One feeling will lead to another in an improvisational way.

An actor can come to the emotion in several ways. The important things to remember are: Don't work too hard to achieve the scene. Don't hold tension in the body (this is a reminder that young actors hear often but don't realize how important it is until they are more experienced.) And whatever way you get there — DON'T HOLD YOUR BREATH WHEN YOU ACT.

I talk a lot about the breath because that is what I use to move emotions back and forth through my mind and body, to keep me from working too hard.

You can find fuller explanations about breath and the way to incorporate thought and emotion in the breath in my book on acting technique, *My Breath in Art: Acting From Within.*

There I talk about the Art of the Start. The art is to start your acting with your breath giving you emotional information before the intellect can interfere.

I introduce the concept of acting with the breath; the breath, bypassing the interfering mind, carries the emotions into the body.

> Breath is always emotional. With the slightest ripple of change, the breath changes. We experience fear, laughter, anxiety... first in the breath. When we perform it's as if our breath hears the cue even before our ears do, as if our breath sees before we see. Images and memories float onto the breath without prompting from the rational mind. The breath touches intuition, that part where our native talent is sheltered. If we know how to breathe, intending our thought to mesh

with the breath is enough. It will.

Using the breath, I notice that my acting is more immediately physical. I feel my body tremble, I feel laughter in my chest. These physical feelings connected to thoughts are honest. They are real. I trust them. They happen for me each time I play the scene.

"Believe what you feel" is the key. Believing in what you are doing and the way you do it, is all that matters. If you feel comfortable in the scene, the breath will flow although you may be unaware of using it.

THE PLACEBO EFFECT

And just when I need the most help to explain these ideas, comes a leading article from the science section of *The New York Times* asserting that the brain/mind is so powerful, that belief is all that's needed for some miraculous thing to happen. According to the *Times*, these new studies have explored the brain's triumph over reality. Doctors call it the placebo effect. The placebo effect may be related to an evolutionary advantage. It allows us to *act first, analyze later*. It seems to be an intuitive strategy for survival.

In the article, a neuroscientist argues that we are misled by the idea that mind and body are separate. Using new techniques of brain imagery, doctors are uncovering biological mechanisms that can turn a thought, belief or desire into an agent of change in cells, tissues and organs. A thought that is a set of neurons firing through complex brain wiring, can activate *emotional centers... memories...* and other *parts of the nervous system involved in producing physical sensations.*

The doctors are learning that much of human perception is based not on information flowing into the brain from the outside world *but what the brain, based on previous experience, expects to happen next.*

This last equates with our knowledge of the script. At one time if we asked actors why they were doing at that moment what they did and they answered, "because the script said so", we would be horrified at having gotten an answer that had no psychological reason. But now I wonder. With my knowledge of the placebo effect and after studying the script and being convinced by the playwright that my character cries at one point and laughs at another, don't I use the script to say why I do something at that moment?

Let's take HAMLET as an example.

The actors have arrived at the castle to perform Hamlet's play. The leading actor does a monologue for his hosts. Hamlet is intrigued by the actor's real tears.

FIRST PLAYER: When she saw Pyrrus make malicious sport
    In mincing with his sword her husbands limbs,
    The instant burst of clamor that she made-...

POLONIUS: Look wh'er he has not turned his colour
    And has tears in's eyes. Prithee, no more.

HAMLET: Is it not monstrous that this player here,
    But in a fiction, a dream of passion,
    Could force his soul so to his own conceit
    That from her working all his visage wanned,
    Tears in his eyes, distraction in's aspect,
    A broken voice, and his whole function suiting
    With forms to his conceit? And all for nothing!
    For Hecuba!
    What's Hecuba to him or he to Hecuba
    That he should weep for her?"

That's what we actors can do. If we believe in the scene, we can cry for real at the thoughts a playwright has laid out for us. This is our "dream of passion", our "Make-Believe."

Belief in my Make-Believe works for me and produces emotions and complexities of emotion far beyond those my studious intentions could provide.

THE GREAT CHARACTERS OF CHARLES DICKENS

It's time we had some new scenes on which to try out these notions, to try out less strenuous ways of acting, thereby allowing our natural talents to take over. The scenes that I've adapted from Dickens are great fun to work on. And the characterizations afforded the actor are endlessly fascinating. Everything from the beautiful, disdainful Lady Dedlock through the hypocrite, Mr. Pecksniff and his two snobs of daughters, through the snide cruelty of Jonas Chuzzlewit, to the con man Montague Tigg.

There are the lovely ladies, Dolly Varden and Kate Nickleby, the skinny Miggs, the ample Mme. Mantalini and the great shrew, Miss Fanny Squeers. There is the stable boy, Hugh, and the arch manipulator, Sir John Chester, the hot tempered but well meaning Nicholas Nickleby and his deadly rival (his own uncle) Ralph Nickleby.

In Dickens we also see endless varieties of the comic character and situation, from old deaf Peg Sliderskew to the surreal Smallweed family to the lighter comedy of Mr. Guppy, so much in love with Esther Summerson. And then there is the inimitably sleazy Uriah Heep and his appallingly humble mother. As you read the scenes you will find many more.

These are wonderful roles, written so that their emotional content is universal, timely and recognizable. They are, for the most part, written in American English and can be considered as American and contemporary.

Once you enter the scene, you should feel natural. You should not feel that you have to be "English". You're not supposed to play cockney, or use an English accent to sound upper class here. That's not what these scenes are meant for.

They are, for you, the actor, to experience a range of emotional responses: to see how wildly funny you dare to be, to find an archness, a constraint in yourself that isn't generally supported in our culture, to explore chilling cruelty and Machiavellian manipulations.

Short but complete scenes are useful in class. Brief but interesting, they can be worked on again and again, to deepen and broaden involvement, to close the gap between yourself and the character.

This anthology is not for purists. I have not strayed far from the original scenes as they appear on Dicken's page. But I have strayed. Victorian phrases such as 'Aye, aye', 'mistress', 'lookee', 'unhand me' etc. are avoided. But every once in a while, the rhythm of a line insists on an English word such as pounds because the word 'money' won't work or a character is called Lord Dedlock although his suffering is like any other man's.

I give the background and temperament of the characters, and summaries of what has happened in the story up to the point where the dialogue begins. I include simple explanations to clarify a place or an event that has been mentioned. But I don't want to overload you with information so that details become burdensome. If there is a glitch and something is left out in my account of the story which puzzles you, then, by all means, go and read the book. Find what is the particular thing the character knows that you, the actor, are supposed to know.

Do not play the scene without the information you need. Many actors will allow themselves to act and not know – that is hack work.

However important in the novel some characters are, if they are not essential to carrying a particular scene forward and have no dialogue and would need a history to validate their presence, I have cut them out of the scene.

Most acting classes and workshops use a modest space with access to a table and a few chairs. As much as possible I have eliminated windows, staircases and second floors. In certain scenes that are too good to leave out but too difficult to stage I simplify the setting. Characters walk out instead of leaving in a carriage. If an elaborate dinner party is called for, wine, plentifully served, can be substituted.

In DAVID COPPERFIELD, a confrontation between the rich bully Steerforth and the impoverished teacher Mr. Mells takes place in front of the whole class. The only purpose in having the students present is to add to the debasement and embarrassment of Mr. Mells. So that the actors can imagine them overhearing, I place the students in the hallway looking into the room.

By the way, I hope actors take to the idea of staging scenes for themselves. We have become so used to taking directions, especially blocking directions from a director, that some of us are terrified to think through a staging problem. Some actors feel unable to act without a director. Get used to it. It's good practice.

CHAPTER 2

DON'T WORK SO HARD — BREATHE EASY

Imagine that every day you drive to Place X. It is bumper to bumper traffic, noisy, honking horns and cops at every turn. Then one day it occurs to you to take a different route. It is quiet, much less traffic, and you get to Place X easily and it has taken much less time than you thought.

That is what using the breath does for me: it takes all the thoughts and emotions, all the material away from the front part of my mind and lets me think, communicate, speak without effort.

So one way of not working so hard – is to let the breath and the imagination do the work for you.

When we are not self conscious, when we are not acting, this is the natural way we use breath. But when we act, under stress, we hold our breath,

First we have to learn how to breathe. The body can go a long time on minimal breath. Enough to keep us alive. We have to learn to breathe from the diaphragm, a space between the ribs and the stomach area. You see, it's the lungs that want the air, and when the diaphragm gets the message it gets out of the way by flattening out and letting the lungs grow large with the air it draws in. (I call it air when it is outside the body and breath when it is inside the body.) When the lungs expel breath, the diaphragm folds up into its resting place.

The next thing we have to do is connect the breath to the words. Words need breath. If you talk without breath, you will say a few words and soon you will choke. Those of you who can keep talking without any breath are actually taking tiny amounts of air but it doesn't leave you feeling good. You breathe high in the chest, it tightens all the muscles in the shoulders, neck, torso, and you get very few vibrations from the voice. It is in the vibrations that all the complex meaning of words reside and that is what we convey to the audience.

After we learn to connect words to breath, we learn this wonderful way of dropping a thought or an image or an emotion into the breath stream and it does for us what taking that quieter route to Place X does. It all happens without so much hard work.

Once you become fascinated by the breath and what it does for you as an actor, you will never take the noisier streets again.

TO BREATHE AND ACT — THREE EXAMPLES

The scenes in To Breathe and Act are wholly dependent on the breath. You can't sob or sit deeply in thought without the breath doing the sobbing or taking you to an unaccustomed psychic place. You will see this in the following three scenes:

1.

In BLEAK HOUSE, a young woman in utmost poverty sits before the fire, her dead baby in her arms. A friend, in rags and impoverished, comes into the hovel and knowing what has happened says only two words: "Jenny. Jenny".

I would have the first actor, Jenny, sink the feeling (through the imagination and the breath) into the body. Breathing in the thought of sadness, hopelessness, the actor can sit quietly for as long as needed.

For the second actor, Liz, it is necessary to use speech techniques in the placement of the words "Jenny, Jenny". If the words are too close to the back of the mouth and if they are not filled with the breath which will fill them with emotion, they will not be felt or heard. Often the actor speaks so quietly that no sound can be heard. No matter what the technical achievements in TV or film are, it is important for the actor, however minimal the sound he or she makes, to speak loudly enough to feel the vibrations.

2.

In BARNABY RUDGE, Dolly has been badly frightened by

Hugh who is a dangerous and lawless young man. Dolly is sobbing with fear and relief because her friend Joe has come in time to rescue her. When he asks her what happened she cannot answer. She is safe but cannot stop crying. End of scene. That is all you need to know to sob. No more analysis than that.

Analysis, where it is not needed, will stop the flow of tears, will make you work too hard trying to justify the emotions. The sobbing can begin with a catch in the breath and the thought of sobbing. Working physically — that is, through the breath — is more honest than bringing the interfering mind into the scene. Dolly is not crying with her intellect.

For actors who are trained to work only with analysis, who are distrustful of acting with spontaneity, this will be a disturbing suggestion. Take a chance.

I offer suggestions as to thoughts you might think but I don't want to be didactic. Natural behavior isn't routine or deliberate. There isn't just one way of doing anything.

You want to bring spontaneity and trust in your physical responses back into acting. When I do the Dolly scene, using my breath brings me to actual physical responses. When I breathe with a catch in my breath, knowing what has happened in the scene, I start to sob. I feel my stomach cramping, my chin trembling. I try to talk and can't. That's because the script says Dolly can't answer, that she just sobs and sobs. What I pick up from the script influences me. When the scene is over I stop.

I have not used memory recall or any other technique for emotional aid. I just breathed with some suggestion of Dolly's terror. I used only the information which was in the scene. I am honest in my emotions: what I am doing is real. I have bypassed the rational mind. The scene doesn't need 'thinking.'

I showed the Dolly scene to two actors. The more experienced actor said: "It is too difficult for a young actor." The younger actor said: "It might help the actor playing Dolly to recall a time when she was terribly frightened, or when her boyfriend..." etc.

These are techniques that are usually taught. For some actors they work. In some mysterious way the actor replaces all the words with an emotional memory and crying becomes easy. For others, it is always a fearful experience: they are afraid the tears won't come. You can't rationalize fear.

I explained to the two actors that that kind of recall was exactly what I didn't want the actor to do. It is unnecessary. It can lead the actor to try too hard to make the sobs come, and to end up "justifying" her behavior.

Although I say it is easy to sob in the scene as Dolly, there is nothing that comes for free. You have to learn to breathe and to have a body released from tension. That takes time. And you have to believe in that thought or emotion which is folded into the breath. If you do, you will respond emotionally.

3.

In DAVID COPPERFIELD, there is a scene in which Steerforth, the wealthy, charming, spoiled (and spoiler) friend of David is having a rare introspective moment. He sits staring at his glass of wine and is so deep in thought that he doesn't hear David come into the room and is noticeably frightened by the disturbance. This is very unusual behavior for the dashing, carefree Steerforth. He is planning to seduce an innocent village girl and take her away from her family with no intention of marrying her. It is one of the few times in his life when he realizes he is doing a terrible thing.

I worked with an actor on the Steerforth scene. It was difficult for him. He wasn't used to this kind of material. We took just the first three steps: sitting deep in thought, being startled, and uttering "oh!".

Often an actor will pretend quietness but it will be only a shallow stillness. On his first try at thinking deeply, the actor's eyelids flickered and there was movement in his brows.

Steerforth is in a very private place; he has gone deep into his body, his psyche has left his normal consciousness. Awake, he is in that place of dreaming; it can be terrifying or visionary. It comes from a part of the psyche rarely inhabited.

The actor and I knew that he had not got there. You can't get there without the breath travelling there, taking you there. After a few tries he deepened into his body and felt removed from the surface life. Being startled came easily. Then came the transition to speech. He felt fake. I explained that you make the transition by the way the breath changes its direction and its pace.

It is almost inexplicable but perhaps the following example is not so intimidating, since it is something we've all experienced.

HE: BOO!

I: I gasp. My breath stops for a second. Then it starts to flow again. I follow the breath. It comes up to my mouth and connects to the word.

I: (relieved) Oh, it's you. You scared me.

After my breath jumped up at hearing someone, it wanted to go back to the place it had been, but it didn't go all the way; it came back up again to daylight, as it were, and I found the words to say, "You frightened me".

Feel the breathing process in your own body, then read the explanation again.

The Steerforth scene may come very easily to you. Let it.

Don't work carefully, don't work slowly "to make sure". That will make you self conscious. Don't take a lot of time to make yourself feel the breath changing. That's counterproductive. Don't be exasperated at what's being asked of you. If this is a new technique, read the suggestions and leave them alone for a while.

BODY OVER MIND IN ACTING II

You will notice that in many of the scenes which follow I go to the body first, along with the breath, to evoke pyschological results.

If you experiment with your breath, you will see that you can make your self breathe in different ways. You don't have to feel the emotion first. It's the kind of breath you are creating that can lead to feeling.

I use the breath and a physical response, like the narrowing of the eyes, for example, to create, oh, let us say, the feeling of anger. *Of course there is psychology involved* but it seems to come in that nanosecond between breath and physical action. We must use the body very subtly. If the narrowed eyes come from the outside of the body, if we merely narrow the eyes, it will be ham acting. It begins in the torso that our facial reactions and body language take place.

The breath carrying thoughts is a natural activity for us. But when it's explained, it sounds obscure, difficult. Don't be afraid of the explanation.

Take Mr. Pecksniff, for example, in MARTIN CHUZZLEWIT:

As Pecksniff is trying to impress the wealthy owner of a mansion by pointing out the archectectural wonders of the building, his hands are especially graceful. His daughters are studies in exquisite attention to what he is saying. Mrs. Todgers, the inn keeper, clutches her purse; she is having a hard time keeping her mind on the subject. The more elaborate Mr. Pecksniff becomes, the greater is the insult that he has to bear from the owner.

In another scene, when he gets drunk, Pecksniff is loutish and vulgar. If you start by unfocussing your eyes, stare at the crumb on your trousers, manage a foolish smile at Mrs. Todgers, and then speak the disjointed sentences, you will have a funny scene.

In meeting the invalid, Martin Chuzzlewit, Pecksniff could

play the first part of the scene with his chin very much forward. It is his attempt to be kindly and understanding. As he is thrust away by Old Martin, Pecksniff's chin comes back to his body and he regains his most royal dignity.

Playing Old Martin with a wheeze and a cough, is to begin to feel like an invalid.

As Mr. Murdstone, in the novel DAVID COPPERFIELD, if you breathe in, you may feel the insides of your mouth pulling together. This brings the corners of your mouth down. It seems to dry out the expression in your eyes. You speak as Mr. Murdstone without moving your lips very much. For his sister, Miss Murdstone, you feel your eyes bulge, which causes you to purse your lips tightly. Murdstone's breathing is long and deliberate. Miss Murdstone's breathing is quick and watchful.

In BARNABY RUDGE, Dennis, the hangman who is now in jail himself, must be utterly sincere in everything he says. His humor is totally unconscious. If Hugh could model himself after an animal, I would suggest a bear. He speaks like one, swats at Dennis like one, and goes back to sleep like a bear as well.

For sickly young Smike, in NICHOLAS NICKLEBY, as you feel the breath leaving the body, the torso getting narrower, make an effort to speak clearly. The effort together with your lack of breath will bring you to feebleness.

You can't go too far in your characterization of Uriah Heep in DAVID COPPERFIELD. As you breathe in, let the thought of pure hatred mix with a thought of imposed humility. What comes out will be utterly malicious. David Copperfield doesn't want to create a more unpleasant scene. It is bad enough. David's breathing reflects his distaste for Uriah. As he breathes, his breath affects his whole body. That will make his feeling obvious without overacting.

Jonas and his wife Mercy, in the novel MARTIN CHUZZLEWIT, are playing out a moment of terror when Jonas thinks his enemy, Montague, has spotted him trying to run away. Mercy's breathing is in short spurts. Her shortness of breath leads her to hysteria.   Jonas is wild-eyed, looking everywhere for Montague. This body behavior lends itself to utter fear.

In BARNABY RUDGE, Dolly, when accosted by Hugh, has already been frightened by the noises she hears in the lonely forest.   She is walking quickly, she begins to take quick gasps of air and this gets her to panting. The panting brings on hysteria.

And finally, for all the examples I will give here, in the scene in DAVID COPPERFIELD between Aunt Betsy and the very pregnant Mrs. Copperfield, the phrase "have some tea" has to be clear and separate from "no,no,no." The clarity comes from a breath that precedes "have some tea." It's as though the breath clears a space in the mind. "Have some tea" then sounds sturdy and reassuring as though battles could be fought and won if the right people had their tea, a good bracing cup of tea, at the right time.

There are other examples of the body inducing emotions throughout the scenes. Use them as they serve you.

Any technique, if overused, is dangerous. Don't luxuriate in the breath, don't become precious about it. Allow for contradictions.

If you are easy with yourself, and let yourself grow familiar with its possibilities, the mind will accept, will wrap itself around the movement of the breath and move with it. Work lightly.

PLAYING A STRAIGHT ROLE

Why is it so hard?

Every actor I've ever met is reluctant to play the straight leading role, which requires charm and believability.   As Rosie O'Donnell said: "Actors would much rather play the best friend."

The actors themselves say it best.

Richard Gere, in an interview: "Playing normal and being

interesting is the hardest thing in the world. Henry Fonda did it all the time. You've got to be transparent. You can't tart it up. You can't hide behind it. You've got to be totally open. It's much easier playing a retarded guy with a limp."

And Meg Ryan said: "It is hard. I think we all need to find out how to play 'simply,' how to be ourselves and be able to come out from behind the character's mannerisms."

Talking about "being ourselves" is dangerous because it can lead to generalization, to sentimentality, to manipulation and every other terrible behavior that we in the acting community have tried to eliminate.

What do you need to play a straight role?

You have to go beyond self interest.

It is simplicity. It is for you, the actor, to listen when you're spoken to, to hear what is said. It is simplicity and courage.

It takes courage to live in the moment. It takes trust to know that the next moment will come out alright; that you will be able to give it what is required.

You have to get rid of tension in the body. Tension is actually a drawing away from others, a pulling in towards yourself. There was a reason early on in your life when you used tension to serve a need, something in the mind that led you to tighten somewhere in the body. By now you have forgotten why you felt you needed tension and have even forgotten the feel of tension. But it's there. Tension is a little neurosis. And you have it all over the body, probably slight, probably unimportant to everyone but you, the actor.

Sometimes when you begin to work on a straight role, you feel flat. As though you are not doing enough to satisfy the role. You feel your inadequacy. You can't find your charisma; you wonder whether you have any. You don't think you are handsome or beautiful enough. Who ever does? Actually this feeling of inadequacy is a good foundation for a straight role because actors who think of themselves as having charisma are going to have too much for the role.

When you are playing a character role, the thoughts are originally written into the role. Then as thought begets thought, you begin to invent; you add more to the character and make it more and more interesting.

In a straight role, the thoughts are not often apparent. But they are there. In a straight role everyone else's part seems more colorful, even though yours may be the leading part. The straight character often seems to be a sounding board for the more "interesting" figures in the play.

Recently I saw a production in which the actor playing the leading straight role was too involved with his own acting. His body was already taking its next step in the scene while his mind pretended to pay attention to what was being said. He displayed anger and resistance but was a bit ahead of the role, just in front of the character and not in the character. He wasn't able to let the script "melt down" into his mind and body so that he was a real person talking to another real person.

If you listen, really listen to the other, and really hear what is said, if the mind is in line with the body, and not secretly thinking of something else while the body seems to be paying attention, you needn't worry: you will hold the audience's attention.

The notion that actors who have charm and stand apart from the character will be forgiven because of their charm is entirely misleading.

I believe that sitting, standing, lying down, listening, and talking when the mind and body are in sync will, if you have it in you, bring out this special natural charm. The role and you have to be one shape. The more closely she is identified with the character, the more we are enchanted with the actor.

If you search for the deepest motivation, find the essence of the character and stay with it, others may play off of you and seem more inventive, but you will register strongly on the audience and attain that transparency Richard Gere talked about.

ABOUT AUTHORS

Most actors and directors I talk to say they immediately black out everything the author writes except the dialogue. I don't agree with this at all. It's not something you should do automatically.

An actor once described the author as a nuisance in rehearsal. This was an author, she said, who didn't allow for the actor's creativity to enhance the script. Admittedly, many of the scripts we get are not written by great writers and their scripts would be much better served if they let the actors alone to do their job.

I sat in on rehearsals of a play I had written. I was very polite. I never interfered with what was going on. There was one whole paragraph that the actress couldn't have known about, that I had the clue to. I offered to explain it to her. She agreed to listen to my explanation. But she never showed up to hear it. She was a talented and typical actress. To her the author was the enemy.

Don't assume that once the author has written the script you know more and it is all up to you.

But we have to know when to ignore the suggestions and when to follow them.

Charles Dickens has so much to offer in terms of stage business, gesture, tone of voice, and emotional response that an actor is a fool not to read his suggestions. His observations of social snobs, low lifes, con men, cowards, bluffers, expectant spinsters, thieves, and cronies are extraordinary and dynamic.

Dickens is also a writer whose straight characters, beautiful, sweet, young girls, handsome, honest men, kindly older folk, are often so sentimental, so overwritten, so saintly and sappy, they are almost unplayable. Here it is best to use our wits to contain the sweetness.

A REMINDER

I'm addressing young actors who have a certain amount of training. The training is needed but it is also at this point that acting becomes effortful. If the work becomes difficult, stop. Don't imprint effort or uncertainty in the body or on the brain. Work simply from the beginning.

CHAPTER THREE

THE SCENES

INTRODUCTION

The scenes range over a wide emotional territory and pose a series of opportunities for the actor. First, I have gathered a set of short scenes that will allow you to further explore the possibilities of acting on the breath. After you have completed them, I have organized another group of scenes according to the following categories: Playing a Straight Role, Fear, Humor, Passion, Manipulation and Scenes For The Young Actor.

In auditions, you are often asked to play with full emotional commitment and aren't given a heavily detailed character background, something that will give you a boost into the emotions. In order to prepare you for these common situations, I have included a few one-minute-scenes for you to prepare yourself for this sort of challenge. You will also find opportunities here to explore characters of different types and ages – young and old, male and female, eccentric and straight. Finally, I have included a section at the end: Scenes For The Young Actor. These parts are often the hardest to act. Most of us find character roles easy because we can hide behind a beard or mannerism. We can get involved with the complexity of character. We don't trust ourselves, our natural selves to show through our initial training.

TO BREATHE AND ACT

THE BRICKLAYER'S WIFE
JENNY AND HER BABY

From the novel *BLEAK HOUSE.*

JENNY AND HER BABY can be played alone or with LIZ COMFORTS JENNY.

CHARACTERS: JENNY: a bricklayer's wife, with a dead infant on her lap.

SETTING: A crowded, filthy hovel, home to the bricklayers and their families.

SUMMARY:

The woman, Jenny, sits motionless with her dead baby on her lap. Her eye is bruised She looks at the baby as it lies on her lap. Tears course slowly down her cheeks, but she makes no sound.

BLACKOUT

Don't worry about real tears. Just breathe, letting all the sadness in the world fill the breath. Follow the breath where it wants to go. It's happening inside the torso. Don't worry about whether tears appear on the face. You need not consciously search for real memories. They may come of their own accord. You can also find one word "sadness," "baby," or another, to think as you breathe.

* * *

THE BRICKLAYER'S WIVES
LIZ COMFORTS JENNY

From the novel *BLEAK HOUSE*

CHARACTERS: JENNY: a bricklayer's wife, with a dead infant on her lap.

LIZ: another bricklayer's wife and Jenny's friend.

SETTING: A crowded, filthy hovel, home to the bricklayers and their families.

SUMMARY:

Jenny, with a bruised eye that she got from her husband and tries to hide, sits motionless, looking at her dead baby. Tears course slowly down her cheeks, but she makes no sound. Liz, poorly clothed and with marks of brutality on her face and arms, comes in the room and embraces her.

LIZ: Jenny. Jenny!

[LIZ *gently removes the baby from* JENNY's *lap, lays it on a table, and covers it with a rag.* JENNY *begins to cry openly. She rises, falters, and falls to her knees.*]

LIZ: [*stroking her hair*] Jenny, Jenny!

BLACKOUT

The bricklayer's wives are in the same room as their husbands. They are used to expressing themselves carefully in order to avoid arousing the men, who are harsh and unsympathetic.

* * *

HUGH FRIGHTENS DOLLY

From the novel *BARNABY RUDGE*

CHARACTERS: DOLLY VARDEN: the pretty daughter of Varden, the locksmith.

HUGH: has but one name. He knows of no other. After a brutal childhood, he is now a stable boy at the Maypole Inn, more at home with the animals than he is with humans.

SETTING: A lonely country road.

SUMMARY:
Dolly, a young woman, is walking through a lonely area. Thinking she hears noises, she becomes frightened and walks decidedly faster. Suddenly a man comes plunging through the bushes. Dolly recognizes Hugh, whose wild, uncouth appearance fills her with alarm. He gazes at her with admiration; he is like a handsome satyr. Dolly is terrified. She is uncertain whether to go forward or retreat. Then, taking courage, she attempts to run past him.

HUGH: [*keeping close at her side*] Why do you avoid me?

DOLLY: I wish to get back as quickly as I can, and you walk too near me.

HUGH: [*so close she can feel his breath on her*] Why too near? You're always proud to me!

DOLLY: I am proud to no one. You mistake me. .

HUGH: [*trying to take her arm*] I'll walk with you.

[DOLLY *hits him as hard as she can.* HUGH *roars with laughter.*]

HUGH: [*his arm around her waist*] Well done! Hit me again. Beat my face, and tear my hair, and welcome, for the sake of your bright eyes. Hit me again, I like it.

DOLLY: [*trying to push him off*] Let go of me! Let go of me this minute.

HUGH: Be kinder to me, Sweetlips. Come. Tell me why are you always so proud? I don't quarrel with you for it. I love you when you're proud. You can't hide your beauty from a poor fellow, that's a comfort!

[DOLLY *walks rapidly. But between hurrying, her terror, and his tight embrace, her strength fails her.*]

DOLLY: [*panting*] Hugh, good Hugh, if you will leave me I will give you anything – everything I have – and never tell one word of this to any living creature.

HUGH: You'd better not, little dove. Everyone around here knows me and what I dare do if I have a mind. I'd sooner kill a man than a dog. If ever you are going to tell, stop when the words are on your lips.

[HUGH *is so savage in his words and looks that* DOLLY'*s great fear gives her new strength. She breaks away from him.*]

HUGH: [*catching her in his arms*] Softly, darling – gently – would you fly from rough Hugh, that loves you as well as any rich fellow?

DOLLY: [*struggling*] I would. I will. Help!

HUGH: [*laughing*] Pay a fine for crying out, Pretty one, from your lips. I pay myself!

[*He tries to kiss her.*]

DOLLY: [*shrieking*] Help! Help! Help!

A VOICE: Dolly, where are you? Dolly?

DOLLY: Joe, Joe, help!

[HUGH, *irresolute for a moment, releases* DOLLY.]

HUGH: [*whispers*] Tell him and see what follows!

[HUGH *runs off.* DOLLY *runs into* JOE WILLET'*s arms.*]

JOE: What's the matter? Are you hurt? What was it? Who was it?

[DOLLY *cannot answer. She sobs.*]

BLACKOUT

As Hugh says in another scene, he wouldn't have been able to approach Dolly if it weren't for the drink. Dolly should smell the drink on Hugh's breath as he gets close to her. Joe and Hugh are both handsome and strong, but Joe has a steadiness and quietness to him. Hugh has a reckless quality. Once again, you can tell it by the way he breathes.

* * *

JOE RESCUES DOLLY

From the novel *BARNABY RUDGE*

This next scene can be played together with the preceding scene or by itself.

CHARACTERS: JOE WILLET: in love with Dolly.

DOLLY VARDEN: a badly frightened girl.

SETTING: The secluded field where Dolly was accosted by the ferocious Hugh.

SUMMARY:

Dolly is in terrible danger from Hugh's advances. Luckily, her screams reach Joe, who rescues her.

JOE: Dolly! Ah, Dolly. What happened? Don't weep so. I'm here now. Nothing to fear, Dolly.

[DOLLY *is breathless and terrified. She is unable to answer him. She hangs upon his shoulder, sobbing and crying.*]

JOE: Dolly, Dolly, don't, don't cry. Ah, poor dear girl...

DOLLY: I...I...

[*She sobs.*]

BLACKOUT

Although Joe loves Dolly, he would not use this moment to be romantic with her.

* * *

THE LITTLE MAID'S ILLNESS

From the novel *BLEAK HOUSE*

CHARACTERS: CHARLEY: the little maid has had a harsh life until she came to work for Esther.

ESTHER SUMMERSON: is a young woman who has managed to be kindly and loving to all despite her own childhood, which lacked any kind of love or nurturing.

SETTING: Esther's sitting room.

SUMMARY:

Esther and Charley have been nursing Jo, a terribly ill, homeless waif. Now Jo has disappeared and they have given up the search for the poor boy. It is evening. Esther and Charley are sitting at a table reading. Suddenly Esther sees Charley shaking and shivering.

ESTHER: Charley, are you so cold?

CHARLEY: I think I am. I don't know what it is. I can't hold myself still. I felt it yesterday at about this same time. Don't be uneasy, I...I... oh,...

[CHARLEY *faints.*]

ESTHER: [*holding* CHARLEY *in her arms*] Charley, my poor dear, you have caught it; you are very ill. My poor dear, dear Charley.

[ESTHER *holds and rocks* CHARLEY *in her arms*.]

BLACKOUT

Charley has the smallpox. It is extremely contagious. Charley's illness comes upon her as soon as the scene opens. The actor has no preparation for it. Letting your hands shake can start the trembling. Try putting your teeth together while you are breathing and think of shaking. This may induce your chattering. It comes with practice. Not forcing. Opening your eyes wide helps to bring on fear. Esther's only concern is to care for Charley.

* * *

YOUNG MARTIN NEAR DEATH

From the novel *MARTIN CHUZZLEWIT*

CHARACTERS: YOUNG MARTIN CHUZZLEWIT: a rather spoiled young man who has the potential for change.

MARK TAPLEY: Martin's servant and so-called partner.

SETTING: The town of Eden.

SUMMARY:

Seeing no way to secure a future for himself and Mary Graham, the girl he loves, Young Martin Chuzzlewit is determined to try his luck in America. Mark Tapley, aware of the good in Martin in spite of Martin's youthful selfishness, accompanies him to the New World. Arriving in

America, Martin is duped into spending all his and Tapley's money on a piece of land called Eden. Martin gradually suspects that he has made a terrible mistake. His worst fears are realized: Eden turns out to be a hideous swamp choked with slime and matted growth. Standing before the hovel that is to be their home, Martin's disappointment and despair are so great that he breaks down and weeps. He becomes deathly ill, both psychically and physically. Mark Tapley is staunch in his support of Martin and will not let him die.

MARK: Don't do that! Don't do that! Anything but that! It never helped anybody over the lowest fence yet and it never will. The least sound of it will knock me flat down. I can't stand up against it!

MARTIN: I ask your forgiveness a thousand times. I couldn't have helped it, if death had been the penalty.

MARK: Ask my forgiveness! The head partner a-asking forgiveness of me? There must be something wrong in the firm when that happens. Ah, we'll soon be having pork and biscuit. And the whiskey we brought. And we've got the tin pot. That's a small fortune in itself! And blankets. And an axe. Who says we ain't got a first-rate outfit? For what we are going to receive, et cetrer. It's like a gypsy party!

[MARTIN *gives no answer. He sits with his head in his hands.*]

MARK: Don't give in.

MARTIN: Oh, Mark, what have I done in all my life that has deserved this heavy fate?

MARK: Hold up. Do something. Couldn't you ease your mind, now, by writing a letter to that scoundrel who sold us the plot.

MARTIN: No, I am past that. Do the best you can for yourself. And then God speed you home, and forgive me for bringing you here! I am going to die in this place.

MARK: I said you must be ill, and now I'm sure of it. Wait half a minute, till I run over to one of our neighbors and ask what's best to take and to-morrow you'll find yourself as strong as ever again. I won't be gone a minute. Don't give in while I'm away, whatever you do!

[MARK *rushes off.* MARTIN, *pale and shaking, his eyesight failing, grows weaker; he tries to stand and with a sudden violent trembling, falls to the ground.*]

BLACKOUT

The actor playing Mark might feel like crying but would not, ever, admit to it. For Martin, it's all in the breath. Don't worry about the stage directions and what impression you are making on the audience. You can't take too long to let the breath have its effect on you: you have a whole scene to get it started. Think a word, like "losing it", "I…I can't". Unfocus your eyes and fall to the ground.

* * *

A FLEETING MOMENT OF CONSCIENCE
FOR STEERFORTH

From the novel *DAVID COPPERFIELD*.

CHARACTERS: DAVID COPPERFIELD: has always thought his friend Steerforth the best of men.

JAMES STEERFORTH: is dashing, charming and the very worst of men.

SETTING: Mr. Peggotty's house
TIME: Dusk

SUMMARY:

Steerforth, a wealthy young man, has become a favorite of the simple and respectable Peggotty family. He is sitting alone in Mr. Peggotty's house and is deep in thought. He has a glass of wine in his hand which he stares at and has forgotten to drink. David enters the room, but Steerforth does not notice him. David puts his hand quietly on Steerforth's shoulder, which startles him.

STEERFORTH: [*almost angrily*] You come upon me like a reproachful ghost!

DAVID: I had to let you know, somehow, I was here. Have I called you down from the stars?

STEERFORTH: No. No.

DAVID: [*sitting beside him*] Up from somewhere?

STEERFORTH: I detest this mongrel time, neither day nor night. You're late! Where have you been?

DAVID: Taking the last of my usual walk.

STEERFORTH: [*glancing around the room*] And I've been sitting, thinking that all the people we found so glad when we came here, might - come to - I don't know what harm. David, I wish to God I had had a judicious father these last twenty years!

DAVID: What's the matter?

STEERFORTH: I wish with all my soul I'd had better guidance! I wish with all my soul I could guide myself better! I would rather be this poor Uncle Peggotty, or his lout of a nephew, than to be who I am, and be the torment to myself that I have been this last half-hour!

DAVID: What's troubling you? I've never seen you like this.

STEERFORTH: [*forcing a laugh*] It's nothing, nothing! I told you, I'm heavy company for myself, sometimes. I've been in a nightmare just now. At odd dull times, nursery tales come up into my memory. I believed I was the bad boy who "didn't care", and became food for lions—[he laughs gaily] What old women call the horrors crept over me from head to foot. I was afraid of myself.

DAVID: But you're afraid of nothing else.

STEERFORTH: Perhaps not, and yet, I may have enough to be afraid of. I am not about to have this happen again, but I tell you, my friend, it would have been well for me [*and for more than me*] if I had had a caring father!

[*A pause.*]

STEERFORTH: [*grinning*] So much for that! All my visions are gone; I am a man again, like Macbeth. And now for dinner! Come on, let's go!

BLACKOUT

David's innocence is obvious in this scene. He is unable to imagine what is in Steerforth's mind. Steerforth, still alone even after David's entrance, does not trouble to hide his mood from David. He brightens up more to assure himself than to please David.

* * *

PLAYING A STRAIGHT ROLE

FANNY SQUEERS MANAGES TO MEET
NICHOLAS NICKLEBY

From the novel *NICHOLAS NICKLEBY*

CHARACTERS:

FANNY SQUEERS: the daughter of Headmaster Squeers is usually as mean and vicious as her parents, but since she fell head-over-heels in love with Nicholas Nickleby, Fanny is momentarily on her best manners.

HER SERVANT: a shrewd girl who has learned how to survive in the hostile atmosphere of the Dotheboys school and who knows how to flatter Fanny.

NICHOLAS: a handsome teacher who, new to the school, wishes to do well.

SETTING: Fanny's bedroom.

SUMMARY:

Fanny is doing her hair. She questions her servant about the new schoolmaster, Nicholas.

FANNY: What does he look like?

SERVANT: Oh, ma'am, he has beautiful dark eyes, and such a sweet smile, and, oh, ma'am, his legs are so straight.

FANNY: [*pretending little interest*] He can't be such a remarkable person as you make out. But if he is something quite out of the common, I shall have to see for myself.

[*She leaves her room to go to the classroom.*]

PART TWO

SETTING: The classroom.

SUMMARY:

Fanny happens to go into the Nicholas's classroom to get a pen mended. Nicholas has just dismissed the students.

FANNY: [*blushing*] I beg your pardon, I thought my father was — or might be — dear me, how awkward!

NICHOLAS: Mr. Squeers is out.

FANNY: [*with bashful hesitation*] Do you know will he be long?

NICHOLAS: He said about an hour.

FANNY: [*showing the pen and murmuring*] Thank you! I am very sorry I intruded. If I hadn't thought my father was here, I wouldn't upon any account have...it is very provoking...must look so strange.

NICHOLAS: [*pointing to the pen*] If that's all you want...— [*he smiles at* FANNY's *affected embarrassment*] — Perhaps I can take his place.

[FANNY, *with a winning mixture of reserve and condescension, sidles up to* NICHOLAS *and gives him the pen*].

NICHOLAS: [smiling to keep from laughing] Do you write with a hard or a soft point?

FANNY: [*murmuring*] He has a beautiful smile.

NICHOLAS: Which did you say?

FANNY: Dear me, I was thinking of something else for the moment, I declare. Oh! I write with a soft as possible point, if you please.

[NICHOLAS *fixes the pen and gives it to* FANNY *who drops it. They both bend to pick it up and knock heads.*]

NICHOLAS: Very awkward of me.

FANNY: Not at all, it was my fault. It was all my foolish ... a...a...good-morning!

NICHOLAS: Goodbye. Take care! You are biting the nib off now.

[*He opens the door for her as she prepares to leave.*]

FANNY: Really, so embarrassing that I scarcely know what I...very sorry to give you so much trouble.

NICHOLAS: Not the least trouble in the world.

[*He turns back to his papers.*]

FANNY: [*at the door*] I have never seen such straight legs in the whole course of my life!

BLACKOUT

If you think of Fanny as a natural shrew — a screaming harradin when enraged – and then observe her affectations when she meets Nicholas, you can imagine how unpleasant her mincing behavior is to him.

Knocking heads has to be practiced until that piece of business is perfect and convincing to the onlooker. Don't accept 'nearly right.'

* * *

URIAH HEEP IS HUMBLE

From the novel *DAVID COPPERFIELD*

CHARACTERS: **URIAH HEEP:** has learned to use his hum- ble beginnings to get himself a good position with Mr. Wickfield, an honorable investment broker.

DAVID COPPERFIELD: before David has learned enough about Uriah to despise him, he has difficulty hiding his impatience at Uriah's humble manners.

SETTING: A desk in Mr. Wickfield's study.

SUMMARY:

David is sitting at the desk with Uriah standing by.

URIAH: [writhing] You had promised to take tea with mother and me but I didn't expect you to keep it, Master Copperfield, we're so very humble.

DAVID: [*hiding his annoyance*] I wasn't being proud, I had only wanted to be asked.

URIAH: Oh, if that's all, Master Copperfield, and it really isn't our humbleness that prevents you, will you come this evening? But if it is our humbleness, I hope you won't mind owning to it, Master Copperfield, for we are well aware of our condition. Mother will be proud, indeed, or she would be proud, if it wasn't sinful, Master Copperfield.

DAVID: Yet you didn't mind supposing I was proud this morning.

URIAH: Oh dear, no, Master Copperfield! Oh, believe me, no! Such a thought never came into my head! I shouldn't have deemed it at all proud if you had thought us too humble for you. Because we are so very humble.

DAVID: Have you been studying much law lately?

URIAH: [*with an air of self denial*] Oh, Master Copperfield, my reading is hardly to be called study. I have passed an hour or two in the evening, sometimes.

DAVID: Rather hard, I suppose?

URIAH: It is hard to me sometimes, but I don't know what it might be to a gifted person.

[*He beats a little tune on his chin with the two forefingers of his skeleton right hand*]

There are expressions, you see, Master Copperfield - Latin words and terms - that are trying to a reader of my humble attainments.

DAVID: [*briskly showing some impatience*] Would you like to be taught Latin? I will teach it to you with pleasure, as I learn it.

URIAH: [*shaking his head*] Oh, thank you, Master Copperfield. I am sure it's very kind of you to make the offer, but I am much too humble to accept it.

DAVID: What nonsense, Uriah!

URIAH: [*shaking his head and writhing modestly*] Oh, indeed you must excuse me, Master Copperfield! I am greatly obliged, and I should like it of all things, I assure you. A person like myself, though, had better not aspire. If he is to get on in life, he must get on humbly, Master Copperfield!

DAVID: I think you are wrong, Uriah. I dare say there are several things that I could teach you, if you would like to learn them.

URIAH: Oh, I don't doubt that, Master Copperfield, not in the least. I won't provoke my betters with knowledge, thank you. I'm much too humble. But we will expect you to tea. Mother and me.

BLACKOUT

It is hardly possible to go too far in a characterization of Uriah Heep — his squirming, writhing, jerking and his especially unpleasant smile. A standing joke when we first meet him, Heep becomes more and more sinister. David doesn't yet have any idea of Uriah's deepest selfishness; at the moment he merely dislikes him. Although every sympathetic character in the novel is aware of Heep, no one — except for the courageous Mr. Micawber, who is finally able to get the goods on Heep — knows what to do about him and his rise to power in the firm of Wickfield ... and Heep.

* * *

KATE IS ACCOSTED BY HER UNCLE'S GUEST

From the novel *NICHOLAS NICKLEBY*

CHARACTERS:	**KATE NICKLEBY:** the younger sister of Nicholas. She is beautiful. She has dignity and a sense of right and wrong.
	SIR MULBERRY HAWKE: a vulgar, wealthy guest at Ralph's dinner party.
	RALPH NICKLEBY: Kate's uncle who has shamelessly hoped to use her to entertain his guests.
SETTING:	Ralph Nickleby's upstairs room.

SUMMARY:

Uncle Ralph, who has been mean-spirited and stingy to his poor relatives, suddenly becomes gentle (as gentle as a man can be who has not spoken a kind word to anyone in years.) He invites Kate to his home for a dinner party. Kate is surprised and shocked to see that she is the only woman at the party. The male guests are sophisticated and coarse and, of course, moneyed. Sir Mulberry Hawke is especially interested in Kate. Looking at Sir Mulberry's repulsive face, she is revolted and hurries from the room. She restrains her tears until she is alone.

Kate stays upstairs, hoping to leave her uncle's house after the guests have all gone. Seated on a sofa, she dozes slightly. Suddenly, she becomes aware that Sir Mulberry Hawke is sitting beside her. Note: The young man referred to as 'the young lord', is Lord Verisopht, another guest who has also been smitten by Kate's charm.

SIR MULBERRY: [*somewhat drunk*] What a delightful study. Were you really asleep or were you displaying your eyelashes?

[KATE *looks anxiously towards the door.*]

SIR MULBERRY: I have looked at them for five minutes. They are perfect. Why did I speak, and destroy such a pretty little picture?

KATE: Please don't speak to me.

SIR MULBERRY: [*moving closer to* KATE] You oughtn't to be so arch. Such a devoted slave of yours, Miss Nickleby, as I am...and to treat him so harshly.

KATE: [*trembling*] Understand that you offend and disgust me. Now please leave me alone.

SIR MULBERRY: Why, why will you keep up this appearance of excessive rigor, my sweet creature? Now, be more natural — my dear Miss Nickleby, be more natural.

[KATE *gets up. But* SIR MULBERRY *catches her dress and forcibly detains her.*]

KATE: Let me go! Do you hear?

SIR MULBERRY: Sit down, sit down. I want to talk to you.

KATE: Let me go!

SIR MULBERRY: Not for the world.

[*He leans over to put* KATE *back in her chair.* KATE *pulls violently away.* SIR MULBERRY *loses his balance and sprawls on the floor*].

[RALPH NICKLEBY *appears in the doorway.*]

RALPH NICKLEBY: What is this?

KATE: [*greatly agitated*] It is this, uncle, that beneath your roof where I should most have found protection, I've been exposed to insult. I don't know why you have done this. Let me pass.

[RALPH *leads her to a chair. He approaches* SIR MULBERRY HAWKE *who has gotten up from the floor.*]

RALPH NICKLEBY: [*with suppressed anger*] There's the door. You know the way.

SIR MULBERRY: [*fiercely*] What do you mean by that?

[RALPH'*s face registers the anger and strain he feels. He again points to the door.*]

SIR MULBERRY: Do you know me, you old madman?

RALPH NICKLEBY: I know you well.

[*Looking at* RALPH NICKLEBY, SIR MULBERRY *gives in and walks to the door, muttering.*]

SIR MULBERRY: [*suddenly*] You wanted the young Lord, didn't you? Dammit, I was in the way, was I?

[RALPH *smiles but does not answer.*]

SIR MULBERRY: You would sell your flesh and blood for money if you've not already made a bargain with the devil. Do you mean to tell me that your pretty niece was not brought here as a decoy for the drunken boy downstairs?

[*Both men are speaking intensely and softly.* RALPH *looks involuntarily round to ascertain that* KATE *has not heard anything.* SIR MULBERRY *sees his advantage.*]

SIR MULBERRY: Do you mean to tell me that if his Lordship had found his way up here instead of me, you wouldn't have been a little more blind, and a little more deaf, than you have been?

RALPH NICKLEBY: I tell you this, that if I brought her here, as a matter of business...[*slowly and firmly*]... As a matter of business, because I thought she might make some impression on the silly youth, I knew... knowing him... that it would be long before he outraged the feelings even of his usurer's niece. I did not think of subjecting the girl to the licentiousness and brutality of so old a hand as you. And now we understand each other.

SIR MULBERRY: Especially as there was nothing to be got by it — eh?

RALPH NICKLEBY: Exactly so.

[*The men look at each other with cynical frankness.* SIR MULBERRY HAWKE *shrugs and walks out.*]

BLACKOUT

Ralph Nickleby and Sir Mulberry Hawke are a strong match. The one is a model of firmness, the other [despite his drunkenness] a model of lucidity. They are more interested in settling scores with each other than in Kate's predicament. Each man knows himself and knows his enemy. There is no pretense, only cynicism and mutual hatred.

* * *

ARTHUR CLENNAM RETURNS HOME

From the novel *LITTLE DORRIT*

CHARACTERS:

ARTHUR CLENNAM: returns from 20 years in China, where he worked with his father. His mother is harsh and religious and it is difficult for Arthur to greet her.

FLINTWINCH: is a dry, cold, reserved man who is Mrs. Clennam's business partner and all around helper.

MRS. CLENNAM: is a mean, rigid woman who adopted Arthur and has never shown him any affection.

SETTING:

An old brick house, dingy, weather-stained, overgrown with weeds.

SUMMARY:

Arthur Clennam has returned home after years of being abroad. He left the unhappy, somber house as a youth and finds the atmosphere of the house and its inhabitants unchanged.

ARTHUR: [*sotto voce*] Nothing changed. Dark and miserable as ever. A light in my mother's window, the same as when I came home twice a year from school. Well, well, well!

[*An old man, bent and dried but with keen eyes, comes to the door holding a lighted candle. He examines* ARTHUR.]

FLINTWINCH: [*with no emotion*] Mr. Arthur? You've come at last? You've gotten heavier, but you don't come up to your father in my opinion. Nor yet your mother.

ARTHUR: How is my mother?

FLINTWINCH: She is as she always is now. Keeps her room when not actually bedridden, and hasn't been out of it in fifteen years, Arthur.

[*The old man puts the candlestick on the table and smoothes his leathern jaws while he looks at* ARTHUR. ARTHUR *offers his hand. The old man takes it coldly.*]

FLINTWINCH: [*shaking his head warily*] I doubt if your mother will approve of your coming home on the Sabbath, Arthur.

ARTHUR: You wouldn't have me go away again?

FLINTWINCH: Oh! I? I? I am not one to say. It's not what I would have. I have stood between your father and mother for a number of years. I don't stand between your mother and you.

ARTHUR: Will you tell her I've come home?

FLINTWINCH: Yes, Arthur, yes. Oh, to be sure! I'll tell her that you have come home. Please wait here. You won't find the room changed.

[*The old man lights another candle and leaves the room.*]

ARTHUR: [*holding back tears*] Still to feel like crying at this reception, but I've never experienced anything else.

[*He looks around the unchanged room.*]

FLINTWINCH: [*coming back*] Arthur, I'll go before and light the way.

PART TWO

SETTING: A dim bed chamber.

SUMMARY:

Mrs. Clennam, in a widow's dress, sits bolstered up on a sofa. At Arthur's approach, she gives him a glassy kiss for an embrace; he sits down at a little table beside her.

ARTHUR: Mother, this is a change from your old active habits.

MRS. CLENNAM: [*in a stern strong voice*] The world has narrowed for me, Arthur. I never did set my heart upon its hollow vanities.

ARTHUR: [*still feeling the chill of his childhood*] Don't you ever leave your room, mother?

MRS. CLENNAM: I have lost the use of my legs. I never leave my room. I have not been outside this door for a dozen years. I am able to attend to my business and I am thankful for the privilege. But no more of business on this day. It's a bad night outside, is it?

ARTHUR: Yes, mother.

MRS. CLENNAM: Does it snow?

ARTHUR: Snow, mother? We're only into September.

MRS. CLENNAM: All seasons are alike to me, shut up here. No more of business on this day. It is nine o'clock. Good night, Arthur. Flintwinch will see to your accommodation.

[ARTHUR *starts towards her, but* MRS. CLENNAM *stops him.*]

MRS. CLENNAM: Only touch me, for my hand is tender.

[ARTHUR *touches the glove she is wearing and follows the old man out of the room.*]

BLACKOUT

Flintwinch and Mrs. Clennam have grown uglier as the house has decayed. Mrs. Clennam is proud of her illness and her ability to work. It is another way to put Arthur in his place.

Here is a case where a character, Arthur, seems less interesting than the old man or his mother. But the actor must believe and follow his thoughts and feelings, even though at this point in his life Arthur is unmoored and at loose ends.

* * *

THE GOOD NATURED LOCKSMITH VARDEN

From the novel BARNABY RUDGE

CHARACTERS: MR. VARDEN: a patient family man.

MIGGS: an interfering spinster, servant-companion to Mrs. Varden.

MRS. VARDEN: a discontented wife.

SETTING: The Varden home.

SUMMARY:

Mr. Varden comes home but finds it difficult to make conversation with his wife.

[GABRIEL VARDEN *enters his living room.*]

MIGGS: [*with a shrill cry*] Who's there?

GABRIEL VARDEN: Me, girl, me.

MIGGS: What, already, sir! We were just getting ready to sit up,— me and Mrs. Varden. Oh, she has been so bad!

[MRS. VARDEN *pays no attention to Varden's homecoming*.]

MIGGS: He's come home, mim. You were wrong, mim, and I was right. I thought he wouldn't keep us up so late, mim. Mr. V. is considerate so far. I'm so glad, mim, on your account. [*simpering*] I'm a little, a little sleepy myself; I'll own it now, mim, though I said I wasn't when you asked me. It ain't of no consequence, mim, of course.

GABRIEL VARDEN: You had better get to bed at once then.

MIGGS: Thanking you kindly, I couldn't take my rest in peace, nor fix my thoughts upon my prayers, except I knew my lady was comfortable in her bed this night; by rights she ought to have been there, hours ago.

GABRIEL VARDEN: [*pulling off his greatcoat and looking at her askew*] You're talkative, miss.

MIGGS: [*flushing*] Taking the hint and thanking you for it most kindly, I will make bold to say, that if I give offence by having consideration for Mrs. Varden, I do not ask your pardon but am content to get myself to suffer.

MRS. VARDEN: [*reading her Protestant Manual*] Miggs, hold your tongue.

MIGGS: [*every little bone in her neck showing*] Yes, mim, I will.

GABRIEL VARDEN: [*rubbing his knees hard*] How do you find yourself now, my dear?

[*He takes a chair near his wife who has resumed her reading.*]

MRS. VARDEN: [*her eyes on the book*] You're very anxious to know, aren't you? You, that have not been near me all day and wouldn't have been if I was dying!

GABRIEL VARDEN: My dear Martha...

[MRS. VARDEN *turns to the next page; then goes back again to the page before to be quite sure of the last words; she then goes on reading with an appearance of the deepest interest and study.*]

GABRIEL VARDEN: My dear Martha, how can you say such things, when you know you don't mean them? If you were dying! Why, if there was anything serious the matter with you, Martha, shouldn't I be in constant attendance upon you?

MRS. VARDEN: [*bursting into tears*] Yes! Yes, you would. I don't doubt it, Varden. Certainly you would. That's as much as to tell me that you would be hovering round me like a vulture, waiting till the breath was out of my body, that you might go and marry somebody else.

[MIGGS *groans in sympathy—a little short groan that changes into a cough.*]

MRS. VARDEN: [*with resignation*] But you'll break my heart one of these days, and then we shall both be happy. My only desire is to see our daughter, Dolly, comfortably settled, and when she is, you may settle me as soon as you like.

MIGGS: Ah!

[*She coughs.*]

GABRIEL VARDEN: [*after a long silence says mildly*] Has Dolly gone to bed?

MRS. VARDEN: [*looking at* MIGGS *over her shoulder*] Mr. Varden is speaking to you.

GABRIEL VARDEN: No, my dear, I spoke to you.

MRS. VARDEN: [*obdurately, stamping her foot*] Did you hear me, Miggs? You are beginning to despise me now, are you?

[MIGGS, *whose tears are always ready on the shortest notice, cries*

*violently; she's holding both her hands tight over her heart mean-
while, as if nothing less would prevent its splitting into small fragments.* MRS. VARDEN, *who likewise possesses that faculty in high
perfection, weeps too — and with such effect that* MIGGS *gives in
after a time. Except for an occasional sob,* MRS. VARDEN *falls into
a quiet melancholy.*]

MRS. VARDEN: Because, because I never interfere or interrupt;
because I never question where anybody comes or goes;
because my whole mind and soul is bent on laboring in this
house;—therefore, they try me as they do.

GABRIEL VARDEN: Martha, what is it you complain of? I really
came home with every wish and desire to be happy. I did,
indeed.

MRS. VARDEN: What do I complain of! Is it natural, that he
should tell me, without my begging and praying him to, what
he has been doing? Is that natural, or is it not?

GABRIEL VARDEN: I am very sorry, Martha, I was really afraid you
were not disposed to talk pleasantly; I'll tell you everything; I
shall only be too glad, my dear.

MRS. VARDEN: [*rising with dignity*] No, Varden, thank you! I'm
not a child to be corrected one minute and petted the next—
I'm a little too old for that, Varden. Miggs, carry the light.—
you can be cheerful, Miggs, at least.

[MIGGS, *who has been in the very depths of compassionate despondency, passes instantly into the liveliest state conceivable. Tossing her
head as she glances towards the locksmith,* MIGGS *carries the light
and escorts* MRS. VARDEN *to bed.*]

GABRIEL VARDEN: Well, well, all of us have our faults. I'll not be
hard on Martha. We have been man and wife too long for that.

GABRIEL VARDEN: [*murmurs*] I wish, I wish somebody would marry Miggs. I wonder whether there's a madman alive who would marry Miggs.

BLACKOUT

Mr. Varden's character is entirely consistent. Even though he may have disturbing news to tell, Mr. Varden is never theatrical. He is always even-tempered.

Until the devastating riots in which the Protestants attack the Catholics and she sees and admits how fine a man Gabriel Varden is, Mrs. Varden always believes herself the injured wife.

Comic that she is, Miggs is much more dangerous. We see this when she tells the rioters clamoring at his door that Varden's gun is not loaded, thus giving him no way of protecting his family and property.

* * *

JOE SAYS GOODBYE TO DOLLY

From the novel *BARNABY RUDGE*

CHARACTERS: **JOE WILLET:** a hard-working young man who is treated badly by his father and his father's cronies.

DOLLY VARDEN: a beautiful young girl who at this stage in her life is a coquette.

SETTING: The locksmith Varden's house.

SUMMARY:

Young Joe Willet has been hounded. He has been kept in his place by his father and teased by his father's cronies. He leaves the Maypole Inn to join the army. Joe comes to say goodbye to Dolly. Dolly loves Joe as much as he loves her but she is very young, a natural coquette, and doesn't realize the consequences of her behavior.

JOE: [*shaking hands with* DOLLY] I have come to say good-bye — to say good-bye for I don't know how many years; perhaps for ever. I am going abroad.

DOLLY: [*releasing her hand*] Indeed!

JOE: I couldn't go without coming to see you. I hadn't the heart to.

DOLLY: I am more sorry than I can say that you have taken so much trouble. You must have such a great deal to do. And how is Mr. Willet? That dear old gentleman...

JOE: Is this all you say!

DOLLY: All! Good gracious, what did you expect!

JOE: You don't ask "Why do you go?"

[DOLLY *plays with the corner of her apron and says nothing.*]

JOE: [*after a long pause*] Good-bye.

DOLLY: [*pleasantly*] Good-bye.

JOE: [*reaching out*] Come, Dolly, dear Dolly, don't let us part like this. I love you dearly, with all my heart and soul. I am a poor fellow, as you know...poorer now than ever, for I have fled from home, not being able to bear it any longer. You are beautiful, loved by everybody. But give me a word of comfort. Say something kind to me. I have no right to expect it of you, I know, but I ask it because I love you, and shall treasure the slightest word from you all through my life. Dolly, dearest, have you nothing to say to me?

DOLLY: No. Nothing. I have said good-bye, twice. Take your arm away directly, Mr. Joseph, or I'll call Miggs.

JOE: I'll not reproach you. It's my fault, no doubt. I have thought sometimes that you didn't quite despise me, but I was a fool to think so. Every one must, who has seen the life I have led...you most of all. God bless you!

[*He goes.* DOLLY *waits a little, thinking he will return. She peeps out the door, and waits a little longer. She hums a tune, sits down and cries as if her heart would break.*]

BLACKOUT

No actress born since the sixties will even begin to understand this behavior unless she has some understanding of the Victorian woman's manners and mores. A Victorian woman was never supposed to show her real feelings towards a man —and certainly not her sexual impulses. She was encouraged to be a coquette, to have many beaus, to be in demand socially, to be pretty, to do needlepoint, to sing a bit. You get the picture. Unless the actress has done research, uncovered this social history, and can believe it, she will not be able to fathom the scene, let alone act it. It may be somewhat difficult to accept the girl's behavior even though we understand that she is a coquette. But if you are cast and the job requires that you do the scene, you must play it with total immersion and belief.

* * *

DOLLY AND JOE AFTER THE RIOTS

From the novel *BARNABY RUDGE*

CHARACTERS: **DOLLY VARDEN:** has suffered and is now able to express her real feelings.

JOE WILLET: has matured and is realistic.

SETTING: Dolly Varden's home.

SUMMARY:

Joe Willet rescues Dolly from her kidnappers, the Protestant rioters. There is much rejoicing. Joe, who has lost an arm in the service but whose simplicity, honesty and lack of bitterness remain untouched, expects nothing from Dolly other than to say a few words to her before he leaves again. Dolly has matured while Joe has been away. She knows now how much she loves — has always loved — Joe, and she is eager for him to speak. Joe has said goodbye to the Vardens. Dolly follows him to the door.

JOE: Good night!

DOLLY: [*tears well up in her eyes*] Good night!

JOE: Don't cry. You are safe now. You are safe and happy now.

   [DOLLY *can't speak.*]

JOE: You must have suffered very much within these few days – but you're not changed — you were always very beautiful, you are more beautiful than ever.

DOLLY: [*lowers her eyes*] I shall bless your name as long as I live. I shall never hear it spoken without feeling as if my heart would burst.

JOE: It makes me, it makes me very glad and proud to hear you say so.

   [DOLLY *cannot stop her tears.*]

JOE: For the moment, I feel as if — there can be no harm in talking of that night now – as if I had come back, and nothing had happened in the mean time. I feel as if I hadn't suffered any hardships, but had come to see you with my bundle on my shoulder before running away. You remember?

[DOLLY *raises her eyes to* JOE*'s and for a moment he can't speak*].

JOE: Well! It was to be otherwise. I have been abroad and I have come back as poor as I went, and crippled for life besides. I did hope once, that I might come back a rich man, and marry you. But I was a boy then, and have long known better than that. I am a poor, maimed, discharged soldier, and I have to be content to rub through life as best I can.

[DOLLY *throws her arms around* JOE'S *neck.*]

Dolly! Dolly!

DOLLY: Dear Joe, I always loved you — in my own heart I always did, although I was so vain and giddy. I hoped you would come back that night. All these long, long years, I have never once forgotten you, or left off hoping that this time might come. You have borne so much from me — you owe your sufferings and pain to my caprice — for you to be so kind—so noble to me, Joe—

JOE: What have I done, Dolly, what have I done to hear you say this?

DOLLY: Ah, Joe, you've taught me to know myself; to be something better than I was. Joe, don't ever leave me!

BLACKOUT

Dolly and Joe have suffered and they have the right to speak "from the heart." In this scene the actors can't go just by the words. It's their maturity that permits them to speak as they do.

***

KATE LOOKS FOR ANOTHER JOB

From the novel *NICHOLAS NICKLEBY*

CHARACTERS:	**MRS. WITITTERLY:** lets her husband tell whoever will listen of her accomplishments.
	KATE NICKLEBY: a modest person who needs work.
	MRS. NICKLEBY: like most mothers, Kate's mother wants the world to know how well her daughter was raised.
	MR. WITITTERLY: a true believer.
	ALPHONSE: a servant.
SETTING:	Mrs. Wititterly's parlor.

SUMMARY:

Having lost her position at the dressmaking studio, Kate applies for a job with a married lady who wants a genteel person as companion. Mrs. Wititterly herself is a genteel lady, so genteel, poetic, and sensitive that she faints easily and has to have her husband and her doctor constantly in attendance upon her.

MRS. WITITTERLY: [to her servant] Place chairs.

ALPHONSE: Yes, Modom.

MRS. WITITTERLY: Leave the room, Alphonse.

ALPHONSE: [*previously know as Bill*] Yes, Modom.

[ALPHONSE *leaves.*]

KATE: [*after an awkward silence*] I have ventured to call, ma'am, from having seen your advertisement.

MRS. WITITTERLY: [*weakly, with a sigh*] Yes, one of my people put it in the paper. Yes.

KATE: I thought, perhaps, that if you had not already made a final choice, you would forgive my troubling you with an application.

MRS. WITITTERLY: Yes.

KATE: If you have already made a selection...

MRS. WITITTERLY: Oh dear no, I am not so easily suited. I really don't know what to say. You have never been a companion before, have you?

MRS. NICKLEBY: [*getting her word in*] Not to any stranger, ma'am, but she has been a companion to me for some years. I am her mother, ma'am.

MRS. WITITTERLY: Oh! I apprehend you.

MRS. NICKLEBY: I assure you, ma'am, that I very little thought, at one time, that it would be necessary for my daughter to go out into the world at all, for her poor dear papa was an independent gentleman, and would have been at this moment if he had but listened in time to my constant entreaties and...

KATE: [*in a low voice*] Dear mother.

MRS. NICKLEBY: My dear Kate, if you will allow me to speak, I shall take the liberty of explaining to this lady...

KATE: I think it is almost unnecessary, mother.

[MRS. NICKLEBY *frowns and winks to* KATE *that she means to say something important, but* KATE *gives her an especially strong look and* MRS. NICKLEBY *stops immediately.*]

MRS. WITITTERLY: [*with her eyes shut*] Do you have a good temper?

KATE: I hope so.

MRS. WITITTERLY: And you have a highly respectable reference for everything, have you?

KATE: I have. Here is my uncle's card.

[*She lays the card on the table.*]

MRS. WITITTERLY: Have the goodness to draw your chair a little nearer, and let me look at you. I am so very nearsighted that I can't quite discern your features.

[KATE *complies, with some embarrassment.* MRS. WITITTERLY *looks at her languidly for some time.*]

MRS. WITITTERLY: I like your appearance.

[*She rings a little bell.* ALPHONSE *appears.*]

MRS. WITITTERLY: Alphonse, request your master to come here.

ALPHONSE: Yes, Modom.

[*He leaves.*]

[MR. WITITTERLY *appears. He leans over* MRS. WITITTERLY *and converses in whispers.*]

MRS. WITITTERLY: I think she'll do. She's plain but pretty.

MR. WITITTERLY: [*to* KATE] Oh! yes. This is a most important matter. Mrs. Wititterly is of a very excitable nature; very delicate, very fragile; a hothouse plant, an exotic.

MRS. WITITTERLY: Oh! Henry, my dear.

MR. WITITTERLY: You are, my love, you know you are; one breath...[*he blows an imaginary feather away*] Pho! you're gone!

[*The lady sighs.*]

MR. WITITTERLY: Your soul is too large for your body. Your intellect wears you out; all the medical men say so; 'Be proud of that woman; she is an ornament to the fashionable world. Her complaint is her soul'.

[*Flourishing his hands*, MR. WITITTERLY *almost knocks* MRS. NICKLEBY's *hat off.*]

MRS. WITITTERLY: [*with a faint smile*] You make me out worse than I am, Henry.

MR. WITITTERLY: I do not, Julia, I do not. Can I ever forget the night you danced at the election ball. It was tremenjous.

MRS. WITITTERLY: I always suffer for these triumphs afterwards.

MR. WITITTERLY: And for that very reason you must have a companion, in whom there is gentleness, sweetness, excessive sympathy, and repose. [*to* MRS. NICKLEBY] Mrs. Wititterly, is sought after and courted by glittering crowds and brilliant circles. She is excited by the opera, the drama, the fine arts, the...uh... the...

MRS. WITITTERLY: The nobility, my love.

MR. WITITTERLY: The nobility, of course. And the military. She expresses a variety of opinions on a variety of subjects. If some people in public life were acquainted with Mrs. Wititterly's real opinion of them, they would not hold their heads, perhaps, quite as high as they do.

MRS. WITITTERLY: Hush, Henry, this is scarcely fair.

MR. WITITTERLY: I mention no names, Julia. And nobody is

injured. It is to show that you are no ordinary person, and that you must be soothed and tenderly. [*to* KATE] We will give you an answer, Miss Nickleby within two days. Alphonse, show the ladies out.

ALPHONSE: Yes, siree.

[*The* SERVANT *leads* KATE *and her mother out of the room.*]

BLACKOUT

There are different speech rhythms in this scene; Mrs. Wititterly's is slow and languishing, Mrs. Nickleby's is nervous and chatty, Kate's is even and controlled.

* * *

FEAR

JONAS TRIES TO ESCAPE

From the novel *MARTIN CHUZZLEWIT*

CHARACTERS: **JONAS:** surly son of a stingy father.

MERCY: his unhappy wife.

SETTING: On a dock.

SUMMARY:

Suspecting that the conniving Montague knows his secret [that Jonas has given pills to his father to cause his death] Jonas dons a disguise and tries to escape. But Jonas sees Montague and realizes that he has been spotted. He looks wildly about for his wife, Mercy.

JONAS: [*in great fear*] Where's that woman!

[*He sees* MERCY *lingering behind him.*]

JONAS: Come here! Come here!

[JONAS *drags* MERCY *to his side.*]

MERCY: [*pale and frightened*] Where are we going? What's the matter? What is it? Good heaven, what is it? Why did you tell me last night to prepare for a long journey, and why are we rushing like criminals? Jonas, be merciful. Whatever this dreadful secret is, be merciful.

JONAS: Hold your tongue, damn you, keep with me, don't question me, or I'll be the death of you!

MERCY: [*unable to suppress her sobs*] Jonas, you are hurting me!

[JONAS *thrusts her ahead of him. She stumbles. He drags her away.*]

BLACKOUT

As I wrote in the chapter on working from the body, Mercy's panting causes her hysteria, and Jonas' wild searching for Montague magnifies his fear.

* * *

WHAT MR. WICKFIELD HAS BECOME

From the novel *DAVID COPPERFIELD*

CHARACTERS:	**AUNT BETSEY:** an honest, no-nonsense woman.
	DAVID: her nephew, generous to most people but resistant to Uriah.
	AGNES: Mr. Wickfield's caring daughter.
	MR. WICKFIELD: a secret alcoholic.
	URIAH HEEP: a conniving, manipulative man who hides his self-aggrandizing plans under a cloak of humbleness.
SETTING:	David's chambers.

SUMMARY:

Mr. Wickfield, an honest business man, has been terribly compromised by Uriah Heep. Heep has discovered Mr. Wickfield's weakness for drinking and has been plying him with liquor. Heep has led Mr. Wickfield to think that he can't do without him. It is painful to those already in the room to see Uriah in a position of power and to note how Mr. Wickfield has submitted himself to someone as loathsome as Uriah Heep.

[MR. WICKFIELD *and* URIAH HEEP *enter the room where* AUNT BETSEY, AGNES *and* DAVID *are waiting for* MR. WICKFIELD.]

AGNES: Papa! Here is Miss Trotwood - and David, whom you have not seen for a long while!

[*As* MR. WICKFIELD *shakes hands with* AUNT BETSEY *and* DAVID, URIAH *manages a smile that is not a smile but two long creases on either side of his closed mouth.*

AUNT BETSEY: [*breaking the silence*] Well, Wickfield! I have been telling your daughter how well I have been disposing of my money for myself, because I couldn't trust it to you, as you were growing rusty in business matters. [addressing Uriah] Hmmf! And how do you find yourself, sir?

URIAH: I am pretty well, thank you, ma'am. I hope you are the same. And you, Master - I should say, Mister Copperfield, I hope I see you well! I am rejoiced to see you, Mister Copperfield.

[URIAH *awkwardly shakes* DAVID*'s hand.*]

URIAH: [*fawning*] And how do you think we are looking, Master Copperfield, - I should say, Mister?   Don't you find Mr. Wickfield blooming?   Years don't tell much in our firm, Master Copperfield, except in raising up the humble, namely, mother and self - and in developing, the beautiful, namely, Miss Agnes.

[URIAH *is jerking and writhing as he insinuates himself into the group so that* AUNT BETSEY *loses her patience.*]

AUNT BETSEY: What is the matter with this man? Don't be galvanic!

URIAH: I ask your pardon, Miss Trotwood, I'm aware you're nervous.

AUNT BETSEY: I am nothing of the sort. If you're an eel, conduct yourself like one. If you're a man, control your limbs! Good God! I am not going to be serpentined and corkscrewed out of my senses!

URIAH: [*abashed, he speaks to* DAVID *meekly*] I am well aware, Master Copperfield, that Miss Trotwood, though an excellent lady, has a quick temper. I only called to say that if there was anything we could do, in present circumstances, mother or self, or Wickfield and Heep, we should be really glad. [He smiles sickly to his partner] I may go so far?

MR. WICKFIELD: [*in a monotonous forced tone*] Uriah Heep is active in the business, David. What he says, I quite concur in. What Uriah says I quite concur in!

URIAH: [*trying not to fidget*] Oh, what a reward it is, to be so trusted! But I hope I am able to do something to relieve him from the fatigues of business, Master Copperfield!

MR. WICKFIELD: [*in the same dull voice*] Uriah Heep is a great relief to me. It's a load off my mind, David, to have such a partner.

[URIAH *smiles in his ugly fashion and watches* DAVID.]

AGNES: Papa, will you not walk back with David and me?

[MR. WICKFIELD *is about to look to* URIAH *for permission.*]

URIAH: [*anticipating him*] I leave my partner to represent the firm. Miss Agnes, ever yours! I wish you good-day, Master Copperfield, and leave my humble respects for Miss Betsey Trotwood.

[*Leering at the group until his face is like a mask,* URIAH *kisses his hand and leaves the room.*]

BLACKOUT

Agnes seems rarely to have anything to do when she is in a scene. She can actually do a great deal by controlling her breathing as she watches her father. When Uriah refers to her, she can feel revolted but she must control her body and not let her feelings show. Aunt Betsey never checks her responses. David controls himself admirably. Mr. Wickfield has muted himself into as monotonously few sentences as possible.

* * *

SMIKE DIES

From the novel *NICHOLAS NICKLEBY*

CHARACTERS: **SMIKE:** ill-begotten, nearly a slave at the Dotheboys school, rescued by Nicholas.

NICHOLAS: a true friend to Smike.

SETTING: A place in the country.

SUMMARY:

Ralph Nickleby's scheme is to send Smike, whom he doesn't actually know, back to the Dotheboys school. To avoid the authorities, Nicholas and Smike must get away. With Smike's death imminent and in the hope of easing his suffering, Nicholas has taken him to a little place in the country where no one can find them. On this day, Nicholas has carried Smike out and laid him on a couch to see the sunset. Nicholas is dozing by his side when he is aroused by Smike's scream of terror.

SMIKE: [*trembling*] Help, Nicholas, help me!

NICHOLAS: What is it? Have you been dreaming?

SMIKE: [*clinging to* NICHOLAS] No, no, no! Hold me tight. Don't let me go. There —there — behind the tree!

NICHOLAS: There is nothing there. Nothing.

SMIKE: There is. Was. I saw as plain as I see now. Say you'll keep me with you — swear you won't leave me!

NICHOLAS: I'm here. I swear I won't leave you. What was it?

SMIKE: [*in a low voice and fearful*] Do you remember, do you remember my telling you of the man who first took me to the school?

NICHOLAS: Yes, surely.

SMIKE: Just now, that tree, there with his eyes fixed on me, he stood!

NICHOLAS: If it is likely he is alive and wandering about a lonely place like this, do you think, from so long ago, you could possibly know that man again?

SMIKE: Anywhere. Just now, he stood leaning on his stick and looking at me, exactly as I remembered him. The wet night, his face when he left me, the parlor I was left in, and the people that were there, all come back together. When he knew I saw him, he started, and shrunk away. I think of him by day, and dream of him by night.

NICHOLAS: Be at peace. I am here and I won't leave your side.

[SMIKE *settles down and closes his eyes. A few minutes pass.* SMIKE *opens his eyes and puts his arm around* NICHOLAS.]

SMIKE: I shall soon be there. I am not afraid to die.

NICHOLAS: Let me hear you say you are happy.

SMIKE: I must tell you something, first. I should not have a secret from you. [*he draws* NICHOLAS *closer*] You will forgive me; I could not help it, but I would have died to make her happy...

NICHOLAS: [*whispers*] Kate.

SMIKE: [*growing more feeble, points to his chest*] I have a lock of her hair and her ribbons. When I am dead, Nicholas, take it off so that no one sees it. When I am laid in my coffin, hang it around my neck again so it is with me in my grave.

NICHOLAS: [*on his knees*] I promise you I'll do it.

[NICHOLAS *and* SMIKE *embrace and kiss each other.* NICHOLAS *holds* SMIKE*'s hand.*]

SMIKE: Now, I am happy.

BLACKOUT

Unable to believe that Smike has seen a man from so long ago, Nicholas questions him very gently. As Smike, when you feel the breath leaving the body, the torso getting narrower, make an effort to speak clearly. That effort combined with your lack of breath, will make you feeble.

* * *

DENNIS THE COWARD IN PRISON WITH HUGH

From the novel *BARNABY RUDGE*

CHARACTERS: DENNIS: a rioter and former hangman now in prison to be hanged.

A JAILOR

HUGH: a rioter, captured and brought to prison because of Dennis' treachery.

SETTING: Hugh's prison cell

SUMMARY:

Dennis, a leader in the Protestant riots against the Catholics, knows when it is time to change sides. To insure his own safety, he points out his former comrades to the military. But he does not escape the law and he too is taken to Newgate jail. Hugh, an attractive but savage type who lost his mother to hanging when he was six, has lived alone all these years. He became a rioter because he had nothing better to do. He has been fingered by Dennis and is now in jail, waiting to be hanged. As we see later in the scene, Dennis was the executioner of Hugh's mother.

Dennis and the Jailor are outside a cell. Dennis is convincing himself that the good hangman he formerly was will certainly help to get him a reprieve. Dennis behaves with nonchalance and sees himself as a member of the jailor's club.

DENNIS: [*to the* JAILOR] I know these corridors well. The government has often praised me for the work I did.

JAILOR: So it's said. We'll see before long which end of the rope...

DENNIS: [*assuming a nonchalant air*] Hush, none of your jailor nonsense talk, Brother. Where are you taking me? Am I going to be rooming along with anybody? I don't object to company, Brother. I rather like company.

JAILOR: That's rather a pity, ain't it? Being cut off in your flower, you know—

DENNIS: Don't talk. Who's a-going to be cut off in their flowers?

JAILOR: I thought you was, perhaps.

[DENNIS'S *face grows very hot.*]

DENNIS: [*in a tremulous voice*] You've always been fond of your joke, I remember that. [*he changes the subject with a laugh*] This is my quarters, is it?

JAILOR: This is the shop, sir.

[DENNIS, *trying to hold on to his casual unworried air, steps inside the cell. He stops and starts back*]

DENNIS: [*greatly alarmed, whispers*] Shut the door. [*whispering*] I can't go in there. I can't be shut up with that man. Do you want me to be throttled, Brother?

JAILOR: I got my orders.

[*He pushes* DENNIS *into the cell and locks the door.* DENNIS *stands trembling with his back against the door. He involuntarily raises his arm as though to defend himself. He stares at a sleeping man. The man is breathing deeply in his heavy sleep. Seeming to wake, the man rolls over on one side, his arm falls down, he murmurs something and falls fast asleep again.*]

[DENNIS *looks around the cell for a place to position himself. He steals on tiptoe to get behind a heavy chair.*]

[DENNIS *stands, looking cautiously over the back of the chair, watching the sleeper with vigilance and caution. The sleeping man is* HUGH *whom he has betrayed. Tired of standing, he crouches down in his corner and rests on the cold floor of the cell.* DENNIS *is so afraid of* HUGH *that every now and then he has to make sure that he won't be attacked by surprise.* DENNIS *rises stealthily and stretches out his neck to peer at the sleeping* HUGH *to assure himself that he is really asleep. After a while, the sleeper turns, sighs, and lazily opens his eyes.*]

[HUGH'*s face is turned directly towards the newcomer. It takes a few seconds for* HUGH *to recognize* DENNIS.]

HUGH: [*jumping up*] Damn you, Dennis!

DENNIS: [*dodging behind the chair*] Keep off, Brother, keep off! Don't do me a mischief. I'm a prisoner like you. I'm an old man. [*whining*] Don't hurt me!

HUGH: [*checks himself*] Get up. You.

DENNIS: I'll get up certainly, Brother. [he stands] I'm up now. What can I do for you? Only say the word, and I'll do it.

HUGH: [*clutching and shaking him by the collar*] What can you do for me! What have you done for me?

DENNIS: The best.

[HUGH *shakes* DENNIS *until his teeth chatter and then, in disgust, throws him to the floor.*]

HUGH: [*flinging himself down on his bench*] If it wasn't for the comfort it is to me, to see you here, also, I'd have crushed your head.

DENNIS: [*whining*] I was forced with two bayonets and I don't know how many bullets on each side of me, to point you out. If you hadn't been taken, you'd have been shot; a fine young man like you!

HUGH: I know you expected to get something by it, or you wouldn't have done it. But it's done, and you're here, and it will soon be all over with both of us. Why should I trouble myself to have revenge on you? To eat, and drink, and sleep, is all I care for.

[HUGH *stretches himself out on his bench once more and closes his eyes.* DENNIS *creeps over to him.*]

DENNIS: Well said, Brother. We'll eat and drink of the best. Anything can be got for money.

HUGH: Where do you find the money?

DENNIS: You must look up your friends – or your relations...

HUGH: [*laughing*] He talks of friends to me — talks of relations to a man whose mother died the death in store for her son, and left him, a hungry brat, without a face he knew in all the world!

DENNIS: [*changes color*] Your mother...you mean...

HUGH: I mean, they hung her up at Tyburn. What was good enough for her, is good enough for me. Say no more to me. I'm going to sleep.

DENNIS: But tell me...

HUGH: [*growling*] Hold your tongue. I told you I'm going to sleep.

DENNIS: I..I..must know...

[HUGH *swipes angrily at* DENNIS, *misses, and then turns to the wall to sleep.*]

BLACKOUT

See the chapter on Body Over Mind for comments on this scene.

* * *

DAVID GOES HOME FOR THE HOLIDAYS

From the novel *DAVID COPPERFIELD*

CHARACTERS: DAVID COPPERFIELD: a young boy in this scene. He can't seem to find the behavior that will suit Mr. Murdstone, his new stepfather.

MR. MURDSTONE: a cruel and exacting man.

MISS MURDSTONE: Mr. Murdstone's sister who carries out Mr. Murdstone's wishes with a vengeance.

SETTING: The living room of David's mother, Clara Copperfield Murdstone.

SUMMARY:

Hounded by Mr. Murdstone the last time he was at home, David bit him on the thumb. He was sent away to school. Now he is home for his vacation. It is difficult for David to greet Mr. Murdstone, who shows no sign of recognizing him.

DAVID: I beg your pardon, sir. I am very sorry for what I did, and I hope you will forgive me.

MR. MURDSTONE: [*with a sinister expression*] I am glad to hear you are sorry, David.

DAVID: [*extending his hand to* MISS MURDSTONE] How do you do, ma'am?

MISS MURDSTONE: [*offering the tea caddy scoop instead of her hand*] Dear me! How long are the holidays?

DAVID: A month, ma'am.

MISS MURDSTONE: Counting from when?

DAVID: From today, ma'am.

MISS MURDSTONE: Oh! Then here's one day off.

[MISS MURDSTONE *has a calendar near her. She checks one day off.*]

MR. MURDSTONE: David, I am sorry to observe that you are still of a sullen disposition.

MISS MURDSTONE: As sulky as a bear!

[DAVID *hangs his head.*]

MR. MURDSTONE: Now, David, a sullen obdurate disposition is, of all tempers, the worst. You must endeavor to change it. We must endeavor to change it for you.

DAVID: I beg your pardon, sir, I have never meant to be sullen since I came back.

MR. MURDSTONE: [*fiercely*] Don't take refuge in a lie, you! You have withdrawn yourself in your sullenness to your own room. You have kept your own room when you ought to have been in the parlor with us here. You know now, once for all, that I require you to be here, and not there. Further, that I require you to be obedient here. You know me, David. I will have it done.

[MISS MURDSTONE *gives a hoarse chuckle.*]

MR. MURDSTONE: I will have you be respectful and prompt towards myself and towards my sister, Jane Murdstone. I will not have this room shunned as if it were infected at the pleasure of a child. Sit down.

[MR. MURDSTONE *commands* DAVID *to sit down, and* DAVID *obeys like a dog.*]

MR. MURDSTONE: One thing more - you are not to associate with servants. I mean Mrs. Peggotty. I disapprove of your preferring such company. Now, David, you understand me, and you know what will be the consequence if you fail to obey me to the letter.

BLACKOUT

In the chapter *Body Before Mind* I talk about breathing techniques for the Murdstones.

HUMOR

THE SMALLWEEDS

From the novel *BLEAK HOUSE*

CHARACTERS:

GRANDFATHER SMALLWEED: a shrewd little old man.

GRANDMOTHER SMALLWEED: as close to a parrot as a human being can be.

THE TWIN GRANDCHILDREN: Judy and Bart Smallweed are chips off the family block.

CHARLEY: a servant.

SETTING:

The Smallweed lodging.

SUMMARY:

AN INTRODUCTION TO THE SMALLWEED FAMILY.
Dickens describes the members of the Smallweed family as bearing a likeness to old monkeys with something depressing on their minds. Seated in two chairs, one on each side of the fire-place, the superannuated Mr. and Mrs. Smallweed while away the rosy hours. Under the venerable Mr. Smallweed's seat and guarded by his spindle legs is a drawer reported to contain property worth a fabulous amount. Beside him is a spare cushion which he throws at his venerable partner whenever she makes an allusion to money — a subject on which he is particularly sensitive. Note: The man referred to as George owes Grandfather Smallweed money. He makes makes regular payments, but Mr. Smallweed plans to call in the note for a sum of money that George will not be able to pay. It's not until the end of the scene when Grandfather Smallweed speaks of liming George that the plot actually moves along. The beginning of the scene is used to show a day in the life of the Smallweeds. Grandmother making sounds that we might hear in an aviary; Grandfather barely putting up with her; Judy, tightlipped and old before her time; brother Bart given mostly to gestures and few words.

GRANDFATHER SMALLWEED: [*to his granddaughter,* JUDY] And where's Bart?

JUDY: He ain't come in yet.

GRANDFATHER SMALLWEED: It's his tea-time, isn't it?

JUDY: No.

GRANDFATHER SMALLWEED: How soon will it be?

JUDY: Ten minutes.

GRANDFATHER SMALLWEED: Hey?

JUDY: TEN MINUTES.

GRANDFATHER SMALLWEED: Ho! Ten minutes.

[GRANDMOTHER SMALLWEED *has been mumbling and shaking her head.*]

GRANDMOTHER SMALLWEED: [*screeching like a parrot*] Ten, ten-pound notes!

[GRANDFATHER SMALLWEED *immediately throws a cushion at her.*]

GRANDFATHER SMALLWEED: Drat you, be quiet!

[*This bounces* MRS. SMALLWEED's *head against the side of her chair and knocks her cap to the side.* MR. SMALLWEED's *exertion throws him back into his chair like a broken puppet.* JUDY *straightens* GRANDMOTHER *up and then shakes and pokes and punches* GRANDFATHER SMALLWEED *until he sits up in his chair.*]

[JUDY, *with a clash and clatter, sets one of the tea-trays on the table and arranges cups and saucers. She puts bread and very little butter on a small plate.*]

GRANDFATHER SMALLWEED: Where's the girl?

JUDY: Charley, do you mean?

GRANDFATHER SMALLWEED: Hey?

JUDY: CHARLEY, DO YOU MEAN?

GRANDMOTHER SMALLWEED: [*chuckling and energetic*] Over the water! Charley over the water, Charley over the water, over the water to Charley, Charley over the water, over the water to Charley!

[GRANDFATHER SMALLWEED *would like to throw the pillow at her but has not recovered full strength.*]

GRANDFATHER SMALLWEED: [*when silence is restored*] Ha! If that's her name. She eats a deal. It would be better to make her pay.

[JUDY *shakes her head and purses up her mouth into NO.*]

GRANDFATHER SMALLWEED: No? Why not?

JUDY: We can do it for less.

GRANDFATHER SMALLWEED: Sure?

[JUDY *nods. She scrapes a thin layer of butter on bread.*]

JUDY: You, Charley, where are you?

[*A little girl in a rough apron appears and curtseys.*]

JUDY: What work are you about now?

CHARLEY: I'm a-cleaning the upstairs back room, miss.

JUDY: Mind you do it thoroughly, and don't loiter. Shirking won't do for me. Go along! You girls are more trouble than you're worth.

[*Brother Bart appears.*]

GRANDFATHER SMALLWEED: Bart! Here you are, hey?

BART: Here I am.

GRANDFATHER SMALLWEED: Been along with your friend again, Bart?

[BART *nods*.]

GRANDFATHER SMALLWEED: Eating with him at his expense, Bart?

[BART *nods*.]

GRANDFATHER SMALLWEED: That's right. Live at his expense as much as you can, and take Warning by his foolish example. That's the use of such a friend. The only use you can put him to.

[*His grandson, honors it with a slight wink and a nod and takes a chair at the tea-table. The four old faces hover over their teacups like a company of ghastly cherubim.* GRANDMOTHER SMALLWEED *twitches and chatters.*]

GRANDFATHER SMALLWEED: Shake me up again, once again. Ah, yes, yes, that's such advice as your father would have given you, Bart. You never saw your father. More's the pity. He was my true son, a good accountant, and died fifteen years ago.

GRANDMOTHER SMALLWEED: Fifteen hundred pound. Fifteen hundred pound in a black box, fifteen hundred pound locked up, fifteen hundred pound put away and hid!

[GRANDFATHER SMALLWEED *discharges the cushion at* GRAND- MOTHER SMALLWEED *crushing her against the side of her chair; he falls back in his chair, overpowered.*]

GRANDFATHER SMALLWEED: [*having recovered*] If your father, Bart, had lived longer, he might have been worth a deal of money — you chatterer...you magpie — but he took ill and died of a low fever,— always being a sparing and a spare man — I should like to throw a cat at you instead of a cushion, and I will too if you make such a confounded fool of yourself! — and your mother, who was a prudent woman as dry as a chip, just dwindled away like touchwood after you and Judy were born – you are an old pig!

[JUDY *collects the unfinished tea from the bottoms of the cups and picks up fragments and worn-down heels of bread for the servant girl's meal.*]

JUDY: Now, if everybody has done, I'll have that girl in to her tea. She would never leave off if she took it by herself in the kitchen.

[CHARLEY *comes in and, under the family's eyes, sits down to her bread and tea.*]

JUDY: Now, don't stare about you all the afternoon. Take your victuals and get back to work.

CHARLEY: Yes, miss.

JUDY: Don't say yes for I know what you girls are. Do it without saying it, and then I may begin to believe you.

[*There is a knock at the door.*]

JUDY: [*to* CHARLEY] See who it is, and don't chew when you open the door!

[CHARLEY *goes to the door without finishing her meal.*]

JUDY: Now! Who is it, and what's wanted?

GRANDFATHER SMALLWEED: [*making a hideous face*] It's George. That damned rogue! I'll lime him this time, that dog, I'll lime him!

BLACKOUT

Judy can have a habit, perhaps, of biting the inside of her lip, which can screw her face up all through the scene. Grandmother can hardly keep her head up, which will give her an imbecilic look. Grandfather can look sideways at whoever talks to him. Brother Bart can hook his thumbs onto his vest and pat himself from time to time.

* * *

ESTHER RELEASES MR. GUPPY FROM HIS PROPOSAL OF MARRIAGE

From the novel *BLEAK HOUSE*

CHARACTERS:	**ESTHER SUMMERSON:** has discovered that she is the illegitimate daughter of Lady Dedlock and must keep that secret.
	MR. GUPPY: in love with Esther.
SETTING:	Mr. Guppy's home.

SUMMARY:

Thinking that Esther was a governess and of his social class, Mr. Guppy, a lowly law clerk, at one time proposed marriage. Having remarked that Esther's resemblance to Lady Dedlock is very strong, he has been poking into Lady Dedlock's affairs and has offered his help to Esther in the hope of finding out something that may be of value to her. But Esther has come to ask Mr. Guppy to stop prying. Esther is wearing a veil, her face disfigured by a case of smallpox from which she has recently recovered. She is ushered into the parlor by Mr. Guppy.

MR. GUPPY: Miss, this is indeed an oasis.

[*He calls to his mother who is eavesdropping outside the room.*]

MR. GUPPY: Mother, will you be so good as to get out of the gangway.

ESTHER: I took the liberty of sending you a note.

[MR. GUPPY *takes the note out of his pocket, puts it to his lips and then back into his pocket, holding his hand over his heart. When* ESTHER *puts up her veil,* GUPPY *is shocked to see her pock-marked face.*]

ESTHER: I asked the favor of seeing you for a few moments, remembering what you said when you spoke to me in confidence, Mr.Guppy.

[MR. GUPPY *falters in confusion and apprehension. His hand grows limp over his heart. After a moment, he gathers his wits.*]

MR. GUPPY: Miss, I—I—beg your pardon, but in our profession— we—we—find it necessary to be explicit. You have referred to an occasion, Miss, when I...when I did myself the honor of making a declaration which...

[MR. GUPPY *coughs and begins to choke.*]

MR. GUPPY: [*continues*] A kind of giddy sensation has come upon me, miss. It rather knocks me over. My intention was to remark, Miss...[he coughs]...something bronchial, I think...[he clears his throat] I..uh...mean to remark that you was so good on that occasion as to repel and repudiate that declaration. You...you wouldn't perhaps object to admit that? Though no witnesses are present, it might be a satisfaction to...uh...to your mind...if you was to put in that admission.

ESTHER: There can be no doubt, that I declined your proposal without any reservation, Mr. Guppy.

MR. GUPPY: Thank you, miss, so far that's satisfactory, and it does you credit. Er—this is certainly bronchial!- must be in the tubes...er...you wouldn't perhaps be offended if I was to mention...not that it's necessary, for your own good sense to men-

tion that such declaration on my part was final, and there terminated?

ESTHER: I quite understand that.

MR. GUPPY: Perhaps—er—it may not be worth the form, but it is
satisfaction to your mind—perhaps you wouldn't object to
admit that, Miss?

ESTHER: I admit it most fully and freely.

MR. GUPPY: Thank you. Very honorable, I am sure. I regret that
my arrangements in life, combined with circumstances over
which I have no control, will put it out of my power ever to
fall back upon that offer or to renew it in any shape or form
whatever, but it will ever be a retrospect entwined...er ...with
friendship's bowers.

[MR. GUPPY's *bronchitis takes over.*]

ESTHER: I may now perhaps mention what I wished to say to you?

MR. GUPPY: I shall be honored, I am sure. I am so persuaded that
your own good sense and right feeling, Miss, will...uh...will
keep you as square as possible...that I can have nothing but
pleasure, I am sure, in hearing any observations you may wish
to offer.

ESTHER: You were so good as to imply, on that occasion...

MR. GUPPY: Excuse me, miss, but we had better not travel out of
the record into implication. I cannot admit that I implied
anything.

ESTHER: You said on that occasion, that you might have the
means of promoting my fortunes by certain discoveries. You
founded that belief upon your knowledge of my being an
orphan girl. What I have come to beg of you is, Mr. Guppy,

that you will have the kindness to relinquish all idea of so serving me.

MR. GUPPY: Nothing can be more satisfactory than such a right feeling, and if I mistook any intentions on your part just now, I am prepared to tender a full apology. I hereby offer that apology - limiting it to the present proceedings.

ESTHER: I come to you as privately as possible because you spoke to me in confidence...

MR. GUPPY: [*ashamed but very earnest*] Upon my word and honor, upon my life, upon my soul, as I am a living man, I'll act according to your wish! I'll take my oath to it if it will be any satisfaction to you, I speak the truth, the whole truth, and nothing but the truth, so...

ESTHER: I am quite satisfied, and I thank you very much.

[ESTHER *prepares to leave.* MR. GUPPY *stands staring, his mouth has fallen open, his eyes are glazed.*]

MR. GUPPY: [*suddenly awake and fervent*] Upon my honor and soul, you may depend on me!

ESTHER: I do. Most assuredly.

[ESTHER *leaves.*]

MR. GUPPY: [running outside after Esther] I beg your pardon, miss. Could we repeat our agreement. It is lacking in specifics, you see - not allowable in a court of...

ESTHER: Of course. So that it is perfectly clear, I shall repeat it: There never has been any engagement -

MR. GUPPY: No proposal or promise of marriage whatsoever.

ESTHER: No proposal or promise of marriage whatsoever.

MR. GUPPY: Between William Guppy, of Penton Place, Pentonville, in the county of Middlesex, if you don't mind, Miss.

ESTHER: Not at all, between you, Mr. William Guppy, of Penton Place, Pentonville, in the county of Middlesex, and myself.

MR. GUPPY: Thank you, thank you, Miss.

[MR. GUPPY *turns and starts towards his house. He turns and runs back again.*]

MR. GUPPY: [*forlorn and despondent*] Touching that matter, you know, I really and truly am very sorry that my arrangements in life, over which I have no control, should prevent a renewal of what was wholly terminated some time back. But it couldn't be. Nor could it, you know! I only put it to you.

ESTHER: It certainly could not.

[MR. GUPPY *sadly agrees. He turns towards his house. Another thought sends him running back to* ESTHER *again.*]

MR. GUPPY: It's very honorable of you, Miss. If an altar could be erected in the bowers of friendship – but, upon my soul, you may rely upon me in every respect - [*he coughs*] save and except the tender passion only!

[ESTHER *is finally on her way.* MR. GUPPY *is still muttering and moving back and forth. He is struggling with the immense burden of legal rightness and relief at having been spared a marriage to a lady with a pock marked face.*]

BLACKOUT

Mr. Guppy's smile might fade slowly as he sees Esther. As his mouth falls open, it could start his choking. Esther remains serene throughout her visit with Mr. Guppy, while he struggles to come to grips with his narrow escape. Once   Esther leaves, the actor playing Mr. Guppy must have some knowledge of the law to mumble to himself.

MR. GUPPY PROPOSES AGAIN

From the novel *BLEAK HOUSE*

CHARACTERS:	**MR. GUPPY:** in love with Esther Summerson.
	ESTHER SUMMERSON: has rejected Mr. Guppy once and is prepared to reject him again.
	MR. JARNDYCE: Esther's fond employer.
	MRS. GUPPY: a proud mother.
	MR. JOBLING: a boyhood friend of Mr. Guppy.
SETTING:	Drawing room at Bleak House.

SUMMARY:

Mr. Guppy was a lowly law clerk who wavered in a previous proposal of marriage to the once beautiful Esther Summerson. Her loss of looks is due to the terrible effects of the smallpox. Upon passing his examinations, Mr. Guppy has changed his mind and come with his mother and a friend to try his suit again. Mr. Guppy does his best, but it is not good enough. Between his winking, jostling mother, his sullen friend, and the presence of Esther's employer, Mr. Jarndyce, Mr. Guppy does not stand a chance to make his case with Esther.

MR. GUPPY: [*embarrassed to find* MR. JARNDYCE *present*] Uh…How de do?

MR. JARNDYCE: How do you do?

MR. GUPPY: Thank you, I am tolerable. Will you allow me to introduce my mother, Mrs. Guppy of the Old Street Road, and my particular friend, Mr.Jobling.

MR. JARNDYCE: Please be seated.

[*The visitors sit.*]

MR. GUPPY: [*after an awkward silence*] Tony, will you open the case?

MR. JOBLING: Do it yourself.

MR. GUPPY: Well, Mr. Jarndyce, I had an idea that I should see Miss Summerson by herself and was not quite prepared for your esteemed presence. But Miss Summerson has mentioned to you, perhaps, that something has passed between us on former occasions?

[MR. GUPPY'*s mother is delighted with her son's presentation. She nudges* JOBLING *with her elbow and blinks and winks at* ESTHER.]

MR. JARNDYCE: Miss Summerson has said something to me, yes.

MR. GUPPY: That makes matters easier. Sir, I have come out of my examinations, and I believe with satisfaction to all parties. I am now admitted (after undergoing an examination that's enough to badger a man blue) I am admitted on the roll of attorneys and have taken out my certificate, if it would be any satisfaction to you to see it.

MR. JARNDYCE: Thank you, Mr. Guppy. I am quite willing — I believe I use a legal phrase — to admit the certificate.

[MR. GUPPY *puts the proffered certificate back in his pocket.*]

MR. GUPPY: I have no capital myself, but my mother has a little property which takes the form of an annuity...

[MRS. GUPPY *rolls her head happily, puts her handkerchief to her mouth, and winks at* ESTHER.]

MR. GUPPY: [*continues*] and a few pounds for expenses out of pocket in conducting business will never be wanting, free of interest, which is an advantage, you know.

MR. JARNDYCE: Certainly an advantage.

MR. GUPPY: I have some connection, and it lays in the direction of Walcot Square, Lambeth. I have therefore taken a house in that locality, which, in the opinion of my friends, is a hollow bargain [taxes ridiculous, and use of fixtures included in the rent], and intend setting up professionally for myself there forthwith.

[MR. GUPPY'*s mother begins to roll her head with extroadinary energy, smiling waggishly at anybody who looks at her.*]

MR. GUPPY: [*continues*] It's a six-roomer, exclusive of kitchens, and in the opinion of my friends, a commodious dwelling. When I mention my friends, I refer principally to my friend Jobling, who I believe has known me, from boyhood's hour.

[MR. JOBLING *confirms this by shifting his weight*].

MR. GUPPY: My friend Jobling will render me his assistance in the capacity of clerk and will live in the house. My mother will likewise live in the house; and consequently there will be no want of society. My friend Jobling is naturally aristocratic by taste, and besides being acquainted with the movements of the upper circles, fully backs me in the intentions I am now developing.

MR. JOBLING: [*avoiding* MRS. GUPPY'*s elbow*] Certainly.

MR. GUPPY: Now, I have no occasion to mention to you, sir, you being in the confidence of Miss Summerson… [Mother, I wish you'd be so good as to keep still], that Miss Summerson's image was formerly imprinted on my heart and that I made her a proposal of marriage.

MR. JARNDYCE: That I have heard.

MR. GUPPY: Circumstances over which I had no control, but quite the contrary, weakened the impression of that image for a time. At which time Miss Summerson's conduct was highly genteel; I may even add, magnanimous.

[MR. JARNDYCE *pats* ESTHER *on the shoulder*].

MR. GUPPY: Now, sir, I have got into that state of mind myself that I wish for a reciprocity of magnanimous behavior. I wish to prove to Miss Summerson that I can rise to a height of which perhaps she hardly thought me capable. I find that the image which I did suppose had been eradicated from my heart is not eradicated. Its influence over me is still tremenjous, and yielding to it, I am willing to overlook the circumstances over which none of us have had any control and to renew those proposals to Miss Summerson which I had the honor to make at a former period. I beg to lay the house in Walcot Square, the business, and myself before Miss Summerson for her acceptance.

MR. JARNDYCE: Very magnanimous indeed, sir.

MR. GUPPY: Well, sir, my wish is to be magnanimous. I do not consider that in making this offer to Miss Summerson I am by any means throwing myself away; neither is that the opinion of my friends.

MR. JARNDYCE: I take upon myself, sir, to reply to your proposals on behalf of Miss Summerson. She is very sensible of your handsome intentions, and wishes you good evening, and wishes you well.

MR. GUPPY: [*with a blank look*] Oh! Is that tantamount, sir, to acceptance, or rejection, or consideration?

MR. JARNDYCE: To decided rejection, if you please.

[MR. GUPPY *looks incredulously at his friend and at his mother.* MRS. GUPPY *turns very angry, looking at the floor and at the ceiling.*]

MR. GUPPY: Indeed? Then, Jobling, if you was the friend you represent yourself, I should think you might hand my mother out of the gangway instead of allowing her to remain where she ain't wanted.

[JOBLING *starts to help* MRS. GUPPY *up.*]

MRS. GUPPY: [*refusing to budge*] Why, get along with you. What do you mean? Ain't my son good enough for you? You ought to be ashamed of yourself. Get out with you!

MR. JARNDYCE: My good lady, it is hardly reasonable to ask me to get out of my own room.

MRS. GUPPY: I don't care for that. Get out with you. If we ain't good enough for you, go and procure somebody that is good enough. Go along and find 'em. Go along and find somebody that's good enough for you. Get out! Why don't you get out? What are you stopping here for?

MR. GUPPY: [*keeping her from* MR. JARNDYCE] Mother, will you hold your tongue?

MRS. GUPPY: No, William, I won't! Not unless he gets out, I won't!

[MR. GUPPY *and* MR. JOBLING *have to close in on* MRS.GUPPY. *They manage to get her out of the room.*]

MRS. GUPPY: [*offstage*] Let them go and find somebody who is good enough for them. Let them get out.

BLACKOUT

Esther sits serenely, Jobling is sullen, Mrs. Guppy is all eyes and elbows, Mr. Jarndyce listens politely, and Mr. Guppy sweats out his proposal which sounded so good when he presented himself before a mirror at home.

* * *

OLD MARTIN AND PECKSNIFF FIND EACH OTHER

From the novel *MARTIN CHUZZLEWIT*

CHARACTERS:

MARTIN CHUZZLEWIT: an old gentleman, suddenly ill, stops at an inn, won't see a doctor, and insists on sitting in a chair. Rigid and inflexible in his determination, he has greatly perplexed the landlady of the inn.

MARY GRAHAM: his companion is very young, reticent but self possessed, and in complete control of her emotions.

MRS. LUPIN: the good-natured lady who runs the inn.

MR. PECKSNIFF: A genteel hypocrite who has fooled many people (but not all.)

SETTING: Evening at the Inn.

SUMMARY:

The scene starts out soberly and rather grimly. Mary and Mrs. Lupin are standing quietly a short way off from the sickly old man.

MARY: Did you call me, Martin?

MARTIN: Call you? No. No. Why do you ask me? If I had called you, what need for such a question? You stand there, Mary, as if I had the plague! [turns away helplessly] They're all afraid of me, even she! There is a curse upon me. What else have I to look for?

MRS. LUPIN: Oh dear, no. Oh no, I'm sure. Be of better cheer, these are only sick fancies.

MARTIN: What are only sick fancies? What do you know about fancies? Who told you about fancies? The old story! Fancies!

MRS. LUPIN: Oh, how you take one up! Dear heart alive, there is no harm in the word. Folks in good health have their fancies, too, and strange ones, every day.

[MARTIN glares at MRS. LUPIN.]

MRS. LUPIN: Dear sir, there are none but friends here.

MARTIN: Oh! Why do you talk to me of friends! Can you or anybody teach me to know who are my friends, and who my enemies?

[MRS. LUPIN looks in great astonishment to MARY.]

MRS. LUPIN: At least, this young lady is your friend, I am sure.

MARTIN: She has no temptation to be otherwise. I suppose she is. Heaven knows.

[He begins to nod.]

[A step is heard in the entry. MR. PECKSNIFF looks sweetly into the room. MRS. LUPIN goes to greet him.]

MR. PECKSNIFF: [in a whisper] Good evening, Mrs. Lupin.

MRS. LUPIN: [drawing him into the room away from the old man's *chair*] Oh dear me! I am so very glad you have come.

MR. PECKSNIFF: And I am very glad I have come, if I can be of service. I am very glad I have come. What is the matter, Mrs. Lupin?

MRS. LUPIN: A gentleman taken ill on the road.

MR. PECKSNIFF: [*affably nodding his head*] A gentleman taken ill on the road, has he? Well, well! And how is he now?

MRS. LUPIN: He is better and tranquil now.

MR. PECKSNIFF: He is better and tranquil now. Very well! Ve-ry well!

MRS. LUPIN: There must be weighty matters on his mind, though, for he talks, sir, in the strangest way you ever heard. He is far from easy in his thoughts, and needs some proper advice.

MR. PECKSNIFF: [*murmuring*] Then, he is the sort of customer for me.

[PECKSNIFF *runs his fingers through his hair, places one hand gently in the bosom of his waist-coat, and walks to a large arm chair near the fire.* MARY *rises from her stool.*]

MR. PECKSNIFF: [*in a whisper*] Be not alarmed. I reside in this village — in an influential manner, however undeserved. I have been summoned here by this kindly lady, as I am everywhere, I hope, in sympathy for the sick and sorry. I will sit and wait his awakening.

[MARY *and* MRS. LUPIN *leave the room.*]

[*Still impressive,* PECKSNIFF *makes himself comfortable. He observes the patient. Gradually his hands tighten upon the arms of the chair, his eyes dilate with surprise, his mouth opens, his hair stands erect upon his forehead. The old man turns in his chair, opens his eyes, and stares at* PECKSNIFF *with horror.*]

MR. PECKSNIFF: You are Martin Chuzzlewit!

MARTIN: I am Martin Chuzzlewit and Martin Chuzzlewit wishes you had been hanged, before you had come here to disturb him in his sleep.

MR. PECKSNIFF: My good cousin...

MARTIN: [*throwing up his hands*] There! His very first words! In his very first words he asserts his relationship! I knew he would. They all do it! Near or distant, blood or water, it's all one. Ugh! What deceit and lying.

[*The old man falls back into his chair.*]

MR. PECKSNIFF: Mr. Chuzzlewit...

MARTIN: Go! Enough of this. I am weary.

MR. PECKSNIFF: I am sorry for that, sir.

[*He walks to the door.*]

MR. PECKSNIFF: [*turning to Old Martin*] Bless you for hating me. And good night! You will regret being hasty, I know you will.

BLACKOUT

See the chapter Body Over Mind, in which I talk about Pecksniff's behavior.

* * *

MR. PECKSNIFF GETS A LITTLE DRUNK

From the novel *MARTIN CHUZZLEWIT*

CHARACTERS: MR. PECKSNIFF: a hypocrite who has dropped his good manners for the moment.

MRS. TODGERS: has known Pecksniff for a long while.

CHARITY and MERCY: Mr. Pecksniff's snobbish daughters.

SETTING: The dining room at Todgers Inn.

SUMMARY:

The lodgers at Mrs. Todgers Inn have insisted on having a party. Mr. Pecksniff was happy to add his presence. The party over, all have gone except for Mr. Pecksniff who is sitting on a chair, his legs sprawled, looking dazedly at a coffee stain on his trousers and unaware that there is a bit of muffin on his knee. Mrs. Todgers comes into the room looking for Mr. Pecksniff with some concern..

MRS. TODGERS: And how have they behaved, Mr. Pecksniff?

MR. PECKSNIFF: Their conduct has been such, my dear madam, as I can never think of without emotion, or remember without a tear. Oh, Mrs. Todgers!

MRS. TODGERS: My goodness! How low you are in your spirits!

MR. PECKSNIFF: [*shedding tears and speaking rather imperfectly*] I am a man, my dear madam, but I am also a father. I am also a widower. My feelings, Mrs. Todgers, will not consent to be entirely smothered.

[MR. PECKSNIFF *suddenly becomes conscious of the bit of muffin and stares at it intently. He shakes his head forlornly; he and looks somewhat imbecilic.*]

MR. PECKSNIFF: She was beautiful, Mrs. Todgers. She had a small property.

MRS TODGERS: [*with great sympathy*] So I have heard.

MR. PECKSNIFF: [*with increasing emotion*] And her daughters, they were her daughters...

MRS. TODGERS: Oh, I have no doubt about it.

MR. PECKSNIFF: Mercy and Charity, Charity and Mercy. Not unholy names, I hope?

MRS. TODGERS: Mr. Pecksniff! What a ghastly smile! Are you ill?

[MR. PECKSNIFF *presses his hand upon* MRS. TODGERS *arm.*]

MR. PECKSNIFF: [*solemn and in a faint voice*] Chronic.

MRS. TODGERS: Cholic?!

MR. PECKSNIFF: Chron-ic. Chron-ic. A chronic disorder. I have been its victim from childhood. It is carrying me to my grave.

MRS. TODGERS: Heaven forbid!

MR. PECKSNIFF: Yes, it is. I am rather glad of it, upon the whole. You are like her, Mrs. Todgers.

[*His arm goes around her waist.*]

MRS. TODGERS: Don't squeeze me so tight, Mr. Pecksniff. If any of the gentlemen should happen to come in.

MR. PECKSNIFF: For her sake. Permit me. In honor of her memory. For the sake of a voice from the tomb. You are very like her Mrs. Todgers! What a world this is!

MRS. TODGERS: Ah! Indeed you may say that!

MR. PECKSNIFF: [*overflowing with despondency*] I'm afraid it is a vain and thoughtless world. These young people about us. Oh! what sense have they of their responsibilities? None. Give me your other hand, Mrs. Todgers.

MRS. TODGERS: [*hesitating*] I don't like...

MR. PECKSNIFF: [*with dismal tenderness*] Has a voice from the grave no influence? This is irreligious! My dear creature.

MRS. TODGERS: Hush! Really you mustn't...

MR. PECKSNIFF: [*his voice thick, husky, stuttering and drunk*] It's not me. Don't suppose it's me. It's the voice; from the grave. It has been a day of enjoyment, Mrs. Todgers, but still it has been a day of torture. It has reminded me of my loneliness. What am I in the world?

MRS. TODGERS: An excellent gentleman, Mr. Pecksniff.

MR. PECKSNIFF: There is consolation in that too. Am I?

MRS. TODGERS: There is no better man living, I am sure.

MR. PECKSNIFF: [*smiling through his tears*] Thank you. It is a great happiness to me, Mrs. Todgers, to make young people happy. The happiness of my pupils is my chief object. I dote upon 'em. They dote upon me too. Sometimes. [he whispers] When they say they haven't improved...[he motions her to bring her ear closer to his mouth] when they say they haven't improved, and the tuition was too high, they lie!

MRS. TODGERS: Base wretches they must be!

MR. PECKSNIFF: Madam, you are right. A word in your ear. This is in confidence, Mrs. Todgers?

MRS. TODGERS: The strictest, of course!

MR. PECKSNIFF: Do you know any parent or guardian, Mrs. Todgers, an orphan would be preferred, who would want this opportunity to be my student? Do you know of any orphan with a sum of money?

[MRS. TODGERS *reflects, and shakes her head no.*]

MR. PECKSNIFF: When you hear of an orphan with some money to…[he falls heavily against Mrs. Todgers] Let's have a little drop of something to drink.

[CHARITY *and* MERCY *enter looking for their pa.*]

MRS. TODGERS: Bless my life, Miss Pecksniffs! Your dear pa's took very poorly!

[MR. PECKSNIFF *straightens himself with a surprising effort; standing on his feet, he regards the ladies with a look of ineffable wisdom. Gradually it gives place to a smile — a feeble, helpless, melancholy smile, bland, almost to sickliness.*]

MR. PECKSNIFF: Do not weep for me. It is chronic.

[*His legs give way and he sprawls on the floor, pulling* MRS. TODGERS *down with him. He smiles serenely.*]

BLACKOUT

See the chapter *Body Over Mind* for more comments on Mr. Pecksniff.

* * *

MR. PECKSNIFF IS SNUBBED ON
THE GRAND SCALE

From the novel MARTIN CHUZZLEWIT

CHARACTERS:

MR. PECKSNIFF: a second rate architect who abuses his pupils in a genteel manner.

CHARITY: the elder of his two daughters.

MERCY: the younger and prettier daughter.

MRS. TODGERS: an innkeeper who has made friends with the snobbish daughters.

VOICE OF THE OWNER: a wealthy owner of the mansion.

SETTING:

Leaving the mansion.

SUMMARY:

Pecksniff's apprentice Tom Pinch has asked Mr. Pecksniff, as a great favor, to look in on his sister Ruth while he is in London. Ruth is a charming girl, governess in a wealthy family. Mr. Pecksniff would like the master of the house to hear him praising its architecture, to know that Pecksniff himself is "in architecture." The daughters take their leave of Ruth Pinch, whom they consider a nobody, with a reluctant curtsey. They flounce out the doors. Mr. Pecksniff and his party are standing in front of the mansion.

MR. PECKSNIFF: [*taking in the proportions of the exterior with great appreciation*] Ah, the exterior, my dears, if you look, if you look, at the cornice which supports the roof, and observe the airiness of its construction, especially where it sweeps the southern angle of the building, you will feel with me...[*He bows to a gentleman at an upper window*] How do you do, sir? I hope you're well?

[PECKSNIFF *feigns pointing out other remarkable aspects with his hand.*]

MR. PECKSNIFF: [*continues*] I have no doubt, my dears, that this is the proprietor. I should be glad to know him. It might lead to something. Is he looking this way, Charity?

CHARITY: He is opening the window, pa!

MR. PECKSNIFF: [*softly*] Ha, ha! All right! He has found I'm professional. He heard me inside just now, I have no doubt. Don't look! With regard to the fluted pillars in the portico, my dears...

VOICE OF THE OWNER: Hallo!

MR. PECKSNIFF: [*taking off his hat*] Sir, I am proud to make your acquaintance.

VOICE OF THE OWNER: Get off the grass, will you!

MR. PECKSNIFF: I...uh... beg your pardon, sir. Did you...?

VOICE OF THE OWNER: Get off the grass!

MR. PECKSNIFF: [*smiling*] We are unwilling to intrude, sir.

VOICE OF THE OWNER: Trespassing. You see a gravel walk, don't you? What do you think it's meant for?

[*The man of the house shuts the window and disappears.* MR. PECKSNIFF, *somewhat dazed, puts on his hat, manages a smile, and leads his daughters and* MRS. TODGERS *out of the garden. Out of earshot, the daughters burst into sounds of indignation.*]

CHARITY: This comes of cherishing such creatures as the Pinches.

MERCY: This comes of lowering ourselves to their level.

CHARITY: We put ourselves in the humiliating position of seeming to know such bold, audacious, cunning, dreadful girls as Ruth Pinch. We had expected this. We had predicted it to Mrs. Todgers, did we not, this very morning?

MRS. TODGERS: I distinctly remember.

CHARITY: The owner, supposing us to be Miss Pinch's friends, had acted, in my opinion, quite correctly. He has done no more than might reasonably be expected.

MERCY: [*breaking into tears*] He is a brute and a bear....

CHARITY: [*breaking into tears*] Oh, he is, he is.

MR. PECKSNIFF: A good action is its own reward.

CHARITY: Mrs. Todgers did not mean, I'm sure, to offend...

MERCY: Heavens no. But, my dear, handing your card to a servant, Mrs. Todgers...

MR. PECKSNIFF: Young ladies, we will all be the better for this adventure and find much to laugh over, I'm sure, at the vulgar rich.

MRS. TODGERS: [*twisting her handkerchief*] Oh, yes, my darlies, such vulgarities are best forgotten.

[*She fans herself.*]

BLACKOUT

See *Body Over Mind* for comments.

* * *

CHARITY - A WOMAN SCORNED

From the novel *MARTIN CHUZZLEWIT*

CHARACTERS:

MR. PECKSNIFF: his younger daughter having married, now Pecksniff has to endure living alone with the jilted Charity.

CHARITY PECKSNIFF: has plans to move from home, and better her chances to find a husband.

SETTING: Mr. Pecksniff's parlor

SUMMARY:

Jonas has led all the Pecksniff's to believe that he was courting the austere Charity.   Expectations were high but Jonas, in the crudest way thinkable, proposed to the younger, prettier sister, Mercy, instead.   Since then, Charity, stung by the insult which has festered in her heart, has forced her dear papa to lead a dog's life. Moreover, Charity is aware that papa is planning to marry the young Mary Graham for the money she will inherit from old Martin Chuzzlewit.

Father and daughter are alone in the parlor.   Here is a nice homey scene that ends up in a pushing and shoving match between father and daughter.   Observing the hostile Charity, with her nose very red and twisted up tight, Mr. Pecksniff screws up his courage.

MR. PECKSNIFF: Cherry, my dear girl, what has happened between us?   My child, why are we disunited?

CHARITY: Oh, bother, Pa!

MR. PECKSNIFF: Bother!

CHARITY: It is too late, Pa, to talk to me like this.   I know what it means, and what its value is.

MR. PECKSNIFF: [*addressing his coffee cup*] This is hard! This is very hard! She is my child. I carried her in my arms when she wore little knitted booties, many years ago!

CHARITY: You needn't taunt me with that, Pa. I am not so many years older than my sister, either, though she is married to your friend!

MR. PECKSNIFF: Ah, human nature. To think that this discord should arise from such a cause! Oh dear!

CHARITY: State the real cause, Pa, or I'll state it myself. Mind! I will!

MR. PECKSNIFF: [*changing to anger*] You will! You have. You did yesterday. You do always. You have no decency; you make no secret of your temper; you have exposed yourself to Mr. Chuzzlewit a hundred times.

CHARITY: Myself! Oh indeed! I don't mind that.

MR. PECKSNIFF: Me too, then. And since we have come to an explanation, Charity, let me tell you that I won't allow it. None of your nonsense, Miss! I won't permit it to be done.

[CHARITY *rocks her chair back and forth*].

CHARITY: [*her voice rising to a high pitch*] I shall do, I shall do, Pa, what I please and what I have done. I am not going to be crushed in everything, depend upon it. I've been more shamefully used than anybody ever was in this world...[she begins to cry and sob] and may expect the worse treatment from you, I know. But I don't care for that. No, I don't!

[MR. PECKSNIFF, *frantic, uncertain, and desperate to shut* CHARITY *up, starts to shake her violently.* CHARITY, *astonished, stops crying.*]

MR. PECKSNIFF: [*catching his breath*] I'll do it again! If you dare to talk in that loud manner. How do you mean about being shamefully used? If Mr. Jonas chose your sister in preference to you, who could help it, what have I to do with it?

CHARITY: [*sobbing and wringing her hands*] Wasn't I made a convenience of? Weren't my feelings trifled with? Didn't he address himself to me first? And oh, good gracious, that I should live to be shook!

MR. PECKSNIFF: You'll live to be shook again. You surprise me. I wonder you have not more spirit. If Mr. Jonas didn't care for you, how could you wish to have him?

CHARITY: I wish to have him?! I wish to have him, Pa?!

MR. PECKSNIFF: Then what are you making all this fuss for? If you didn't wish to have him?

CHARITY: Because I was treated with duplicity, and because my own sister and my own father conspired against me. I am not angry with her —[*looking very angry*] I pity her. I'm sorry for her. I know the fate that's in store for her, with that Wretch.

MR. PECKSNIFF: Mr. Jonas will survive your calling him a wretch, my child, I dare say, but call him what you like and make an end of it.

CHARITY: Not an end, Pa, no, not an end. It's better you should know that at once. No. Pa! I am not quite a fool, and I am not blind. All I have got to say is, I won't submit to it!!

[CHARITY *is carried away and begins to shake* PECKSNIFF.]

PECKSNIFF: [*mild and fawning*] My dear, if in an angry moment I resorted to unjustifiable physical behavior doing injury to you as well as myself — I ask your pardon. A father asking pardon of his child, is, I believe, a spectacle to soften the most rugged nature.

CHARITY: I'm not quite a fool, and not blind, and I won't submit to it. I won't, I won't!

MR. PECKSNIFF: You labor under some mistake, my child! But I will not ask you what it is; I don't desire to know. No! Let us avoid the subject, my dear, whatever it is!

CHARITY: It's quite right that the subject should be avoided between us. But I wish to be able to avoid it altogether, and consequently must beg you to provide me with a home. Another home, papa. Place me at Mrs. Todgers's or somewhere, on an independent footing; but I will not live here.

MR. PECKSNIFF: [*managing a few tears*] One of my birds. One of my birds. But I have ever sacrificed my children's happiness to my own — I mean my own happiness to my children's. If you can be happier at Mrs. Todgers's than in your father's house, my dear, go to Mrs. Todgers! Do not think of me, my girl! I shall get on pretty well, no doubt.

CHARITY: [*concealing her pleasure*] Let us negotiate the terms.

BLACKOUT

In this scene, Pecksniff's voice goes to its highest range as he reveals his frustration. It is Charity who first gives up the blather when she says: "Oh, bother, Pa". Mr. Pecksniff hangs on to his delicacy as long as he can, but then he gets down to shouting in earnest.

* * *

DAVID AND THE WAITER WHO EATS HIS FOOD.

From the novel *DAVID COPPERFIELD*

CHARACTERS: **DAVID:** a young boy on his way to a boarding school for the first time.

WAITER: who seems kind to David.

SETTING: An inn on the way to school.

SUMMARY:

David is made miserable by his stepfather, Mr. Murdstone. One day, after months of abuse, when he is provoked to the extreme, David bites Mr. Murdstone. He is subsequently sent away from his mother and faithful servant, Peggotty, to a boarding school. During the trip, the coach stops at an inn where David is scheduled to take his meal [it has been paid for in advance.] A waiter ushers David into the dining room and sets a table for him with great flourish while David waits, shyly, at the side. Then the waiter brings in chops and vegetables.

WAITER: [*affably*] There you are. Come on!

DAVID: [*taking his seat*] Thank you.

[DAVID *tries to use the knife and fork to cut his meat and not to splash gravy on himself, aware that the waiter is staring at him.*]

WAITER: There's half a pint of ale for you. Will you have it now?

DAVID: Yes, thank you.

WAITER: [*holding up the poured ale against the light*] My eye! It seems a good deal, don't it?

DAVID: [*relieved to find the waiter so pleasant*] It does seem a good deal.

WAITER: There was a gentleman here, yesterday, a stout gentleman, by the name of Topsawyer - perhaps you know him?

DAVID: No, I don't think... No, I haven't the pleasure...

WAITER: He came in here, ordered a glass of this ale - would order it - I told him not to - drank it, and fell dead. It was too stale for him. It oughtn't to be drawn; that's the fact.

DAVID: I think I had better have some water.

WAITER: The owner don't like things being ordered and left. It offends 'em. But I'll drink it, if you like. I'm used to it. I don't think it'll hurt me, if I throw my head back, and take it off quick. Shall I?

DAVID: You would very much oblige me by drinking it, if you can do it safely. But by no means otherwise!

[*The* WAITER *throws his head back and swiftly takes in the ale.*]

WAITER: [*putting a fork into a chop*] What have we got here? Not chops?

DAVID: Chops.

WAITER: Lord bless my soul! I didn't know they were chops. Why, a chop's the very thing to take off the bad effects of that beer! Ain't it lucky?

[*The* WAITER *takes a chop in one hand and a potato in the other and eats with a good appetite. He takes another chop and another potato; then a third portion of each. He eats heartily.*]

WAITER: Now, ah, let us get you your dessert.

[*The* WAITER *comes with a pudding and sets it on the table.*]

WAITER: [*ruminating*] Hmn. Let me think now, hmn...

DAVID: Is anything the matter?

WAITER: [*rousing himself*] How's the pie?

DAVID: It's a pudding.

WAITER: Pudding! Why, so it is! [*he looks at it closer*] You don't mean to say it's a bread-pudding!

DAVID: Yes, it is indeed.

WAITER: [*taking up a tablespoon*] A bread-pudding is my favorite pudding! Ain't that lucky? Come on, little one and let's see who'll get most. Here, here's your spoon. [*hands* DAVID *a teaspoon*] Come on, now, make it that you win.

DAVID: [*to himself*] I'm afraid I can't keep up with him. He enjoys a pudding!

WAITER: [*with much laughter and good humor*] Young friend, that was a delicious pudding.

DAVID: Would you be good enough to bring me pen and paper? I must write Peggotty, my friend.

[*The* WAITER *brings pen and paper and stands over* DAVID*'s shoulder while he writes.*]

WAITER: Where are you going to school?

DAVID: Near London.

WAITER: Oh! I am sorry for that.

DAVID: Why?

WAITER: Oh, Lord! that's the school where they broke the boy's ribs - two ribs - a young boy he was - let me see – about as old as you are. They broke his first rib; when they broke his second, that did it for him.

DAVID: How did they...break his rib?

WAITER: By whipping.

VOICE FROM OUTSIDE: All aboard!

DAVID: [*rising*] Is there anything to pay?

WAITER: There's a sheet of letter-paper. Did you ever buy a sheet of letter-paper?

DAVID: No, I don't think I have.

WAITER: It's expensive, on account of the duty. That's the way we're taxed in this country. There's nothing else, except the waiter. Never mind the ink. I lose by that.

DAVID: [*blushing*] What should you...what should I...how much ought I to, uh, what would it be right to pay the waiter, if you please?

WAITER: If I hadn't a family, and that family hadn't the cowpock, I wouldn't take a cent. If I didn't support a aged parent, and a lovely sister...[*he is greatly agitated*] I wouldn't take the slightest amount. If I had a good place, and was treated well here, I should beg you to accept something from me, instead of taking it from you. But I live on broken bits of food - and I sleep on the coals.

[*The* WAITER *bursts into tears.*]

DAVID: I am sorry to hear...here, take this!

WAITER: Ah, how good of you, my whole family thanks you and will remember this for a long time to come. [*he knicks the coin with his thumb*] Ah, it's a good one it is!

BLACKOUT

If you start out as the waiter with a broad smile and flourish the table-cloth a few times as you lay it on the table, you can get right into the spirit with a pace that never slows down. This is a vaudeville bit that comedians would put into their acts — and repeat over and over again as the audience called for it. In the role of David as a youngster, don't get cute by trying too hard to cut your food. Attitude is the safer way to go.

* * *

DAVID IS BORN. 'TIZ A PITY HE'S A BOY

From the novel *DAVID COPPERFIELD*

CHARACTERS:	**MRS. COPPERFIELD:** a widow pregnant with David.
	AUNT BETSEY TROTWOOD: a formidable relative of Mr. Copperfield.
	PEGGOTTY: the faithful servant
SETTING:	Mrs. Copperfield's parlor.

SUMMARY:

David's father had been a favorite of Aunt Betsey, but she was mortally affronted by his marriage because David's mother was 'a wax doll,' not yet twenty and far younger than his father. After the marriage, David's father and Aunt Betsey never met again. David's mother is in poor health, recently widowed, pregnant, and low in spirits.

[MRS. COPPERFIELD *sees a strange lady in the doorway.*]

MRS. COPPERFIELD: [*to herself*] Oh, dear God, I believe that is Miss Betsey. Oh, goodness.

[MISS BETSEY *looks round the room slowly.*]

MISS BETSEY: Mrs. David Copperfield, I think.

MRS. COPPERFIELD: [*faintly*] Yes.

MISS BETSEY:: Miss Trotwood. You have heard of her, I dare say?

MRS. COPPERFIELD: I have had the pleasure.

MISS BETSEY: Now you see her.

MRS. COPPERFIELD: Please sit.

[MISS BETSEY *sits and says nothing.*]

MRS. COPPERFIELD: I... I... oh, dear...

[*She begins to cry.*]

MISS BETSEY: Oh tut, tut, tut! Don't do that! Come, come!

MRS. COPPERFIELD: Forgive me. I didn't mean to. I won't again.

MISS BETSEY: Bless my heart! You are very young.

MRS. COPPERFIELD: I am a childish widow and I'm afraid I'll be a childish mother.

[*She begins to cry.*]

[MISS BETSEY *sits with her skirt tucked up, hands on one knee and frowning.*]

MISS BETSEY: Well? and when do you expect...

MRS. COPPERFIELD: I don't know what's the matter. I'm trembling. I shall die, I am sure!

MISS BETSEY: No, no, no. Have some tea.

MRS. COPPERFIELD: [*helplessly*] Do you think it will do me any good?

MISS BETSEY: Of course it will. It's nothing but your imagination. What do you call your girl?

MRS. COPPERFIELD: I don't know that it will be a girl, yet, ma'am.

MISS BETSEY: I mean your servant-girl.

MRS. COPPERFIELD: Peggotty.

MISS BETSEY: [*calling into the kitchen with authority*] Here! Peggotty! Tea. The lady is a little unwell. Don't dawdle.

[MISS BETSEY *sits down.*]

MISS BETSEY: You were speaking about its being a girl. I have no doubt it will be a girl. I have a presentiment that it must be a girl. Now child, from the moment of the birth of this girl –

MRS. COPPERFIELD: [*taking the liberty*] Perhaps boy.

MISS BETSEY: I tell you I have a presentiment that it must be a girl. Don't contradict. From the moment of this girl's birth, I intend to be her friend. I intend to be her godmother, and I beg you'll call her Betsey Trotwood Copperfield. There must be no mistakes in life with this Betsey Trotwood.

[MISS BETSEY'*s head begins to twitch.*]

MISS BETSEY: [*continues*] There must be no trifling with her affections, poor dear. She must be well brought up, and well guarded from giving any foolish confidences where they are not deserved. I must make that my care.

[MISS BETSEY *becomes silent and stops twitching.*]

MISS BETSEY: [*continues*] And was David good to you, child? Were you comfortable together?

MRS. COPPERFIELD: We were very happy. Mr. Copperfield was only too good to me.

MISS BETSEY: Poor young thing! Do you know anything?

MRS. COPPERFIELD: I beg your pardon, ma'am?

MISS BETSEY: About keeping house, for instance.

MRS. COPPERFIELD: Not much. But Mr. Copperfield was teaching me…

MISS BETSEY: Much he knew about it himself!

MRS. COPPERFIELD: And I am sure we never had a word of difference, except when Mr. Copperfield objected to my threes and fives being too much like each other, or to my putting curly tails to my sevens and nines…

[*She bursts into tears again.*]

MISS BETSEY: You'll make yourself ill, and you know that will not be good either for you or for my god-daughter. Come! You mustn't do it!

[*There is an interval of silence.* PEGGOTTY *enters with the tea things*].

PEGGOTTY: Oh, dear little ma'am, you are not well. Let me help you upstairs.

BLACKOUT

Mrs. Copperfield has to be enormously pregnant and protective of her baby at all times. She is frightened by Aunt Betsey to begin with, and Aunt Betsey's turning up so unexpectedly has intimidated her considerably.

* * *

PART TWO

CHARACTERS:	MR. CHILLIP: the doctor brought in for the birthing. He is a meek, mild mannered little man.
	MISS BETSEY: by now sitting in the parlor

with a wad of cotton in her ear.

MR. CHILLIP: [*touching his ear*] Some local irritation, ma'am?

MISS BETSEY: [*pulling the cotton out*] What!

MR. CHILLIP: [*sweetly*] Some local irritation, ma'am?

MISS BETSEY: Nonsense!

[*She puts the cotton back in.*]

[MR. CHILLIP, *totally intimidated, sits and looks at Miss Betsey.*]

PEGGOTTY: [from upstairs] Mr. Chillip. I think we need you.

MR. CHILLIP: [*leaning towards her cottoned ear*] Excuse me.

[*He leaves.* MISS BETSEY *remains as she is, saying "Hah" every once in a while.*]

[MR. CHILLIP *comes back into the parlor.*]

MISS BETSEY: [takes the cotton out of her ear] Well?

[*She leans her hearing ear towards him.*]

MR. CHILLIP: We are - we are progressing slowly, ma'am.

MISS BETSEY: Ba—a—ah!

[*She puts the cotton back in her ear.*]

MR. CHILLIP: I...uh...may be called shortly. I had better sit near the door. [to himself] It's dark and drafty but anything rather than to sit and look at that, that...dragon.

[*Now there are noises from upstairs; cries and footsteps and* PEG-GOTTY *calling.*]

PEGGOTTY: Mr. Chillip. Do come. I think we have got something.

MR. CHILLIP: Oh, do excuse me. Yes, coming!

[*Hearing the noise,* MISS BETSEY *becomes agitated. She walks back and forth. She takes a pillow from the sofa and pounds and pummels it. This is not enough. She takes another pillow and smashes them together.*]

[*Finally,* MR. CHILLIP *comes down.*]

MR. CHILLIP: [*meekly*] Well, ma'am, I am happy to congratulate you.

MISS BETSEY: [*sharply*] What upon?

[MR. CHILLIP *makes a little bow and smiles sweetly.*]

MISS BETSEY: What's the matter with the man, can't he speak?

MR. CHILLIP: Be calm, my dear ma'am. There is no longer any occasion for uneasiness, ma'am. Be calm.

[MISS BETSEY *restrains herself from further mayhem on the doctor but grabs the doctor's lapels and draws him closer.*]

MR. CHILLIP: Of course, of course. I am happy to congratulate you. All is now over, ma'am, and well over.

MISS BETSEY: [*Her hat is dangling from her folded arms.*] How is she?

MR. CHILLIP: Ma'am, she will soon be quite comfortable, as comfortable as we can expect a young mother to be, under these melancholy domestic circumstances. There cannot be any objection to your seeing her presently, ma'am. It may do her good.

MISS BETSEY: [*sharply*] And she. How is she?

MR. CHILLIP: [*still sweetly smiling*] How is she?

MISS BETSEY: The baby. How is she?

MR. CHILLIP: Ma'am, it's a boy.

[*Hearing this*, MISS BETSEY *pauses for a split second, takes her hat by the strings, aims a blow at* MR. CHILLIP's *head with it, puts the crushed hat on her head, walks out, and never comes back.*]

BLACKOUT

See the chapter on *Body Over Mind* for further comments on this scene.

* * *

MICAWBER CAN NO LONGER CONTAIN HIMSELF

From the novel *DAVID COPPERFIELD*

CHARACTERS:

DAVID: has known and befriended the impecunious Mr. Micawber and his family for several years.

MR. MICAWBER: always in debt and always cheerful but not this time. He has been working for Uriah Heep at the law firm of Wickfield and Heep.

SETTING: David's quarters.

SUMMARY:

A letter from Mrs. Micawber has alerted David to Mr. Micawber's recent disturbing and elusive conduct. David has invited Micawber to visit and, hoping to make him feel at home, has asked Micawber to prepare his favorite punch. Mr. Micawber is peeling lemons. After some time, David engages him in conversation.

DAVID: Are you doing well at your new job? How is our friend Heep, Mr. Micawber?

MR. MICAWBER: [*turning pale*] My dear Copperfield, if you ask after my employer as your friend, I am sorry for it; if you ask after him as my friend, I sardonically smile at it. In whatever capacity you ask after my employer, I beg, without offence to you, to limit my reply to this - that whatever his state of health may be, his appearance is foxy: not to say diabolical.

DAVID: I didn't mean to upset you. I had no idea that you had come to know Heep as well as I....

[MR. MICAWBER *is plunged into gloom. He vacillates between wanting to reveal something, then wanting to reveal nothing. At times he whistles a gay tune to offset his mood, but that only seems to make him feel more troubled. Finally he bursts into tears. He stops peeling lemons.*]

MR. MICAWBER: My dear Copperfield, this is an occupation, of all others, requiring an untroubled mind, and self-respect. I cannot perform it. I cannot peel another lemon.

DAVID: Mr. Micawber, what's the matter? I am your friend. Tell me.

MR. MICAWBER: Good heavens, it is principally because we are friends that my state of mind is what it is. What is the matter? What is not the matter? Villainy is the matter; baseness is the matter; deception, fraud, conspiracy, are the matter; and all in the name of - HEEP!

[MR. MICAWBER *involves himself with his handkerchief. For the moment it is his only means of expression.*]

MR. MICAWBER: The struggle is over! I will lead this life no longer. I have been under a Taboo in that infernal scoundrel's service.

DAVID: I've been outraged myself at Uriah Heep, but you must be rational.

MR. MICAWBER: [*gasping, puffing, sobbing but ever the great speech-maker*] I'll not rest -until I have - blown to fragments – the - a - detestable - serpent - HEEP! Refreshment - a - underneath this roof - particularly punch - would - a - choke me - unless - I had - previously - choked the eyes - out of the head - a - of - interminable cheat, and liar - HEEP! I - a- I'll know nobody - and - a - say nothing - and - a - live nowhere - until I have crushed - to - a - undiscoverable atoms - the immortal hypocrite and perjurer - HEEP!

DAVID: Mr. Micawber, I need to know...

MR. MICAWBER: [*in his frenzy*] No, Copperfield! - No communication - Inviolable secret - a - from the whole world - a - no exceptions – meet me next week - a - at breakfast-time - a – bring everyone, your aunt, everybody – come to the office - a - where - and –I a – will expose intolerable ruffian - HEEP! No more to say - a - or listen to persuasion – I must, must go - I am upon the track of a doomed traitor - HEEP!

BLACKOUT

Playing Micawber, you must make him large and theatrical. Micawber is a man of words. Indulge yourself.

* * *

MR. MICAWBER EXPOSES URIAH HEEP

From the novel *DAVID COPPERFIELD*

CHARACTERS: DAVID: a friend of Mr. Micawber.

                        AUNT BETSEY: a friend and client of Mr. Wickfield.

                        TRADDLES: a lawyer who was a schoolmate of David's.

                        MR. MICAWBER: about to make an important announcement.

                        URIAH HEEP: as evil as ever.

                        AGNES WICKFIELD: the loving daughter of the unfortunate Mr. Wickfield.

                        MRS. HEEP: the always humble mother of Uriah.

SETTING: The office of Wickfield and Heep.

SUMMARY:

Forced to become Uriah Heep's accomplice in defrauding Mr. Wickfield, Mr. Micawber has decided to expose Heep to David and his Aunt Betsey Trotwood. At Micawber's urging, they have come to Wickfield's office accompanied by David's lawyer friend, Traddles.

David, Aunt Betsey, and Traddles find Mr. Micawber at the door with a large desk-ruler stuck in the belt of his trousers.

DAVID: [*as planned*] How do you do, Mr. Micawber?

MR. MICAWBER: [*gravely*] Mr. Copperfield, I hope I see you well?

DAVID: Is Miss Wickfield at home?

MR. MICAWBER: Mr. Wickfield is unwell in bed, sir, of a rheumatic fever, but Miss Wickfield, I have no doubt, will be happy to see old friends. Will you walk in?

[MICAWBER *points to the corner of the room where* URIAH HEEP *is sitting at his desk.* URIAH *looks up in surprise.*]

MR. MICAWBER: [*sonorously*] Miss Trotwood, Mr. David Copperfield, Mr. Thomas Traddles.

[URIAH *Heep at first shows trepidation but immediately changes into his habitual fawning behavior.*]

URIAH: Well, I am sure, this is indeed an unexpected pleasure! To have, as I may say, all friends at once, is a treat unlooked for! Mr. Copperfield, I hope I see you well, and - if I may humbly express myself so - friendly towards them as is ever your friends, whether or not.

[DAVID *lets his hand be shaken by* URIAH.]

URIAH: [*with his sickliest smile*] Things are changed in this office, Miss Trotwood, since I was an humble clerk, ain't they? But I am not changed, Miss Trotwood.

AUNT BETSEY: Well, to tell you the truth, I think you are pretty constant to the promise of your youth; if that's any satisfaction to you.

URIAH: [*writhing*] Thank you, Miss Trotwood, for your good opinion! Micawber, tell 'em to let Miss Agnes know - and mother. Mother will be quite in a state, when she sees the present company!

TRADDLES: You are not busy, Mr. Heep?

URIAH: Not so much as I could wish. Not but what myself and Micawber have our hands pretty full, in general, on account of Mr. Wickfield's being hardly fit for any occupation, sir. But it's a pleasure as well as a duty, I am sure, to work for him.

[TRADDLES *quietly leaves as* MICAWBER *ushers* AGNES *into the room.*]

URIAH: You may go now, Micawber. [MICAWBER *does not move*] Don't wait, Micawber.

[MR. MICAWBER, *with his hand upon the ruler still tucked in his trousers, stands erect before the door.*]

URIAH: What are you waiting for? Micawber! Did you hear me tell you not to wait?

MR. MICAWBER: [*immovable*] Yes!

URIAH: Then why do you wait?

MR. MICAWBER: Because I - in short, choose!

URIAH: [*losing color, attempts a smile*] You are a dissipated fellow, as all the world knows. And I am afraid you'll oblige me to get rid of you. Go along! I'll talk to you presently.

MR. MICAWBER: If there is a scoundrel on this earth, with whom I have already talked too much, that scoundrel's name is - HEEP!

[URIAH *looks slowly around.*]

URIAH: Oho! This is a conspiracy! You have met here by appointment! Now, take care, Copperfield. You'll make nothing of this. We understand each other, you and me. There's no love between us. You were always a puppy with a proud stomach; and you envy me my rise, do you? None of your plots against me; I'll counterplot you! Micawber, you be off. I'll talk to you presently.

DAVID: Mr. Micawber, there is a sudden change in this fellow. Deal with him as he deserves!

URIAH: You are a precious set of people, ain't you? To buy over my clerk, who is the very scum of society, - as you yourself were, Copperfield, you know it, before anyone had charity on you, - to buy over my clerk, to defame me with his lies? Miss Trotwood, old lady, you had better stop this. Miss Wickfield, if you have any love for your father, you had better not join this gang. I'll ruin him. Think twice, you, Micawber, if you don't want to be crushed. I recommend you to take yourself off, you fool! While there's time to retreat.

[*He notices* TRADDLES *is missing.*]

URIAH: Where's mother? Fine doings in a person's own house!

TRADDLES: [*returning with* MRS. HEEP] Mrs. Heep is here, sir. I have taken the liberty of making myself known to her. I am the agent and friend of Mr. Wickfield, sir. And I have a power of attorney from him in my pocket, to act for him in all matters.

URIAH: The old ass has drunk himself into a state of dotage, and it has been got from him by fraud!

MRS. HEEP: [*anxiously*] Ury -!

URIAH: You hold your tongue, mother. Least said, soonest mended.

MRS. HEEP: But, my Ury -

URIAH: Will you hold your tongue, mother, and leave it to me? [*half whining and half abusive to* DAVID] You think it justifiable, do you, Copperfield, to sneak about my place, eaves-dropping with my clerk? If it had been me, I shouldn't have wondered; for I don't make myself out a gentleman.

[*No longer able to contain himself,* MICAWBER *reads from a long letter he has composed for the occasion.*]

MR. MICAWBER: Dear Miss Trotwood and gentlemen – I am appearing before you to denounce the most consummate Villain that has ever existed. [MICAWBER *points the ruler at* URIAH]

MR. MICAWBER: [*continues*] I, I entered the office – of the Firm Wickfield and - HEEP, but in reality, it is HEEP alone. HEEP, is the Forger and the Cheat.

[URIAH *makes a dart at the letter as if to tear it in pieces.*   MR. MICAWBER, *with perfect dexterity, raps his knuckles with the ruler and disables* URIAH'*s right hand. It drops at the wrist as if it were broken.*]

URIAH: [*writhing in a new way with pain*] I'll be even with you.

MR. MICAWBER: Approach me again, you - you - you HEEP of infamy, and if your head is human, I'll break it. Come on, come on!

[MR. MICAWBER, *using the ruler as a broad-sword, is urging* URIAH *to fight. Finally,* DAVID *and* TRADDLES *restraining him, he returns to reading from the letter.*]

MR. MICAWBER: [*continues to read*] I was paid a miserable salary and need I say, that it soon became necessary for me to solicit from - HEEP - pecuniary advances towards the support of Mrs. Micawber, and our blighted but rising family. Need I say that this necessity had been foreseen by - HEEP? That those advances were secured by I.O.U.'s and that I thus became immeshed in the web he had spun for my reception?

[MICAWBER *pauses long enough to refresh his grand elocutionary style.*]

MR. MICAWBER: [*continues to read*] Then it was that I began, if I may so Shakespearianly express myself, to dwindle, peak, and pine. I found that my services were constantly called upon for the falsification of business, and the mystification of an individual we shall call, Mr. W. That Mr. W. was imposed upon, kept in ignorance, and deluded, in every possible way. No longer able to abide these conditions, I entered on a laborious task of clandestine investigation. My charges against – HEEP – are as follows:

[MICAWBER *holds the ruler in a convenient position under his left arm, in case of need.*]

MR. MICAWBER: [*continues*] First: When Mr. W.'s faculties and memory for business became, weakened and confused, - HEEP - complicated the transactions. When Mr. W. was least fit to do business, - HEEP was always at hand to force him to do it. He obtained Mr. W.'s signature to documents of importance, representing them to be documents of no importance.

URIAH: You shall prove this, you Copperfield! All in good time!

MRS. HEEP: Ury, Ury! Be humble, and make terms, my dear!

URIAH: Mother, you're in a fright and don't know what you say or mean. Humble! I've humbled some of them, humble as I was!

MR. MICAWBER: Second. HEEP has systematically forged the signature of Mr. W. Mr. W. being infirm, his possible decease might lead to some discoveries, and to the downfall of - HEEP'S - power over the W. family, - unless his daughter could be secretly influenced from allowing any investigation of the partnership to ever be made. And I have a document, in my possession....

[URIAH HEEP, *with a start, takes out of his pocket a bunch of keys and opens a safe. He realizes that he is being watched. He straight-*

ens up and doesn't look further.]

MRS. HEEP: Ury, Ury! Be humble and make terms. I know my son will be humble, gentlemen, if you'll give him time to think. Mr. Copperfield, I'm sure you know that he was always very humble, sir!

URIAH: Mother, you had better take and fire a loaded gun at me.

MRS. HEEP: But I love you, Ury, And I can't bear to hear you provoking the gentlemen, and endangering of yourself more. I told the gentleman that I would answer for your being humble, and making amends. Oh, see how humble I am, gentlemen, and don't mind him!

URIAH: Mother, Copperfield would have given you a hundred pound to say less than you've blurted out!

MRS. HEEP: I can't help it, Ury, I can't see you running into danger, through carrying your head so high. Better be humble, as you always was.

URIAH: [*to Micawber*] What more have you got to bring forward? If anything, go on with it.

MR. MICAWBER: Third. And last. I am now able to show, by - HEEP'S - false books, and - HEEP'S - real memoranda, that Mr. W. has been for years deluded and plundered. [*gravely*] I have concluded. Now, with my ill-starred family, it may be reasonably inferred that our baby will first expire of exhaustion, as being the frailest member of our circle; and that our twins will follow next in order. So be it! For myself, imprisonment and want, will soon do more. Let it be merely said of me, that what I have done, I did, in despite of mercenary and selfish objects. For England, home, and Beauty. Remaining always, &c. &c., WILKINS MICAWBER.

[MR. MICAWBER *folds the letter and hands it to* AUNT BETSEY *as a memento.* URIAH *remembers the safe. The key is in it. he goes to it, throws the door open. It is empty!*]

URIAH: Where are the books? Some thief has stolen the books!

MR. MICAWBER: [tapping himself with the ruler] I did, when I got the key from you as usual - but a little earlier - and opened it this morning.

TRADDLES: Don't be uneasy, they have come into my possession. I will take care of them, under the authority I mentioned.

URIAH: You receive stolen goods, do you?

TRADDLES: Under such circumstances, yes.

[AUNT BETSEY, *who has been exceptionally quiet, darts at* URIAH HEEP *and seizes him by the collar with both hands!*]

AUNT BETSEY: You know what I want?

URIAH: A strait-jacket.

AUNT BETSEY: No. My property! Agnes, my dear, as long as I believed it had been made away with by your father, I would-n't breathe a syllable about it. But, now I know this fellow's answerable for it, and I'll have it! Trot, come and take it away from him!

[*At the same time that* AUNT BETSEY *is shaking* URIAH, MRS. HEEP *has been going down on her knees to everyone in succession, making the wildest promises.* URIAH *sits her down in his chair and holds her there.*]

URIAH: [*to Traddles*] What do you want done?

TRADDLES: What must be done...

URIAH: Has that Copperfield no tongue? Perhaps somebody has cut it out. I would hope.

MRS. HEEP: My Uriah means to be humble! Don't mind what he says, good gentlemen!

TRADDLES: The deed of relinquishment, that we have heard of, must be given over to me now - here.

URIAH: Suppose I haven't got it.

TRADDLES: But you have.

URIAH: I must have time to think about that.

TRADDLES: Certainly. But, in the meanwhile, we shall compel you – to keep to your own room, and hold no communication with anyone.

URIAH: I won't do it! Damn you!

TRADDLES: Maidstone jail is a safer place of detention. Copperfield, will you go round to the Guildhall, and bring a couple of officers?

[MRS. HEEP *breaks out again, crying on her knees to Agnes to interfere in their behalf.*]

MRS HEEP: He is very humble and it is, it was all true, and if Ury doesn't do what you want, I will!

URIAH: Mother, hold your noise. [*to* DAVID] Don't go. Don't get the police. Mother, let 'em have that deed. Go and fetch it!

[MRS. HEEP *scurries out and returns carrying the box which holds the deed and several other valuables.*]

TRADDLES: Now, Mr. Heep, you can retire to think.

[URIAH, *without lifting his eyes from the ground, shuffles across the room and pauses at the door.*]

URIAH: Copperfield, I have always hated you. You've always been an upstart, and you've always been against me. [*turning to* MICAWBER] As for you, Micawber, I'll pay you!

BLACKOUT

Traddles has proven to be a calm and confident lawyer, working carefully and methodically to protect Mr. Wickfield.

The scene should culminate in a 3-ring circus: Aunt Betsey is shaking Uriah, Mrs. Heep kneeling to everyone and anyone, and Micawber is guarding himself and the others with the ruler.

* * *

FANNY SQUEERS OVERHEARS

From the novel *NICHOLAS NICKLEBY*

CHARACTERS:

JOHN BROWDIE: newly married to Tilda.

TILDA BROWDIE: soon to be a former friend to Fanny.

NICHOLAS NICKLEBY: a friend of the Browdies.

FANNY SQUEERS: a passionate shrew.

MR. SQUEERS: her father, the cruel headmaster of the Dotheboys school.
WACKFORD SQUEERS: Fanny's little brother.

SETTING:

An Inn in London. In Nicholas's room.

SUMMARY:

John and Tilda are married. Fanny Squeers was Tilda's bridesmaid. At the Dotheboys school, Fanny's imagination led her to believe Nicholas was in love with her. Now she hates him because she has realized that it is not so. John and Tilda make sure Fanny will be gone when they arrange a visit with Nicholas.

TILDA: John fixed tonight because Fanny would drink tea with her father. Now, I must say, although you had good reason to leave that dreadful Dotheboys school, I can hardly call it a school, I really think Fanny Squeers was very fond of you.

NICHOLAS: I am very much obliged to her. But I swear, I never tried or wanted to make any impression on her virgin heart.

TILDA: But do you know, really – that I was given to understand by Fanny herself, that you had made an offer to her, and that you two were going to be engaged quite solemn and regular.

A SHRILL FEMALE VOICE: [*outside*] Was you, ma'am — was you? Was you given to understand that I — I — was going to be engaged to an assassinating thief that shed the blood of my pa? Do you — do you think, ma'am — that I was very fond of such dirt beneath my feet? Do you, ma'am - do you? Oh! base and degrading Tilda!

[*The three are astonished to hear* FANNY *screaming outside the door.* FANNY *flings the door open, and there beside her, stand her father and brother, the* WACKFORD SQUEERS, *Sr. and Jr.*]

FANNY: [*frothing*] This is the end, is it, of all my forbearance and friendship for that double-faced thing - that viper, that — that — mermaid? [*screaming*] This is the end, is it, of bearing with her deceitfulness, her lowness, her falseness, laying herself out to be admired by such vulgar... It makes me blush for my...for my...

MR SQUEERS: [*with a malevolent eye*] Gender.

FANNY: Yes. But I thank my stars that my ma is of the same...

MR SQUEERS: Hear, hear! And I wish your ma was here to have a scratch at this company.

FANNY: [*with contempt*] This is the end, is it? Of my noticing her, that...that rubbish, that creature...

TILDA: Oh, come, don't talk such nonsense as that.

FANNY: I don't expect you to blush given your ignominiousness and red-faced boldness.

JOHN: I say, draw it mild, draw it mild.

FANNY: You, Mr. John Browdie, I pity. I have no feeling for you, sir, but one of unliquidated pity.

JOHN: Oh.

FANNY: No, although I am a queer bridesmaid, as you say, and shan't be a bride in a hurry, I feel nothing towards you, sir, but sentiments of pity.

MR SQUEERS: [*to FANNY*] There you have him.

FANNY: [*her curls bouncing violently*] I know what a life is there for you, Mr. Browdie, and if you was my deadliest enemy, I could wish you nothing worse.

TILDA: Couldn't you wish to be married to him yourself, if that was the case?

FANNY: [*with a low curtsy*] Oh, ma'am, how witty you are. Almost as witty, ma'am, as you are clever. How very clever it was in you, ma'am, to choose a time when I had gone to tea with my pa. What a pity you never thought that other people might be as clever as yourself and spoil your plans!

TILDA: You won't vex me, child, with such airs as these.

FANNY: Don't Missis me, ma'am, if you please. I'll not bear it.

JOHN: Dang it all! Say your say out, Fanny, and make sure it's the end, and don't ask nobody whether it is or not.

FANNY: Thanking you for your advice which was not required, Mr. John Browdie. Have the goodness not to meddle with my name. [*with sudden ferocity*] Tilda, I renounce you! [solemnly] I wouldn't have a child named Tilda...not to save it from its grave.

JOHN: As for that, it'll be time enough to think about naming it when it comes.

TILDA: John! Don't tease her.

FANNY: Oh! Tease, indeed! Hehehe! No, don't tease her. Consider her feelings, pray!

TILDA: I will say, Fanny, that times out of number I have spoken so kindly of you behind your back, that even you could have found no fault with what I said.

FANNY: [*with a curtsy*] Oh, I dare say not, ma'am! Best thanks to you for your goodness!

TILDA: I don't know that I have said anything very bad of you, even now. But if I have, I am very sorry for it, and I beg your pardon. I have never borne any malice to you, and I hope you'll not bear any to me.

[FANNY *surveys her former friend from top to toe. She tilts her nose.*]

FANNY: [*mutters*] Puss, minx, contemptible creature.

[FANNY *bites her lips, has great difficulty swallowing, and is short of breath.* MR. SQUEERS *takes* FANNY's *arm, drags little Wackford by the hand, and retreats to the door.*]

MR SQUEERS: Miss Fanny, come along!

FANNY: I leave such society, with my pa, for ever. I am defiled by breathing the air with such creatures. Poor John Browdie! He! he! he! I do pity him; he's so deluded. He! he! he! Artful and designing Tilda!

[FANNY *sweeps from the room in majestic wrath. She sustains her dignity until the last possible moment, and then she is heard sobbing and screaming and stamping her feet in the hallway.*]

BLACKOUT

If Fanny, hiding in the hallway, listens intently to every word that's spoken and lets her breath respond to what's being said, when it's time to scream and rant at her former friends she will have no trouble leaping into the scene and continuing her frenzy until she is out in the hall and completely hysterical.

* * *

MR. MANTALINI IS SUICIDAL AGAIN

From the novel *NICHOLAS NICKLEBY*

CHARACTERS: **MR. MANTALINI:** has a fatal charm for the ladies, especially if they have not yet caught on to his numerous schemes.

MME. MANTALINI: newly married to Mr. Mantalini and adoring of him.

SETTING: Mr. Mantalini's dressing room.

SUMMARY:

The bill collectors have taken over Mme. Mantalini's business because Mr. Mantalini has accumulated so many debts. Mme. Mantalini is distraught; she cannot pay them. At first saucy in the face of the bill collectors, Mr. Mantalini flees the room when Mme. Mantalini refuses to be placated. He leaves the door of his dressing room open. He can be seen sharpening a butter knife. Mme. Mantalini, hooked once again by his desperate love of her, rushes to comfort him.

MR MANTALINI: [*seeing her*] Ach! Interrupted!

[*He thrusts the butter knife into his pocket. He rumples his hair into a wild disorder and rolls his eyes wildly.*]

MME. MANTALINI: [*flinging her arms around him*] Alfred! I didn't mean to say it, I didn't mean to say it!

MR. MANTALINI: [*raving*] Ruined! Have I brought ruin upon the best and purest creature that ever blessed a vagabond! Damn it, let me go.

[MR. MANTALINI *lets his wife restrain him from seizing the butter knife. He attempts to dash his head against the wall — taking care to be too far to reach it.*]

MME MANTALINI: Compose yourself, my own angel. It is nobody's fault. It is mine as much as yours, we shall do very well yet. Come, Alfred, come.

MR. MANTALINI: [*somewhat mollified*] Poison! Give me poison! Please won't someone have pity on me and blow my brains out...

[*He breaks down and weeps pathetically. He lets* MME. MANTALINI *take away the knife, helping her a bit to untangle it from his pocket lining.*]

MME. MANTALINI: [*murmuring as she leads him away*] Come, dear, come, my love... Its sweetness will take its precious boy to breakfast, no more knives. He must not give his sweetness such a fright.

BLACKOUT

Mme. Mantalini is so infatuated with Mr. Mantalini that she is completely taken in by his mighty theatrics. Love is sweet. She is unashamed to talk baby talk to him and to pet him as though he were a spoiled child.

* * *

MR. MANTALINI, HIS LAST SUICIDE

From the novel *NICHOLAS NICKLEBY*

CHARACTERS: **MR. MANTALINI:** found out at last.

                     MRS. MANTALINI: enlightened.

                     MISS KNAG: always knew it.

                     RALPH NICKLEBY: surprised by nothing.

SETTING: Mrs. Mantalini's fitting room.

SUMMARY:

Ralph Nickleby enters the Mantalini studio to find Mr. Mantalini on the floor, with his eyes closed, his face pale, his teeth clenched. He is holding a bottle in his right hand and a little tea-spoon in his left. He is stiff and powerless. Mme. Mantalini is in tears. Miss Knag is also in tears.

RALPH NICKLEBY: What is the matter here?

MME. MANTALINI: Mr. Nickleby, by what chance you came here, I don't know. [*drying her eyes*] I will, however, say before you, and before everybody for the first time, and once for all, that I never will supply that man's extravagances and viciousness again. I have been a dupe and a fool to him long enough. In future, he shall support himself if he can, and then he may spend what money he pleases, upon whom and how he pleases; but it shall not be mine, and therefore you had better pause before you trust him further.

MR. MANTALINI: [*gurgling*] Sweetness! The apothecary has not mixed the prussic acid strong enough, and that I must take another bottle or two to finish the work I...I...

MME. MANTALINI: This amiable fellow, this gallant, with his deceptions, his extravagances, and his infidelities! has poisoned himself in private no less than six times in the last two weeks and I have not once interfered to save his life. I no longer have the least regard for him! Ugh, not the least! And I insist on being separated and left to myself. [sobbing] If he dares to refuse me a separation, I'll have one in law — I can!

MISS KNAG: It would be a warning to me, certainly.

RALPH NICKLEBY: [*in a low voice*] You know you are not in earnest.

MME. MANTALINI: Oh, I am in earnest.

RALPH NICKLEBY: Well, but consider, it would be well to reflect. A married woman has no property.

MR. MANTALINI: [*raising himself on his elbow*] Not a solitary single individual, my darling.

MME. MANTALINI: I am quite aware of that. I have none. The business, the stock, this house, and everything in it, all belong now to Miss Knag.

MISS KNAG: That's quite true, Madame Mantalini. Very true,

indeed, Madame Mantalini, very true. And I never was more glad in all my life, that I had strength of mind to resist matrimonial offers, no matter how advantageous...

MR. MANTALINI: Damn it! Will my adored one not slap and pinch the envious spinster?

MME. MANTALINI: I mind you not! Miss Knag is my particular friend.

[MR. MANTALINI *leers at his wife until his eyes show strain but* MME. MANTALINI *shows no signs of softening.*]

MME. MANTALINI: [*weeping piteously*] You called me old and ordinary to one of your paramours. How could you?

MR. MANTALINI: [*in tears*] Nickleby, you have been made a witness to this cruelty, on the part of an enslaver and captivator that she is, such as never was, oh damn! I forgive that woman.

MME. MANTALINI: Forgive!

MR. MANTALINI: I do forgive her, Nickleby. You will blame me, the world will blame me, the women will blame me; everybody will laugh, and scoff, and smile, and grin. They will say, 'She had a blessing. She did not know it. He was too weak; he was too good; he was a damned fine fellow, but he loved too strong; he could not bear her to be cross, and call him wicked names. But I forgive her.

[MR. MANTALINI *falls down. He is senseless and motionless. When the women leave the room, he comes to a sitting posture. He sits holding the little bottle still in one hand and the tea-spoon in the other.*]

RALPH NICKLEBY: You may put away those fooleries now, and live by your wits again.

MR. MANTALINI: Dammit, Nickleby, you're not serious?

RALPH NICKLEBY: I seldom joke. Good-night.

[RALPH NICKLEBY *puts on his hat and leaves the studio.*]

BLACKOUT

Love is sweet...and short. Mme. Mantalini must make it clear it was what she overheard Mr. Mantalini say about her to one of his paramours — that she was old and ordinary — which caused this final outrage. Having little to say but breathing sympathetically with her sudden best friend, Miss Knag suffers along with Mme. Mantalini. Ralph Nickleby's dryness is a balance to the hysteria in the room.

* * *

MR. WILLET KNOWS ALL ABOUT THE RIOTS IN LONDON

From the novel BARNABY RUDGE

CHARACTERS: **JOHN WILLET:** the owner of the Maypole Inn, as stubborn as the mule in his stable.

SOLOMON DAISY: One of his cronies.

MR. COBB: another crony.

MR. PARKES: a third crony.

SETTING: The Maypole Inn owned by John Willet. A time of rioting between Protestants and Catholics.

SUMMARY:

John Willet, is used to having his opinions respected by his three cronies. They have sat many a long hour keeping warm at John Willet's fire and agreeing with each other that John's opinion is the hardest to disagree with. Today is different. The cronies want to walk into town to see the riots and find out what's happening next between the Protestants and the beleaguered Catholics.

MR. WILLET: [*red in the face*] Do you think, do you think, that I'm a born fool?

SOLOMON DAISY: No, no, Johnny. We all know better than that. You're no fool, Johnny. No, no!

MR. COBB AND MR. PARKES: [*muttering*] No, no, Johnny, not you!

MR. WILLET: Then what do you mean by coming here, and telling me that this evening you're going to walk up to town together-you three—you—and have the evidence of your own senses? Ain't, ain't the evidence of my senses enough for you?

MR. PARKES: [*humbly*] But we haven't got it, Johnny.

MR. WILLET: [*eyeing him from top to toe*] You haven't got it, sir? You haven't got it, sir? You have got it, sir. Don't I tell you that the Government will not stand a rioting and rollicking in the streets?

MR. PARKES: [*daring*] Yes, Johnny, but that's your sense—not your senses.

MR. WILLET: [*with great dignity*] How do you know? You're contradicting pretty free, you are. How do you know which it is? I'm not aware I ever told you.

MR. PARKES: [*in over his head stammers an apology*] Well, uh... If you look at it uh... Sorry John.

[*After quite a long pause* MR. WILLET *shakes with laughter.*]

MR. WILLET: [*to* PARKES] I hope I have tackled you enough.

[MESSRS COBB *and* DAISY *laugh and nod.*]

MR. COBB: Well, that puts you, Parkes, fitting close into your chair.

SOLOMON DAISY:: They do say that the rioters won't go more than two miles, or three out into the countryside, at the farthest. At least, so the story goes.

MR. WILLET: The story goes! The story goes that you saw a ghost last March. But nobody believes it.

SOLOMON DAISY: [*rising*] Well! Believed or disbelieved, it's true; and true or not, if we mean to go to town, we must be going at once. So shake hands, Johnny, and good night.

MR. WILLET: I shall shake hands with no man that goes on such — such a nonsensical errand.

[*He puts his hands in his pockets. The three cronies are reduced to shaking his elbows.*]

MR. PARKES: We'll tell you how it is exactly in the city, Johnny.

MR. COBB: And if you're right, you can claim total victory.

SOLOMON DAISY: If you're right, that is, Johnny.

BLACKOUT

It's tempting to use an Irish brogue for these characters but they are not Irish. I refrain from calling them English because, as I said in my introduction, you can find the quality of each character using American English. You can play Mr. Willet broadly; few characters would put their hands in their pockets and receive handshakes on their elbows. The cronies can fiddle with their pipes and their short beers [which they took because they weren't staying long enough to drink leisurely as they usually do.] The cronies are used to giving Mr. Willet the benefit of any doubt since it is his bar they sit in hour after hour. Today is different, however. They defy him, but it takes some doing. For Mr. Willet to laugh, the actor can start with a 'hah, hah' in the front of the mouth. This will generate as much of the laugh as he needs to start talking again.

* * *

MIGGS IS WATCHING

From the novel *BARNABY RUDGE*

CHARACTERS:	MIGGS: a skinny Olive Oyl type, a companion to Mrs. Varden, a bit above servant status.
	SIM TAPPERTIT: an apprentice locksmith to Mr. Varden, the master locksmith. He has the imagination to see himself in a better setting but his vanity will be his downfall.
SETTING:	The locksmith's home. Miggs' bedroom window, downstairs.

SUMMARY:

Tonight, after the Varden family are all in bed, Miggs is in no mood for sleep. She sits at her window and gazes pensively at the wild night sky. As always, she thinks of the 'prentice Simmun,' wondering if he is thinking of her.

Note: Sim is actually in love with Dolly Varden, of whom Miggs is jealous.

MIGGS: [*suddenly alert*] Is that a creaking? A shuffling? A creaking again. Of...of his door? Are those his footsteps outside my door?? [*she turns pale and shudders*] Oh! what a Providence it is, that I am bolted in! [*she listens intently*] Oh, footsteps have passed my door. Whose are they? [*she gasps*] Thieves? A

Murderer? Where are those footsteps going?

[MIGGS *knows it is* SIM, *her Simmun. She sees* TAPPERTIT *swagger off.*]

MIGGS: [*in amazement*] Mr Tappertit! Fully dressed, stealing away with his shoes in his hand! Here's mysteries! [pause] What did he put in his pocket? Goodness gracious me!

[*She takes her candle and leaves her bedroom and goes to the workshop. She peeps and peers about, and considers greatly what* TAPPERTIT *was up to.*]

MIGGS: [*making a delicious discovery*] Why I wish I may only have a walking funeral, and never be buried decent, if the boy hasn't been and made a key for his own self! Oh the little villain!

[MISS MIGGS *deliberates for some time, looking hard at the shopdoor. She takes a sheet of paper from a drawer, twists it into a long thin spiral tube. She fills it with coal-dust from the forge. She drops on one knee and blows into the keyhole as much of these fine ashes as the lock will hold. When she fills it to the brim, she creeps to her room.*]

MIGGS: [*chuckling and rubbing her hands*] There! now let's see whether you won't be glad to take some notice of me, mister! You'll have eyes for somebody besides Miss Dolly now, I think. A fat-faced puss she is, as ever I come across!

[*She glances at herself in the mirror.*]

MIGGS: I thank my stars that can't be said of me! Well, I don't go to bed this night!

[*She wraps herself in a shawl and draws a couple of chairs near the window. She flounces down upon one chair and puts her feet up on the other.*]

MIGGS: I'll watch you come home, my lad. I wouldn't, no, not for anything! not sit up and wait and listen.

BLACKOUT

The spinster Miggs lets no one get away with anything. Her body is distorted into odd positions as she prepares for Sim's surprise when he comes home and finds he cannot put his key into the keyhole. She settles down comfy and sits with perfect composure all night.

* * *

CAPTAIN TAPPERTIT'S HOMECOMING

From the novel *BARNABY RUDGE*

CHARACTERS: **MIGGS:** a spinster, mistress of all moods.

SIMON [SIM, SIMMUN] TAPPERTIT: has come home after having been the head of a secret group of angry apprentices who swear revenge on their masters. It is time now for him to take up his regular duties.

SETTING: The locksmith's house. Early morning.

SUMMARY:

Miggs has waited up all night to see her Simmun come home. At break of day, she hears him stop at the door and try his key. Tappertit is having trouble with it. He blows into the lock. He knocks the key on a post to beat the dust out. He takes it under a lamp to look at it. He pokes bits of stick into the lock to clear it. He peeps into the keyhole, first with one eye and then with the other. He tries the key again. He can't turn it. It bends and sticks. He gives it a mighty twist and a great pull. The key comes out so suddenly that he falls backwards. He kicks the door. He shakes it. Finally, after beating his forehead, he sits down on the step in despair.

MIGGS: [*faintly*] Who is there?

TAPPERRTIT: [*in a frenzy*] Hush!

[*He motions her to secrecy and silence.*]

MIGGS: Tell me one thing. Is it thieves?

TAPPERTIT: No—no—no!

MIGGS: [*even more faintly*] Then, it's fire. Where is it, sir? It's near this room, I know. I've a good conscience, sir, and would much rather die than climb out a window. All I wish is, send my love to my married sister, Golden Lion Court, number twenty-sivin.

TAPPERTIT: Miggs! Don't you know me? Sim, you know — Sim —

MIGGS: Oh! what about him! Is he in any danger? Is he in the midst of flames and blazes! Oh gracious, gracious!

TAPPERTIT: [*beating on his chest*] Why I'm here, ain't I? Don't you see me? What a fool you are, Miggs!

MIGGS: There! Why...so it...Goodness, what is the meaning of...If you please, mim, here's...

TAPPERTIT: No, no! Don't! I've been out without leave, and something or other's the matter with the lock. Come and undo the shop door.

MIGGS: I dursn't do it, Simmun, I dursn't do it, indeed. You know as well as anybody, how particular I am. And to come to the door in the dead of night, when the house is wrapped in slumbers.

[*She shivers in modesty.*]

TAPPERTIT: But Miggs... My darling Miggs...[MIGGS *screams slightly*] ...That I love so much, and never can help thinking of, do...for my sake, do.

MIGGS: Oh Simmun, this is worse than all. I know if I do come, you'll go, and...

TAPPERTIT: And what, my precious?

MIGGS: [*hysterically*] And try, to kiss me, or some such dreadfulness; I know you will!

TAPPERTIT: [*quite in earnest*] I swear I won't. Upon my soul I won't. It's getting broad daylight, and the watchman's waking up. Angelic Miggs! If you'll only come and let me in, I promise you faithfully and truly I won't.

[MISS MIGGS, *comes lightly over and opens the workshop door.* TAP-PERTIT *enters the room.*]

MIGGS: [*faintly*] Simmun is safe!

[*She faints.*]

TAPPERTIT: If I hadn't eyed her over, she wouldn't have come at all. Here, keep up a minute, Miggs. What a scraggy figure she is! There's no holding her comfortably. Do keep up a minute, Miggs, will you?

[MIGGS *is deaf to all entreaties.* TAPPERTIT *leans her against the wall like an umbrella. Changing position, he takes her in his arms again. In short stages and with great difficulty he carries and plants her, in the same umbrella fashion, against the wall next to her door and escapes.*]

MIGGS: [*recovering*] He may be as cool as he likes, but I'm in his confidence and he can't help himself, nor couldn't if he was twenty Simmunses!

BLACKOUT

The pratfall comedy is obvious as Miggs faints. But the comedy is also Simmun's having to adore Miggs as she wishes.

* * *

SIMON TAPPERTIT WARNS SIR JOHN CHESTER

From the novel BARNABY RUDGE

CHARACTERS: **SIR JOHN CHESTER:** a man of high society who deals with lower class creatures to get him the information he wants.

SIMON TAPPERTIT: one who aspires to more than he is and finds Sir John Chester a man who understands him.

SERVANT

SETTING: Sir John Chester's bedroom.

SUMMARY:

John Chester, accepted and admired in the best circles, is a manipulative, scheming, and cunning man. His private company consists of thieves and snitches who have an axe to grind and whom he uses to accomplish his cruelest purposes.

Simon [Sim] Tappertit has dreams and ambitions beyond his station as an apprentice to a locksmith. He has imagination enough to have created the society of Knight 'Prentices, making himself the Captain of a group that is determined to get even on everyone who is not a member. He sees himself as a moody, introspective Genius waiting to find someone to understand him and appreciate his potential.

[SIR JOHN, *in his dressing gown, is seated before his mirror. His* SERVANT *enters and hands him a very small scrap of dirty paper, tightly sealed*]

SIR JOHN CHESTER: [*reads aloud*] A friend. Desiring of a conference. Immediate. Private. Burn it when you've read it. Where did you pick this up?

SERVANT: [*with obvious distaste*] It was given me by a person waiting outside.

SIR JOHN CHESTER: With a cloak and dagger?

SERVANT: Sir, with a leather apron and a dirty face. Shall I tell him to leave?

SIR JOHN CHESTER: [*amused*] No, bring him here.

[SIMON TAPPERTIT *enters. He carries a great lock which he places on the floor.* SIR JOHN *looks on him as some maniac, who has not only broken open the door of his place of confinement, but has brought away the lock.* MR. TAPPERTIT *bows, displaying his legs to best advantage.*]

TAPPERTIT: [*bowing low again*] You have heard, sir, of G. Varden, Locksmith and repairs neatly executed in town and country, London?

SIR JOHN CHESTER: What then?

TAPPERTIT: I'm his 'prentice.

SIR JOHN CHESTER: And what then?

TAPPERTIT: [*clearing his throat*] Would you permit me to shut the door and will you further give me your honor bright, that what passes between us is in the strictest confidence?

[*At a nod,* TAPPERTIT *shuts the door and returns to the center of the room.*]

SIR JOHN CHESTER: I beg you to speak out and be as rational as you can without putting yourself to any very great personal inconvenience.

TAPPERTIT: [*shaking out a handkerchief gracefully*] In the first place, sir, as I have not a card about me (for the envy of our masters debases us below that level) allow me to offer the best substitute that circumstances will admit of. If you will take that in your own hand and cast your eye on the right-hand corner, you will meet with my credentials.

SIR JOHN CHESTER: Thank you. I see it well enough.

TAPPERTIT: Your name is Chester, I suppose? I observe the initials on your robe. You needn't straighten it, thank you. We will take the rest for granted.

SIR JOHN CHESTER: Mr. Tappertit, perhaps, because it has a strong flavor of oil, you will oblige me to put that huge lock outside the door?

TAPPERTIT: By all means. [*muttering*] This is something like the respect I am entitled to. A courteous demeanor and that from a stranger.

[TAPPERTIT *takes the lock outside and returns.*]

SIR JOHN CHARLES: You'll excuse my mentioning it, I hope?

TAPPERTIT: Don't apologise, sir, I beg. And now, if you please, to business. I am aware that your son keeps company with a young lady against your inclinations. Sir, your son has not used me well.

SIR JOHN CHARLES: Mr. Tappertit, you grieve me beyond description.

TAPPERTIT: Thank you. I'm glad to hear you say so. He's very proud your son; very haughty.

SIR JOHN CHESTER: I am afraid he is haughty. Do you know I was really afraid of that before. And you confirm me?

TAPPERTIT: To recount the menial offices I've had to do for your son. The chairs I've had to hand him, the numerous degrading duties that I've had to do for him, would fill a family Bible. Besides which he is but a young man himself and I do not consider "thank you, Sim," a proper form of address on those occasions.

SIR JOHN CHESTER: Mr. Tappertit, your wisdom is beyond your years. Please go on.

TAPPERTIT: [*much gratified*] I thank you for your good opinion. Now, on this account (and perhaps for another reason or two which I needn't go into) I am on your side. And what I tell you is this — that as long as Dolly Varden goes backwards and forwards, to and fro, up and down, to that there jolly old Maypole Inn, sending letters, and messages, and fetching and carrying, you couldn't prevent your son keeping company with that young lady, Miss Emma, — not if he was minded night and day by a battery of guards in fullest uniform. [*stops to take a breath*] Now, I am a coming to the point. You will inquire of me, "how is this to be prevented?" I'll tell you how. If an honest, civil, smiling gentleman like you –

SIR JOHN CHESTER: Mr. Tappertit — really...

TAPPERTIT: No, no, I'm serious, I am, upon my soul. If an honest, civil, smiling gentleman like you, was to talk but ten minutes to the old lady, the locksmith's wife and mother to Dolly Varden — that's Mrs. Varden — and flatter her up a bit, you'd gain her over for ever. Then there's this point got — that her daughter Dolly...[*a flush comes over his face*] ...wouldn't be allowed to bring messages between Miss Emma and your son. Mind that.

SIR JOHN CHESTER: Mr. Tappertit, your knowledge of human nature...

TAPPERTIT: [*deadly calm at first and increasingly wild*] Wait a minute. Now I come to the point. Sir, there is a villain at that Maypole Inn, a monster in human shape that unless you get rid of and have kidnapped and carried off – nothing less will do — he will marry your son to that young woman, as certainly as if he was the Archbishop of Canterbury himself. He will for the hatred and malice that he bears to you. If you knew how this chap, this Joe Willet — that's his name — comes libelling, and denouncing, and threatening you, and how I shudder when I hear him, you'd hate him worse than I do — worse than I do,...if sich a thing is possible.

SIR JOHN CHESTER: A little private vengeance in this, Mr. Tappertit?

TAPPERTIT: Private vengeance, sir, destroy him. Miggs says so too. Miggs and me both say so. We can't bear the plotting and undermining that takes place. Our souls recoil from it. Barnaby Rudge and Mrs. Rudge are in it likewise. But Joe Willet, is the ringleader. Put Joe Willet down. Destroy him. Crush him. And be happy.

[SIMON TAPPERTIT *takes his leave silently like a lone, mysterious stranger.*

BLACKOUT

Simon has good looking legs, and he displays them as his best feature. He has rehearsed his speech many times, but always calmly. He didn't expect to be carried away with his vehemence. Determining his hearer to be stunned and dumbfounded by the eloquence of his delivery, Simon seems satisfied with his performance.

* * *

TAPPERTIT, THE CONQUEROR

From the novel *BARNABY RUDGE*

CHARACTER: **SIMON TAPPERTIT:** very proud of his legs.

SETTING: The locksmith Varden's house

SUMMARY:

Simon Tappertit, the locksmith's apprentice who has dreams of greatness, is in love with Dolly Varden, the locksmith's daughter. Simon has been hiding and eavesdropping on Joe Willet and Dolly, as Joe [who is leaving to go into the army] says goodbye to Dolly. Dolly, who loves Joe but is too frivolous to show it, has been off-handed with him. Simon interprets Dolly's coldness to Joe as a sign of his own attractiveness to her.

TAPPERTIT: [*emerging from his hiding place*] Have my ears deceived me or do I dream! Am I to thank Thee, oh Fortune or to cus' thee? Which?

[*He takes down his piece of broken mirror and looks closely at his legs.*]

TAPPERTIT: If they're a dream, let sculptures have such visions, and chisel 'em out when they wake. This is reality. Sleep has no such limbs as them. Tremble, Joe Willet, and despair. She's mine! She's mine!

[*He seizes a hammer and gives the table a huge blow. He can't contain a peal of laughter.*]

BLACKOUT

The acting suggestions are all in the scene itself.

* * *

ARTHUR GRIDE AND DEAF PEG

From the novel *NICHOLAS NICKLEBY*

CHARACTERS: **ARTHUR GRIDE:** a revolting old skinflint.

PEG SLIDERSKEW: his faithful, very deaf housekeeper.

SETTING: Gride's house.

SUMMARY:

This is the morning of Arthur Gride's wedding to a girl fifty years younger than he. It is a sordid business arrangement between three men: two usurers, Gride and Ralph Nickleby, and Bray, the girls father.

[PEG *enters* GRIDE'*s parlor.*]

GRIDE: Ah, Peg, what is it? What is it now, Peg?

PEG: [*holding up a small skinny fowl*] It's the fowl.

GRIDE: [*knowing how little she paid for it*] A beautiful bird! With a bit of ham, and an egg made into sauce, and potatoes, and greens, and an apple pudding, Peg, and a little bit of cheese, we shall have a dinner for an emperor. There'll only be she and me — and you, Peg, when we've done.

PEG: [*sulkily*] Don't you complain of the expense afterwards.

GRIDE: [*with a groan*] I am afraid we must live expensively for the first week. And then we must make up for it. I won't eat more than I can help, and I know you love your old master too much to eat more than you can help, don't you, Peg?

PEG: Don't I what?

GRIDE: Love your old master too much...

PEG: No, not a bit too much.

GRIDE: I wish the devil had this woman! Love him too much to eat more than you can help at his expense.

PEG: At his what?

GRIDE: [*whining*] She can never hear the most important word, and she hears all the others! At his expense — [he whispers] You catamaran!

[*The door bell is heard.*]

GRIDE: There's the bell.

PEG: I know, I know. I know that.

GRIDE: [*bawling*] Then why don't you go?!

PEG: [*with a growl*] Go where? I ain't doing any harm here, am I?

GRIDE: [*as loud as he can roar*] Bell! Bell!

[GRIDE *pantomimes ringing at a street-door.*]

PEG: Why hadn't you said there was a ring, instead of talking about all manner of things that has nothing to do with it. And keeping my half-pint of beer waiting on the steps.

[PEG *hobbles out.*]

GRIDE: [*watching her*] There's a change come over you, Mrs. Peg. What it means I don't quite know; but, if it lasts, we shan't agree together long I see. You are turning crazy, I think. If you are, you must take yourself off, Mrs. Peg — or be taken off. All's one to me.

[*He returns to his account book.* PEG, *wiping her hands on her apron, looks back at* GRIDE.]

PEG: Faugh! Wedding indeed! A precious wedding! He wants somebody better than his old Peg to take care of him, does he? And what has he said to me, many and many a time, to keep me content with short food, and small wages? 'My last will, Peg! My last will and testament! I'm a bachelor — no friends — no relations, Peg.' Lies! And now he's to bring home a baby-faced chit of a girl! If he wanted a wife, the fool, why couldn't he have one suitable to his age, and that knew his ways? She won't come in my way, he says. No, that she won't, but you little think why, Arthur boy!

BLACKOUT

Anything you can do to make Peg uglier, like blacking out your teeth, or even wearing your shoes on the wrong foot will work. Anything you can do to make Gride either fatter or skinnier or older or uglier will also do.

* * *

MR. SQUEERS AND PEG SLIDERSKEW

From the novel *NICHOLAS NICKLEBY*

CHARACTERS: MR. SQUEERS: the owner of Dotheboys school. Out of his greed, Squeers will do the most repulsive errands for Ralph Nickleby, who pays well.

PEG SLIDERSKEW: a deaf old woman. Although she is illiterate, Peg knows that she has stolen some important papers from her employer, Gride.

NEWMAN NOGGS: works for Ralph Nickleby, hates him, and does as many good deeds for the other Nicklebys as he can.

FRANK CHEERYBLE: a member of the goodly and generous Cheeryble family.

SETTING:	An Inn where Peg is hiding.
PART ONE:	Squeers'room.
PART TWO:	Peg's room.
PART THREE:	Peg's room.

SUMMARY:

At Ralph Nickleby's persuasion and for a large amount of money, Mr. Squeers has reluctantly agreed to trap the deaf and illiterate Peg Sliderskew into showing him what she has stolen from her employer, Arthur Gride. Squeers has been staying in a desolate room at this Inn in order to make himself a companion to Peg. He is disconsolate, uncomfortable, and drinking heavily.

MR. SQUEERS: I've been six weeks getting to know this blessed old hag. That's the worst of being in with a fellow like Nickleby. You never know when he's done with you, and if you're in for a penny, you're in for a pound. [*chuckles*] But I'm in for a hundred pound at any rate...Oh, joy, here's to money!

[*He drinks happily.*]

MR. SQUEERS: I never seen such a one as that old Nickleby. Never! To see how sly and cunning he grubbed on, day after day, till he found out where this precious Mrs. Peg was hid, and cleared the ground for me to work on her and...and......and, well, I'll think of the rest, and say it when convenient. [*he drinks*] I don't mind a little extra work for good money. [he looks at the clock] It's pretty near the time to wait upon the dear old woman. So I'll have half a glass more, to wish myself success. [he drinks] I'm feeling more cheerful by the minute! I'll take the bottle with me and the glass! In case I need to lift my spirits!

* * *

PART TWO

SETTING: Peg's room

[PEG SLIDERSKEW, *an old deaf woman, is bending over a wretched fire to keep warm.*]

MR. SQUEERS: [*tapping her on the shoulder*] Well, my Slider!

PEG: [*she jumps*] Hah! Is that you?

MR. SQUEERS: Yes, it's me.

[SQUEERS *sits on a stool near* PEG, *and places the bottle and glass on the floor between them.*]

MR. SQUEERS: [*very loud*] Well, my Slider!

PEG: [*graciously*] I hear you.

MR. SQUEERS: [*roaring*] I've come according to promise.

PEG: [*complacently*] So they used to say in that part of the country I come from. But I think oil's better.

MR. SQUEERS: [*roaring*] Better than what? [*in an under-tone*] You foolish old hag...

PEG: No. Of course not.

MR. SQUEERS: [*looking very amiable, he mutters*] I never saw such a monster as you are!

[PEG *is looking at* MR. SQUEERS *and chuckling fearfully at her clever repartee.*]

MR. SQUEERS: Do you see this? This is a bottle.

PEG: I see it.

MR. SQUEERS: [*yelling*] Well, and do you see this? This is a glass.

PEG: I see that, too.

MR. SQUEERS: See, I fill the glass from the bottle, and I say 'your health, Slider' and I empty it; then I rinse it with a little drop and fill it again, and hand it over to you.

[*He hands her the glass.*]

PEG: Your health.

[*She drinks.*]

MR. SQUEERS: [*muttering*] She understands that, anyways.

[PEG *drinks, chokes and gasps.*]

MR. SQUEERS: Now then, let's have a talk. How's the rheumatics?

[PEG SLIDERSKEW *blinks and chuckles, admiring* MR. SQUEERS: *his person, manners, and conversation.*]

PEG: The rheumatics is better.

MR. SQUEERS: [*inspired by the liquor*] What's the reason of rheumatics? What do people have 'em for, eh?

PEG: I don't know. Maybe because they can't help it.

MR. SQUEERS: Measles, rheumatics, hooping-cough, is all philosophy; that's what it is. The heavenly bodies is philosophy, and the earthly bodies is philosophy. If there's a screw loose in a heavenly body, that's philosophy; and if there's a screw loose in a earthly body, that's philosophy too.

[MR. SQUEERS *and* PEG *drink and* MR. SQUEERS *talks, keeping an eye on* PEG.]

MR. SQUEERS: Peg, you look twenty pounds better than you did.

[PEG *chuckles modestly at the compliment.*]

MR. SQUEERS: Twenty pounds better than you did that day when I first introduced myself, don't you know?

PEG: Ah! but you frightened me that day.

MR. SQUEERS: Well, it was rather a startling thing for a stranger to come and say that he knew all about you, and what you had stolen, and who you stolen it from, wasn't it?

PEG: Oh, yes!

MR. SQUEERS: I'm a sort of a lawyer, Peg Slider. I'm the friend and adviser of every person that gets themselves into trouble by being too nimble with their fingers, I'm...

PEG: [*interrupts him*] Ha,ha,ha! And so he wasn't married after all, wasn't he? Not married after all?

MR. SQUEERS: No, that he wasn't!

PEG: And a young lover come and carried off the bride, eh?

[MR. SQUEERS *is plying* MRS. SLIDERSKEW *freely with liquor; under the exertion of speaking so loud, he is drinking heavily..*]

PEG: Tell me all about it again. Let's hear it all again, beginning at the beginning now, as if you'd never told me. Let's have it every word. Now. Now. Beginning at the very first, you know, when he went to the house that morning!

MR. SQUEERS: The young lover carried off the bride from under his very nose. And I'm told the young fellow cut him up rough, and forced him to swaller his wedding flower that he wore in his lapel which nearly choked him.

[PEG's *natural hideousness is even more fearsome as she relishes hearing of her master's defeat. She is in an ecstasy of delight, rolling her head about, drawing up her skinny shoulders, and wrinkling her cadaverous face into such complicated forms of ugliness that it stirs the astonishment and disgust even of* MR. SQUEERS.]

PEG: He's a treacherous old goat. But never mind. I'm even with him. I'm even with him!!

MR. SQUEERS: And that reminds me, if you want me to give you my opinion of them deeds, and tell you what you'd better keep and what you'd better burn, why, now's your time, Slider.

PEG: [*winking knowingly*] There ain't no hurry for that.

MR. SQUEERS: Oh! very well! It don't matter to me; you asked me, you know. I shouldn't charge you nothing, being a friend. You're the best judge of course; but you're a bold woman, Slider, that's all.

PEG: How do you mean, bold?

MR. SQUEERS: Why, I only mean that if it was me, I wouldn't keep papers as might hang me, when they might be turned into money. But everybody's the best judge of their own affairs. All I say is, Slider, I wouldn't do it.

PEG: Come, then you shall see 'em.

MR. SQUEERS: I don't want to see 'em. Don't talk as if it was a treat. Show 'em to somebody else, and take their advice.

[PEG SLIDERSKEW, *in her anxiety to restore herself to her former high position in his good graces, becomes so extremely affectionate that* MR. SQUEERS *stands at some risk of being smothered by her caresses.*]

MR. SQUEERS: No, no. I was only joking. I'm ready to examine the deeds at once, if that will afford you any relief of mind, my fair friend.

[PEG *rises to fetch the papers.*]

MR. SQUEERS: [*bawling*] And now you're up, my Slider, bolt the door!

PEG: It don't bolt. But nobody comes this way.

[PEG *goes to her bed and gets a small box. She places this on the floor at* SQUEERS'*s feet. She takes a small key from under her pillow. She gives it to* SQUEERS *to open.*]

MR. SQUEERS: [*opens the box*] Ah. Oh. Ah...

[*He reaches for a sheet.*]

PEG: [*holding back his impatient hand*] What's of no use we'll burn; what we can get any money by, we'll keep; and if there's any we could get him into trouble by, and fret and waste away his heart to shreds, those we'll take particular care of; for that's what I want to do.

MR. SQUEERS: I thought that you didn't bear him any particular good-will. But, I say, why didn't you take some money besides!

PEG: Some what?

MR. SQUEERS: [*roaring*] Some money. I do believe the woman hears me, and wants to make me break a vessel, so that she may have the pleasure of nursing me. Some money, Slider — money!

PEG: [*with some contempt*] Why, what a man you are to ask! If I had taken money from Arthur Gride, he'd have scoured the whole earth to find me — and he'd have smelt it out, some-how, even if I had buried it at the bottom of a well. No, no! I knew better than that. I took what I thought his secrets were hid in and them he couldn't afford to make public, let 'em be worth ever so much money. He's an old dog; a sly, old, cunning, thankless dog! He first starved, and then tricked me; and if I could I'd kill him.

MR. SQUEERS: All right. But, first and foremost, Slider, burn the box. [*he hands her the box*] You should never keep things as may lead to discovery — always mind that. So while you pull it to pieces and burn it in little bits, I'll look over the papers and tell you what they are.

PEG: Yes, that's good. You do that.

[SQUEERS *tumbles its contents upon the floor and hands the box back to her.*]

MR. SQUEERS: [*keeping* PEG *busy and away from the papers*] You poke the pieces between the bars, and make up a good fire, and I'll read the while. [SQUEERS *eagerly examines the papers*] Let me see, let me see...

* * *

PART THREE

[*In the darkened room, neither* PEG *nor* SQUEERS *are aware that two men have silently entered. They are Newman Noggs and Frank Cheeryble. They stand behind* SQUEERS *while he is reading the papers and* PEG *is feeding the fire. Newman raises a rusty old bellows over* SQUEERS *head. Frank stays his hand.*]

MR. SQUEERS: Here seems to be some deed of sale, some old bills no use to anybody, burn that...here, throw all this into the fire.

[*He hands* PEG *these papers.* PEG *throws them into the fire.*]

PEG: [*chuckling*] What's the next?

MR. SQUEERS: Here you are, bonds — take care of them. Warrant of attorney — take care of that. Hmn...

PEG: What's the matter?

MR. SQUEERS: Nothing. Only I'm looking for...

[*He searches through papers. Newman raises the bellows again. Frank stays his hand again.*]

MR. SQUEERS: [*snatches up one page*] Ah! 'Madeline Bray...come of age or marry...the said Madeline...' Peg, old girl, here, burn this!

[SQUEERS *throws her a useless parchment. While* PEG'*s back is turned,* SQUEERS *stuffs the will into his pocket.*]

SQUEERS: I've got it! I've got it! I've got it! The plan was a good one, a good one, a...

PEG: What are you laughing at? Huh? What, what?

[NEWMAN *brings the bellows down on* SQUEERS' *head.* SQUEERS *is stretched out, flat and senseless.*]

BLACKOUT

There will probably be much laughter during the scene, so you must be careful to not lose some funny dialogue. Find business to cover for the laughter or repeat your lines as though you are trying to make Peg hear. Peg and Squeers are a good team; they get on well together. Their dialogue should have a bouncing quality and they should actually enjoy the scene. Newman and Frank must have large and expressive gestures that will show up in the near darkness.

SQUEERS TURNS ON RALPH NICKLEBY

From the novel *NICHOLAS NICKLEBY*

CHARACTERS:	**MR. SQUEERS:** has been injured doing Ralph Nickleby's dirty work.
	RALPH NICKLEBY: begins to feel that he is losing his power over people.
SETTING:	A jail where Squeers is being held without bail.

SUMMARY:

Squeers is turned over to the police after the will he was looking for among deaf Peg's papers is found in his pocket. This is the will that makes Madeleine Bray a rich woman. It is the will that Ralph Nickleby desperately wants to find. Ralph Nickleby comes to get Squeers out of jail. It is difficult to rouse him. [Not only is he drunk, Squeers is also recovering from being knocked out by Newman Noggs.] Regaining his faculties at length, he sits upright. His face is yellow, his nose very red, and his beard is bristly. He has a dirty white handkerchief, spotted with blood, over the crown of his head and tied under his chin. Squeers stares at Ralph in silence.

SQUEERS: I say, young fellow, you've been and done it now, you have!

RALPH NICKLEBY: What's the matter with your head?

SQUEERS: Why, your man, your informing kidnapping employee, has been and broke it. That's what's the matter with it. You've come at last, have you?

RALPH NICKLEBY: Why have you not sent to me? How could I come till I knew what had happened to you?

SQUEERS: My family! My daughter, my son – the pride of the

Squeerses   Gone! All gone.

RALPH NICKLEBY: You have been drinking, and have not yet slept yourself sober.

SQUEERS: [*his manner altered and insolent*] I haven't been drinking your health, you old rascal.

RALPH NICKLEBY: [*aware of Squeers' change in tone*] Why didn't you send for me?

SQUEERS: What should I get by sending to you? To be known to be in with you wouldn't do me a deal of good, and they won't take bail till they know something more of the case, so here I am hard and fast: and there are you, loose and comfortable.

RALPH NICKLEBY: [*pretending good humor*] So you are in for a few days. They can't hurt you, man.

SQUEERS: Why, I suppose they can't do much to me, if I explain how it was that I got into the good company of that there ca-daverous old Slider, who I wish was dead and buried, and res-urrected and dissected, and hung upon wires in a anatomical museum. I can say to the judge, 'I am the Wackford Squeers as is therein named, sir. I was not aware that anything was wrong. I was merely employed by a friend — my friend Mr. Ralph Nickleby. Send for him, sir, and ask him what he has to say — he's the man; not me!'

RALPH NICKLEBY: What deed was it that you had?

SQUEERS: What deed? Why, the deed. The Madeline What's-her-name one. It was a will; that's what it was.

RALPH NICKLEBY: Of what nature, whose will, when dated, how benefiting her, to what extent?

SQUEERS: A will in her favor; that's all I know. And that's more than you'd have known, if you'd had them bellows on your head. It's all owing to your precious caution that they got hold of it. If you had let me burn it, and taken my word that it was gone, it would have been a heap of ashes instead of being whole and sound, inside of my pocket.

RALPH NICKLEBY: [*muttering*] Beaten at every point! [after a pause] I tell you, once again, they can't hurt you. You shall have an action for false imprisonment, and make a profit of this, yet. We will devise a story for you that should carry you through twenty times such a trivial scrape as this; and if they want security of a thousand dollars for your reappearance in case you should be called upon, you shall have it. All you have to do - is to keep back the truth. And you'll need all your senses about you; for a slip might be awkward.

SQUEERS: [*with cunning, his head to one side*] Oh! That's what I'm to do, is it? Now then, just you hear a word or two from me. I ain't a-going to have any stories made for me, and I ain't a-going to stick to any. If I find matters going against me, I shall expect you to take your share, and I'll take care you do. I don't mean to take it as quiet as you think. The only number in all arithmetic that I know of is number one!

[SQUEERS *is interrupted by the arrival of an attendant who is to take him to another confinement. With great dignity,* SQUEERS *perches his hat on the top of the handkerchief that is binding his head. He thrusts one hand into his pocket, takes the attendant's arm with the other, and suffers himself to be led away.*]

BLACKOUT

The bloody handkerchief around Squeers' head, his besotted appearance, and his great dignity in taking the attendant's arm makes the comedy. Otherwise, Squeers is shrewd and calculating. He knows that Ralph is caught.

PASSION

TULKINGHORN AND HORTENSE

From the novel *BLEAK HOUSE*

CHARACTERS: **TULKINGHORN:** a lawyer

HORTENSE: Lady Dedlock's former French maid.

SETTING: Tulkinghorn's rooms.

SUMMARY:

Hortense has been hovering around the living quarters of Tulkinghorn, waiting for him. Finally, she knows that he is at home. She knocks at his door. It is late. Tulkinghorn is about to enjoy a bottle of good wine. He opens the door with a candle in his hand. Note: 'the man' that Hortense refers to is Detective Bucket; 'that boy' is Jo, a homeless waif who showed the disguised Lady Dedlock [wearing Hortense's clothing] the way to the cemetery where her former lover, Captain Hawdon, is buried. Hortense's hatred for Lady Dedlock matches that of the cool impassive lawyer Tulkinghorn.

TULKINGHORN: It's you, is it? Now! What do you want?

[*He stands the candle on the mantel and taps his cheek with the key to his liquor cabinet. With her eyes almost shut , HORTENSE looks at him sideways like a dangerous feline creature and softly closes the door*].

HORTENSE: I have had great deal of trouble to find you, sir.

TULKINGHORN: Have you?

HORTENSE: I have been here very often, sir. It is always said to me, he is not at home, he is engage, he is this and that, he is not for you.

TULKINGHORN: Quite right, and quite true.

HORTENSE: [*suddenly loud*] Not true. Lies!

[*Feral in her gestures,* HORTENSE *startles* TULKINGHORN *so that he involuntarily and, for a second only, falls back. With her eyes almost shut [but still looking out sideways], she is smiling contemptuously and shaking her head.*]

TULKINGHORN: [*tapping the key rapidly on the mantel*] Now, if you have anything to say, say it!

HORTENSE: Sir, you have not use me well. You have been mean and shabby.

TULKINGHORN: [*rubbing his nose with the key*] Mean and shabby, eh?

HORTENSE: Yes. You know you have. You have tttrapped me — catched me — to give you information; you have ask me to show you the dress of mine my Lady must have wore that night, you have prayed me to come in it - here to meet that man...

TULKINGHORN: Well, I paid you.

HORTENSE: [*fiercely*] You paid me! Two sovereign! I have not change them, I re-fuse them, I des-pise them, I throw them from me!

[*She takes them out of her bosom and flings them violently on the floor.*]

HORTENSE: [*continues*] [*her eyes darkening*] Now! You have paid me? Eh, my God, oh yes!

[TULKINGHORN *rubs his head with the key.* HORTENSE *laughs sarcastically.*]

TULKINGHORN: You must be rich, my fair friend, to throw money about in that way.

HORTENSE: I hate my Lady. You know that.

TULKINGHORN: Know it? How should I know it?

HORTENSE: [*clenching her hands, setting her teeth*] You prayed me give you that information. Because you know perfectly that I was en-r-r-r-raged!

TULKINGHORN: [*examining his key*] Oh! I knew that, did I?

HORTENSE: Yes, without doubt. I am not blind. You have made sure of me because you knew that. You had reason! I det-est her.

TULKINGHORN: Having said this, have you anything else to say, mademoiselle?

HORTENSE: I am not yet placed. Place me well. Find me a good situation! If you cannot, or do not choose to do that, employ me to pursue her, to chase her, to disgrace and to dishonor her. I will help you well, and with a good will. It is what you do. Do I not know that?

TULKINGHORN: You appear to know a good deal.

HORTENSE: Do I not? Is it that I am so weak as to believe, like a child, that I come here in that dress to dec-cive that boy only to decide a little bet, a wager? Eh, my God, oh yes!

TULKINGHORN: [*imperturbably taps his chin with the key*] Now, let us see how this matter stands.

[HORTENSE *angrily nods her head again and again.*]

TULKINGHORN: Let us see. You come here to make a remarkably modest demand, which you have just stated, and it not being conceded, you will come again.

HORTENSE: [*with tight nods of her head*] And again, and yet again. And yet again. And many times again. In effect, for ever!

TULKINGHORN: Very well. Now, Mademoiselle Hortense, let me recommend you to pick up that money of yours.

[HORTENSE *laughs and stands her ground with folded arms.*]

TULKINGHORN: You will not, eh?

HORTENSE: No, I will not!

TULKINGHORN: So much the poorer you; so much the richer I! Look, lady, this is the key of my wine-cabinet. It is a large key, but the keys of prisons are larger. I am afraid a lady of your spirit and activity would find it an inconvenience to have one of those keys turned upon her for any length of time. What do you think?

HORTENSE: [*calmly*] I think, that you are a miserable wretch.

TULKINGHORN: [*blowing his nose*] Probably. But I don't ask what you think of me; I ask what you think of the prison.

HORTNESE: Nothing. What does it matter to me?

TULKINGHORN: [*carefully putting away his handkerchief*] Why, it matters this much: the law takes hold of the troublesome lady and shuts her up in prison. Turns the key on her.

[TULKINGHORN *illustrates his point with his cabinet key.*]

HORTENSE: [*pleasantly*] Truly? That is droll! But, still, what does it matter to me?

TULKINGHORN: My fair friend, make another visit here and you shall learn.

HORTENSE: In that case you will send me to the prison, perhaps?

TULKINGHORN: If you ever present yourself uninvited here again, I will give you over to the police. They carry troublesome people through the streets, strapped down on a board, my good wench.

HORTENSE: [*whispering*] I will prove you. [she stretches out her hand] I will try if you dare to do it!

TULKINGHORN: [*ignoring her*] And if I place you in jail, it will be some time before you find yourself at liberty again.

HORTENSE: [*still in a whisper*] I will prove you.

TULKINGHORN: [*still ignoring her*] And now, you had better go. Think twice before you come here again.

HORTENSE: Think you - twice two hundred times!

TULKINGHORN: [*opening the door for Hortense to leave*]You were dismissed by your lady, you know, as the most unmanageable of women. Now take warning by what I say to you. For what I say, I mean; and what I threaten, I will do.

[HORTENSE *leaves without answering or looking behind her. When she is gone,* TULKINGHORN *goes to his liquor cabinet, chooses a cob-web-covered bottle, and settles down to enjoy his wine.*]

BLACKOUT

You must find the exact French accent that serves Hortense's angry, murderous character. You can't speak in just any French dialect. The physical directions that Dickens gives for her body behavior are very good ones. Hortense experiences different emotions as she speaks. She is ironically polite and tender, then bitter with defiant scorn. Her eyes seem nearly shut and staringly wide open. If you can't manage Dicken's suggestions, take them as a clue and become your own kind of menace.

* * *

THE MURDERESS

From the novel *BLEAK HOUSE*

CHARACTERS: **LORD LEICESTER DEDLOCK:** an elderly man who is very much in love with his wife, Lady Dedlock.

DETECTIVE BUCKET: a well known detective with a sense of style and humor, all in the service of the job he has to do.

HORTENSE: an intense, passionate woman who would get away with murder. If she can't, 'tant pis.'

BUTLER

SETTING: Lord Dedlock's drawing room.

SUMMARY:

Lord Dedlock's physical condition has weakened since the disappearance of his beloved wife, Lady Dedlock. He has asked Detective Bucket to do all he can to clear his wife's name. Detective Bucket has solved the murder of the lawyer Tulkinghorn. He is about to explain how it happened. The scene opens as Lord Dedlock, with his eyes wide open, looks intently at Mr. Bucket.

DETECTIVE BUCKET: [*looks at his watch*] The party to be apprehended is now in this house. And I'm about to take her into custody in your presence. Sir Leicester Dedlock, Baronet, don't you say a word. Don't stir. You shall see the whole case clear, from first to last.

[DETECTIVE BUCKET *goes to the door and whispers to the butler.*

Then he shuts the door, and stands behind it with his arms folded. After a minute, the door slowly opens and the Frenchwoman, Mademoiselle Hortense, enters.]

[*The moment she is in the room* DETECTIVE BUCKET *claps the door shut and puts his back against it. She turns at the noise and sees* SIR LEICESTER DEDLOCK *in his chair.*]

HORTENSE: [*muttering hurriedly*] I ask you pardon. They tell me there was no one here.

[*She steps to the door and is confronted by* DETECTIVE BUCKET. *A spasm shoots across her face and she turns deadly pale.*]

DETECTIVE BUCKET: This is my lodger, Sir Leicester Dedlock. This foreign young woman has been my lodger for some weeks.

HORTENSE: [*straining to be jocular*] What do Sir Leicester care for that, you think, my angel?

DETECTIVE BUCKET: Why, my angel, we shall see.

HORTENSE: You are very mysterieuse. Are you drunk?

DETECTIVE BUCKET: Tolerable sober, my angel.

HORTENSE: I come from arriving at this so detestable house with your wife. Your wife have left me since some minutes. They tell me downstairs that your wife is here. I come here, and your wife is not here.

[*Her arms are crossed casually, but a nerve in her cheek is twitching.*]

HORTENSE: [*continues*] What is the intention of this fool's play, say then?

[DETECTIVE BUCKET *shakes his finger at her.*]

HORTENSE: [*with a laugh*] Ah, my God, you are an unhappy idiot! Leave me to pass downstairs, great pig.

DETECTIVE BUCKET: Now, mademoiselle, you go and sit down upon that sofa.

HORTENSE: [*with many nods*] I will not sit down upon nothing.

DETECTIVE BUCKET: [*pointing his finger*] Now, mademoiselle, you sit down upon that sofa.

HORTENSE: Why?

DETECTIVE BUCKET: Because I take you into custody on a charge of murder, and you don't need to be told it.

[*Mademoiselle complies.*]

HORTENSE: [*her cheek twitching*] You are a devil.

DETECTIVE BUCKET: Now, you see, you're comfortable and conducting yourself as I should expect a foreign young woman of your sense to do. So I'll give you a piece of advice, don't you talk too much, the less you parley anglais, the better, you know.

HORTENSE: [*sitting rigid and looking fierce*] Oh, you Bucket, you are a devil!

DETECTIVE BUCKET: [*his finger moving*] Now, Sir Leicester Dedlock, Baronet, this young woman, my lodger, besides being extraordinary vehement and passionate against her ladyship after being discharged...

HORTENSE: Lie! I discharge myself.

DETECTIVE BUCKET: Now, why don't you take my advice? I'm surprised at the indiscreetness you commit. You'll say something that'll be used against you, you know.

HORTENSE: [*furiously*] Discharge, too, by her ladyship! Eh, my faith, a pretty ladyship! Why, I r-r-r-ruin my character by remaining with a ladyship so infame!

DETECTIVE BUCKET: I thought the French were a polite nation, I did, really. Yet to hear a female going on like that before Sir Leicester Dedlock, Baronet!

HORTENSE: [*spitting on the carpet*] He is a poor abused! I spit upon his house, upon his name, upon his imbecility. Oh, that he is a great man! Oh, yes, superb! Oh, heaven! Bah!

DETECTIVE BUCKET: Well, Sir Leicester Dedlock, this intemperate foreigner also angrily took it into her head that she had established a claim upon Mr. Tulkinghorn, deceased, though she was liberally paid for her time and trouble.

HORTENSE: Lie! I ref-use his money all togezzer.

DETECTIVE BUCKET: If you will parley anglais, you know, you must take the consequences. She lived in my house in that capacity at the time that she was hovering about the chambers of the deceased Mr. Tulkinghorn.

HORTENSE: Lie! All lie!

DETECTIVE BUCKET: The murder was committed, Sir Leicester Dedlock, Baronet, and you know under what circumstances. Now, I beg of you to follow me close with your attention for a minute or two. I was sent for, and the case was entrusted to me. Now, observe!

[DETECTIVE BUCKET *bends forward, beating the air with his fore-finger.* HORTENSE *fixes her black eyes upon him with a dark frown and sets her dry lips closely and firmly together.*]

DETECTIVE BUCKET: [*continues*] I went home, Sir Leicester Dedlock, Baronet, at night and found this young woman having supper with my wife, Mrs. Bucket. It occurred to me that she overdid her respect, for the lamented memory of the deceased Mr. Tulkinghorn. It flashed upon me, as I sat opposite to her at the table and saw her with a knife in her hand, that she had done it!

HORTENSE: [*hardly audible through clenched teeth*] You are a devil.

DETECTIVE BUCKET: I laid a trap for her — such a trap as I never laid yet. I worked it out in my mind while I was talking to her at supper. When I went upstairs to bed, our house being small and this young woman's ears sharp, I stuffed the sheet into Mrs. Bucket's mouth that she shouldn't say a word of surprise and told her all about it. [*He interrupts his explanation*] My dear, don't you give your mind to that again! or I shall link your feet together at the ankles...

[*He goes over to* HORTENSE *and lays his hand on her shoulder.*]

HORTENSE: What is the matter with you now?

DETECTIVE BUCKET: Don't you think any more of throwing yourself out of the window. That's what's the matter with me. Come! Just take my arm. You needn't get up; I'll sit down by you. Now take my arm, will you? I'm a married man, you know. Just take my arm.

[*Mademoiselle* HORTENSE *moistens her dry lips and complies.*]

DETECTIVE BUCKET: Now we're all right again. Sir Leicester Dedlock, Baronet, to throw this young woman off her guard, I have never set foot in our house since, though I've communicated with Mrs. Bucket putting notes to her in loaves of bread and bottles of milk as often as required. My whispered words to Mrs. Bucket when she had the sheet in her mouth were, "Can you do without rest and keep watch upon her

night and day? Can you undertake to say, 'She shall do nothing without my knowledge, she shall be my prisoner without
suspecting it, she shall no more escape from me than from
death, and her life shall be my life, and her soul my soul, till I
have got her, if she did this murder?' Mrs. Bucket says to me,
as well as she could speak on account of the sheet, 'Bucket, I
can!' And she has acted up to it glorious!

HORTENSE: Lies! All lies, my friend!

DETECTIVE BUCKET: Sir Leicester Dedlock, Baronet, what does
our friend here try to do? Don't let it give you a turn. To
throw the murder on her ladyship.

[SIR LEICESTER *rises from his chair and staggers down again.*]

DETECTIVE BUCKET: Now, open that pocket-book of mine, Sir
Leicester Dedlock, if I may take the liberty of throwing it
towards you, and look at the letters sent to me, each with the
two words 'Lady Dedlock'. Open the one directed to yourself, and read the three words 'Lady Dedlock, Murderess'.
These letters have been falling about like a shower of lady-
birds.

HORTENSE: These are very long lies. You speak prose a great
deal. Is it that you have almost all finished, or are you speaking always?

DETECTIVE BUCKET: Sir Leicester Dedlock, Baronet, my prisoner here proposed to Mrs. Bucket, to take tea at a restaurant in
the country. There's a brook nearby. At tea, my prisoner got
up to fetch her handkerchief and was rather a long time gone.
Mrs. Bucket reported to me her suspicions. I had the brook
dragged by moonlight, and the pistol was brought up. Now,
my dear, put your arm a little further through mine, and hold
it steady, and I shan't hurt you!

[DETECTIVE BUCKET *quickly snaps a handcuff on her wrist.*]

DETECTIVE BUCKET: That's one. Now the other, darling. Two, and all told!

[*He rises.* HORTENSE *rises also.*]

HORTENSE: Where, where is your false, your treacherous, and cursed wife?

DETECTIVE BUCKET: She's gone forward to the Police Office. You'll see her there, my dear.

HORTENSE: [*panting like a tiger*] I would like to kiss her!

DETECTIVE BUCKET: You'd bite her.

HORTENSE: [*her eyes very large*] I would! I would love to tear her limb from limb.

DETECTIVE BUCKET: Bless you, darling. I'm fully prepared to hear that. Your sex have such a surprising animosity against one another when you do differ. You don't mind me half so much, do you?

HORTENSE: No. Though you are a devil still.

DETECTIVE BUCKET: Angel and devil by turns, eh? Let me make your shawl tidy. I've been lady's maid to a good many before now. And how about the hat? There's a cab at the door.

[*In one shake, Mademoiselle* HORTENSE *shakes herself perfectly neat and now looks uncommonly genteel.*]

HORTENSE: [*with several sarcastic nods*] Listen then, my angel. You are very spiritual. But can you restore him back to life?

DETECTIVE BUCKET: Not exactly.

HORTENSE: That is droll. Listen yet one time. You are very spiritual. Can you make a honorable lady of her? Or a haughty gentleman of him? Eh! Oh, then regard him! The poor infant! Ha! Ha! Ha!

DETECTIVE BUCKET: Don't be so malicious, why this is worse parleying than the other. Come along!

HORTENSE: You cannot do these things? Then you can do as you please with me. It is but the death, it is all the same. Let us go, my angel. Adieu, you old man, grey. I pity you, and I despise you!

[DETECTIVE BUCKET *somehow enfolds Mademoiselle in his grasp and spirits her out of the room.*]

[SIR LEICESTER, *left alone, remains as though he were still listening and his attention were still occupied. At length, he gazes round the empty room. Finding it deserted, he rises unsteadily to his feet, pushes back his chair, and walks a few steps, supporting himself by the table. He stops, makes inarticulate sounds, lifts up his eyes and seems to stare at something. He extends his arms and tears at his white hair. He sinks to the ground. Oblivious of his suffering, and* SIR LEICESTER *speaks his lady's name with something like distinctness in the midst of his inarticulate sounds, His tone is one of mourning and compassion rather than reproach.*]

BLACKOUT

In Hortense we see a trapped animal. In Detective Bucket we see her trapper. First, feel Hortense's rage by feeling the anger in her breath as she draws it in. Finally, when she says "death is no threat to her," fill the breath with a sneer. Just think it and it will be there.

For Lord Dedlock, follow the direactions and you will have the first signs of a stroke. By looking up vaguely, gazing around an empty room, seeming to stare at something or nothing, tearing at your hair, and sink ing to the ground, you will help to create the emotions that Lord Dedlock feels.

* * *

LADY DEDLOCK FIRST SEES HAWDON'S HAND-WRITING

From the novel *BLEAK HOUSE*

CHARACTERS:

LADY DEDLOCK: the bored, elegant lady of the house.

TULKINGHORN: ever the lawyer, always aware of nuance in behavior.

LORD DEDLOCK: the dull nobleman who, by birthright, has earned the right to be dull.

SETTING:

Lord Dedlock's drawing room.

SUMMARY:

Mr. Tulkinghorn has come to Lord Dedlock's estate as he does very often. This day he brings news of a minor legal matter pertaining to the property Lady Dedlock brought to her marriage. As with all suits before the British courts, this matter has dragged on for years. Lord Dedlock is in his usual chair. Lady Dedlock is sitting in her chair near the fire. Note: The handwriting that Lady Dedlock notices is that of her lover before her marriage, Captain Hawdon. Their affair ended disastrously, and Lady Dedlock has lived with a terrible secret for all these years.

LORD DEADLOCK: My Lady's cause has been again before the Chancellor, has it, Mr. Tulkinghorn?

MR. TULKINGHORN: Yes. It has been on again to-day.

[MR. TULKINGHORN *shakes* LORD DEDLOCK'*s hand and makes one of his quiet bows to* LADY DEDLOCK.]

LADY DEDLOCK: [*in her usual bored manner*] It would be useless to ask whether anything has been done.

MR. TULKINGHORN: Nothing that you would call anything has been done to-day.

LADY DEDLOCK: Nor ever will be.

MR. TULKINGHORN: [*with his usual caution*] As a few fresh affidavits have been put upon the file, and as they are short, and as I see you are going to Paris, I have brought them with me.

[MR. TULKINGHORN *takes out his papers and places them on a table near* LADY DEDLOCK. *He begins to read.*]

MR. TULKINGHORN: Between John Jarndyce —'

LADY DEDLOCK: You may dismiss as many of the formal horrors as you can.

[MR. TULKINGHORN *begins to read lower down on the page.* LADY DEDLOCK *carelessly and scornfully displays her inattention. The fire has become too hot.* LADY DEDLOCK *changes her position. The papers on the table catch her attention. She looks at them nearer – and nearer still.*]

LADY DEDLOCK: [*impulsively*] Who copied that?

[MR. TULKINGHORN *stops short. He is surprised by her animation and tone.*]

MR. TULKINGHORN: Why do you ask?

LADY DEDLOCK: [*resuming her disdain*] Anything to vary this detestable monotony. Oh, go on, do!

[MR. TULKINGHORN *reads again. He sees a change in* LADY DED-

LOCK's *position and in her face. He rises quickly.*]

LORD DEDLOCK: [*starting up from a doze*] Eh? What do you say?

MR. TULKINGHORN: I say I am afraid that Lady Dedlock is ill.

LADY DEDLOCK: [*murmurs*] Faint, only that; but it is like the faintness of death. Don't speak to me. Ring, please, and take me to my room!

[*She falls back in her chair.*]

BLACKOUT

One of the most difficult techniques is to 'accidentally' see something that is of great importance. It is one thing to play Lady Dedlock in her boredom, her alienation from her surroundings, and another to have her see a letter in a handwriting that she hasn't seen for some twenty years. Due to the submerged feelings of guilt and memory, Lady Dedlock's faints "almost to death." The way this can be done is through the breath. If you try to "happen" to see something with the external self, [i.e. using your eyes or an expression on your face] the moment will be jarring. It will not be believed. The moving breath brings the action inside of you.

* * *

MERCY'S NEW HOME

From the novel *MARTIN CHUZZLEWIT*

CHARACTERS:

JONAS: has revenged himself on his wife for her saucy behavior before they were married.

MERCY: is frightened by her new husband.

MRS. GAMP: a nurse for hire who can be

anything else she is asked to be so long as the money is provided.

OLD CHUFFEY: a long time employee of the Chuzzlewits.

SETTING: Jonas Chuzzlewit's home.

SUMMARY:

Jonas and Mercy have been married a month. Jonas has tamed Mercy, and now she is meek and frightened. Old Chuffey still sits near the stove, seemingly unaware of any intrusion.

JONAS: So there you are, Mr. Chuff, still in the land of the living, eh?

MRS. GAMP: Still in the land of the living, sir. And Mr. Chuffey may thank you for it, as many and many a time I've told him.

JONAS: [*in ill humour*] We don't want you any more, Mrs. Gamp.

MRS. GAMP: I'm a-going immediate, sir, unless there's nothink I can do for you, ma'am. Ain't there nothink I can do for you, my little bird?

[MRS. GAMP *rummages in her pocket.*]

MERCY: [*nervously*] No. You had better go away, please!

MRS. GAMP: [*sweet and sly in a low voice*] Would you be so good, my darling dovey of a dear young married lady, as to put my card some-wheres where you can keep it safe? I'm well beknown to many ladies. Gamp is my name, an livin' quite near, I will make so bold as call in now and then, and make inquiry how your health and spirits is, my precious chick!

[*Leering, winking, coughing, nodding, smiling,* MRS. GAMP *curtseys herself out of the room.* MERCY *sits. Looking about the dreary room, she cannot hide her desperation.*]

JONAS: [*watching her*] It ain't good enough for you, I suppose?

MERCY: [*bravely*] Why, it is dull.

JONAS: It'll be duller before you're done with it, if you give me any of your airs. You're a nice article, to turn sulky on first coming home! By god, you used to have life enough, when you could plague me with it. The gal's down-stairs. Ring the bell for supper, while I take my boots off!

[MERCY *looks after him as* JONAS *leaves the room. She rouses herself to call the servant.*]

OLD CHUFFEY: [*lays his hand on her arm*] You are not married? Not married?

MERCY: Yes. A month ago. Good Heaven, what is the matter?

OLD CHUFFEY: [*turning from her and raising his hands*] Oh! woe, woe, woe, upon this wicked house.

BLACKOUT

Mercy is in a stupor. She rouses herself with effort to do what Jonas orders her to do. For Old Chuffey, a line is crossed in marriage from which there is no turning back. He knows what Jonas is like and what is in store for Mercy.

* * *

OLD CHUFFEY'S PASSION

From the novel *MARTIN CHUZZLEWIT.*

CHARACTERS: OLD CHUFFEY: seems dazed and confused.

JONAS: on edge and seems worried about something.

SERVANT: this is a house where even the servant is surly.

SETTING: Jonas' home.

SUMMARY:

Jonas [to our present knowledge and his belief] has killed his father. What does old Chuffey know? Jonas keeps constant watch over him, afraid to leave him alone. Old Chuffey, who rarely speaks and seems to be absent even when he is physically in the room, sits as usual in his corner. Mercy has been gone for some time. Presently, Jonas fears for his wife's absence.

JONAS: By god! Chuffey, you old miser, she's not home yet.

OLD CHUFFEY: She went to her good friend, Mrs. Todgers.

JONAS: To be sure! Always stealing away into the company of that woman. That Todgers is no friend of mine. Who can tell what devil's mischief they are hatching. I want her fetched home directly.

[OLD CHUFFEY, *muttering, rises as if to go after her.*]

JONAS: Sit down, damn old fool. I'll send the servant. [*calls to the servant*] Bring my wife back from Todgers. Drop what you're doing and go!

[JONAS *paces the room, waiting. It is twilight, no candles are yet lit.*]

JONAS: [*muttering*] At Todgers, always some plan against me. If she has been waylaid... what that idiot of a wife could blurt out...

[*The* SERVANT *arrives back quickly.*]

JONAS: Well! Where was she? Has she come?

SERVANT: No. She left there, three hours ago.

JONAS: Left there! Alone?

SERVANT: I didn't know to ask. You didn't say.

JONAS: Curse you for a fool. Bring candles!

[*The* SERVANT *leaves.*]

OLD CHUFFEY: [*coming suddenly upon* JONAS] Give her up! Come! Give her up to me! Tell me what you have done with her. Quick! I have made no promises on that score. Tell me what you have done with her. [*grabs* JONAS *by the collar*] I am strong enough to cry out to the neighbours, and I will, unless you give her up. Give her up to me!

[JONAS, *dismayed and conscience-stricken, stands in the darkness, looking at* CHUFFEY, *unable to unclench the old man's hands.*]

JONAS: [*short of breath*] What do you mean?

OLD CHUFFEY: I will know what you have done with her! If you hurt a hair of her head, you shall answer for it. Poor thing! Poor thing! Where is she?

JONAS: [*trembling and in a low voice*] Why, you old madman! What crazy fit has come on you now?

OLD CHUFFEY: It is enough to make me mad, seeing what I have seen in this house! Where is my dear old master! Where is his only son that I have nursed upon my knee, a child! Where is she, she who was the last; she that I've seen pining day by day, and heard weeping in the dead of night! She was the last, the last of all my friends! Heaven help me, she was the very last!

JONAS: [mustering the courage to push him off] Did you hear me ask for her? Did you hear me send for her? How can I give up what I haven't got, idiot! By god, I'd give her up to you and welcome, if I could; and a precious pair you'd be!

OLD CHUFFEY: If she has come to any harm, mind! I'm old; but I have my memory sometimes; and if she has come to any harm...

JONAS: [*in a low voice*] Devil take you, what harm do you suppose she has come to? I know no more where she is than you do; I wish I did. Wait till she comes home, and see; she can't be long. Will that content you?

OLD CHUFFEY: [*stammering, threatening and feeble*] I...I...have borne it too long, Jonas. I am silent, but I...I...I can speak. I...I can speak.

[*He creeps back to his chair.*]

JONAS: [*muttering*] You can speak, can you! So, so, we'll stop your speaking. It's well I knew of this in good time.

[JONAS *is afraid of the old man, at once bullying and conciliating him; he stands there with sweat breaking out on his face.*]

BLACKOUT

Jonas manages a sneer, but there is fear in his breath. The old man shows strength by clutching Jonas's collar, but then he grows weak, breathing heavily.

* * *

DAVID'S ENCOUNTER WITH THE TINKER

From the novel *DAVID COPPERFIELD*

CHARACTERS: **DAVID COPPERFIELD:** a young boy at this point and quite afraid of the Tinkers he meets on the road.

THE TINKER: a thief and anything else he can be if need be.

THE WOMAN: the Tinker's companion, used to his rough and brutal treatment.

SETTNG: On the road.

SUMMARY:

David is on his desperate journey to find his aunt, Miss Trotwood. He has had his money taken and has been cheated in trying to sell his clothes. Most of all, the trampers and tinkers that he meets on the road frighten him. They are a dangerous lot and David dreads them. One tinker, who has a woman with him, calls to David. David is afraid to run away.

TINKER: Come here, when you're called, or I'll rip your young body open.

[DAVID *goes to him.*]

TINKER: [*gripping* DAVID's *shirt*] What's what you do? Pickpockets?

DAVID: N-no.

TINKER: You don't, eh? If you brag of your honesty to me, I'll knock your brains out.

[*The* TINKER *is about to strike* DAVID.]

TINKER: Have you got the price of a pint of beer about you? If you have, out with it, before I take it away!

[*The Woman, with a bruised eye, looks at* DAVID *and shakes her head slightly and forms the word No! with her lips.*]

DAVID: [*attempting a smile*] I am very poor, and have got no money.

TINKER: What do you mean?

DAVID: Beg pardon?

TINKER: What do you mean by wearing my brother's silk scarf! Give it here!

[*The* TINKER *grabs the scarf from* DAVID's *neck and throws it to the Woman. The Woman laughs, thinking this a joke, and tosses the scarf back to* DAVID, *mouthing the word Go! with her lips. The* TINKER *grabs the scarf out of* DAVID's *hand and ties it around his own neck. He turns to the Woman.*]

TINKER: Damn you!

[*He knocks her down. She falls backward on the hard road and lies there with her hair all whitened from the dust.* DAVID *gets away as fast as he can. He looks back and sees the Woman sitting in the road wiping the blood from her face.*]

BLACKOUT

This could be a funny scene, but it shouldn't be. The Tinker should present a real threat. David should be really frightened. It shows in his breathing. Only the Woman misreads the Tinker's intentions.

* * *

HAM'S MESSAGE TO EM'LY

From the novel *DAVID COPPERFIELD*.

CHARACTERS: DAVID: through his love for his old nurse Peggotty, David has become a trusted friend of the Peggotty family.

HAM: an adopted son of Mr. Peggotty.

SETTING: On the beach.

SUMMARY:

Ham, a simple fisherman, and Em'ly were to be married. Ham's remains devoted to Em'ly even after she has run away with Steerforth. Now Uncle Peggotty has found Em'ly and brought her back to their village, where they will stay until it is time to sail for Australia. David walks with Ham and waits discreetly for him to talk. Note: In referring to 'him,' Ham is referring to his uncle, Mr. Peggotty.

HAM: Davy, have you seen her?

DAVID: Only for a moment, when she was in a swoon.

HAM: Davy, shall you see her, do you think?

DAVID: It would be too painful to her, perhaps.

HAM: I have thought of that. So it would, so it would.

DAVID: But, Ham, if there is anything that I could write to her, for you, if there is anything you wish to make known to her through me I should consider it a sacred trust.

HAM: I am sure of it. I thank you most kind! I think there is something I could wish said or wrote.

[*A pause.*]

HAM: It ain't that I forgive her. It ain't that so much. 'Tis more as I beg of her to forgive me, for having pressed my affections on her. Odd times, I think that if I hadn't had her promise to marry me, she was that trustful of me, in a friendly way, that she'd have told me what was struggling in her mind, and would have counselled with me, and I might have saved her.

[*There is another pause while* HAM *collects himself.*]

HAM: There's yet something else. If I can say it, Davy.

[HAM *collects himself again to speak plainly.*]

HAM: I loved her - and I love the mem'ry of her - too deep - to be able to lead her to believe as I'm a happy man. I could only be happy - by forgetting of her - and I'm afraid I couldn't hardly bear as she should be told I done that. But if you, being so full of learning, Davy, could think of anything to say as might bring her to believe I wasn't greatly hurt: still loving of her, and mourning for her: anything as might bring her to believe as I was not tired of my life, and yet was hoping to see her without blame, - anything as would ease her sorrowful mind, and yet not make her think as I could ever marry, or that it... was possible that anyone could ever be to me what she was - I should ask of you to say that - with my prayers for her - that was so dear.

DAVID: Ham, I will do this as well as I can with all my heart.

HAM: I thank you. It was kind of you to come down here to meet me. It was kind of you to bear him company down. Davy, I am not like to see him again. I feel sure of it. We don't say so, but so it will be, and better so. The last you see on him - the very last – will you give him the lovingest duty and thanks of the orphan, as he was ever more than a father to?

DAVID: Ham, I promise faithfully.

HAM: [*shaking hands heartily*] I thank you again. Good-bye!

[*With a slight wave of his hand and slightly shaking his head,* HAM *reveals that he can not enter* MR. PEGGOTTY'*s home. He leaves in the other direction.*]

BLACKOUT

Find a quality of speech for Ham that feels untutored but sensitive. The note that he has asked David to write is something that Ham has thought about since Em'ly was brought back. It is the best that he has in him.

* * *

MARTHA ALONE IN THE STREETS

From the novel DAVID COPPERFIELD

CHARACTERS: MARTHA: Em'ly's friend when they were girls.

DAVID COPPERFIELD: helping Mr. Peggotty.

MR. PEGGOTTY: searching for Em'ly, who has run away with James Steerforth. He follows any clue he can find.

SETTING: The worst part of the city. The street, alongside the river and covered with refuse, is dark and lonely.   .

SUMMARY:

By now, the passion felt by David and Mr. Peggotty is muted. They are rational and searching for Em'ly in the city. David and Mr. Peggotty have followed Martha in her solitary walk, hoping she might help them find Em'ly. Martha, whose life is worse than it ever was in the fishing village where she grew up, is struggling alone in a heartless city and is close to madness and suicide. The men are careful not to frighten her. They wait for the right moment to speak to her. Martha stands looking at the water as if she were a part of the refuse and decay. Like a sleepwalker, her hands twist around in her shawl. She seems to be talking to herself.

MARTHA: [*mumbling*] Oh, the river! The dreadful river! I must go with it! ... fit for... for me. Oh, the dreadful river!

DAVID: [*taking her arm*] Martha!

[MARTHA *screams in terror and struggles fiercely to get away.* MR. PEGGOTTY *comes to her side.* MARTHA *recognizes him, gives up, and drops down between the two men, crying and moaning. They seat her on the stones nearby and wait for her to become calm.*]

MARTHA: [*holding her head*] Oh, the river! The river! I know it's like me! I belong to it. And it goes away, like my life, to a great sea. And I must go with it! It's the only thing in all the world I am fit for, or that's fit for me. Oh, the dreadful river!

DAVID: Martha, do you know who this is, who is with me?

MARTHA: [*faintly*] Yes.

DAVID: Do you know we have followed you a long way tonight?

[*She shakes her head no. She looks neither at* MR. PEGGOTTY *nor at* DAVID, *but sits humbly.*]

DAVID: Could we speak about that snowy night?

MARTHA: [*sobbing and murmuring*] You didn't drive me away. [*A pause*] I want to say nothing for myself. I am bad, I am lost. I have no hope at all. But tell him that I never was in any way the cause of his misfortune.

DAVID: We know that.

MARTHA: [*in a broken voice*] It was you that came into the kitchen, the night she took such pity on me; didn't shrink away from me like all the rest. Was it you?

DAVID: It was.

MARTHA: I should have been in the river long ago, if any wrong to her had been upon my mind.

DAVID: We know why she fled. We know you are innocent.

MARTHA: She was always good to me! Is it likely I would try to make her what I am myself. And when I heard what had happened the bitterest thought was, that the people would say I had corrupted her! When I would have died to have brought back her good name!

[MARTHA's *remorse and grief is terrible for* MR. PEGGOTTY *to see.*]

MARTHA: To have died would not have been much - I would even have lived to be old, - and to wander about these streets...oh... - I would have done even that, to save her!

[MARTHA *writhes in the pain of her agony.*]

MARTHA: [*to* MR.PEGGOTTY] When she was your pride, you would have thought I had done her harm if I had brushed against her in the street. I love her. Oh, don't think that all the power I had of loving is worn out! Don't think that of me!

MR. PEGGOTTY: Martha, God forbid as I should judge you. You don't understand how we wish to speak to you. Listen now!

[MARTHA *is shaking;* MR. PEGGOTTY *picks up her shawl and puts it around her shoulders.*]

MR. PEGGOTTY: I know, for though Em'ly ain't no call to doubt my love, – there's shame steps in, between us. Our reckoning is, she is like, one day, to make her own poor solitary way to the city. Help us all you can to find her, and may Heaven reward you!

MARTHA: You would trust me to speak to her, if I should ever find her? Shelter her, if I have any shelter?

DAVID: Yes!

MARTHA: How will I reach you?

[DAVID *gives* MARTHA *a card.*]

DAVID: Where can we find you?

MARTHA: [*after a pause*] In no place for long. It is better not to know.

DAVID: Let us give you some money.

MARTHA: No, no! No money.

[MARTHA *wanders away.* DAVID *and* MR. PEGGOTTY *watch her go.*]

BLACKOUT

When Martha sits down at first, she is still talking to herself about the river. Martha's agony is that she knows she should throw herself into the river, but she can't. It turns her stomach to fight for her wretched life.

* * *

ROSA DARTLE'S CRUELTY

From the novel *DAVID COPPERFIELD*

CHARACTERS: ROSA DARTLE: has known and loved James
                       Steerforth since they were children. It was
                       Steerforth who, in a moment of petu-
                       lance,threw a hammer at her and gave her
                       the scar over her lip.

                       EM'LY: an innocent young girl from a small
                       fishing village who was seduced by Steer-
                       forth and ran away with him. Martha has
                       found her in the city.

SETTING: Martha's room.

SUMMARY:

Martha, who left the village because she had to hide her shame, has
found Em'ly. She is keeping Em'ly hidden in her room until David and
Mr. Peggotty come for her. In Martha's absence, Rosa Dartle comes into
the room. Em'ly is huddled in a corner.

EM'LY If you please, Miss, Martha is not at home.

ROSA DARTLE: It matters little to me her not being at home. I
    know nothing of her. It is you I come to see.

EM'LY: Me?

ROSA DARTLE: Yes. I have come to look at you.

    [ROSA DARTLE *speaks with unrelenting hatred. Her scar, with its
    white track cutting through her lips, quivers and throbs as she
    speaks.*]

ROSA DARTLE: I have come to see James Steerforth's fancy; the girl who ran away with him. I want to know what such a thing looks like.

[EM'LY *runs to the door, but* ROSA DARTLE *stands in her way.*]

ROSA DARTLE: Stay here! If you try to evade me, I'll stop you, if it's by the hair. I'll raise the very stones against you!

EM'LY: [*murmuring*] Please, who are you?

ROSA DARTLE: So! I see her at last! To be taken by that delicate mock-modesty, and that hanging head!

EM'LY: Oh, for Heaven's sake, spare me! Whoever you are. I deserve this. But it's dreadful! Dear, dear lady, think what I have suffered, and how I am fallen! Oh, Martha, come back!

[EM'LY *is crouched on the floor.* ROSA DARTLE *sits in a chair.*]

ROSA DARTLE: Listen to what I say! Do you hope to move me by your tears? No more than you could charm me by your smiles, you purchased slave.

EM'LY: Oh, have some mercy on me! Show me some compassion, or I shall die mad!

ROSA DARTLE: It would be no great penance for your crimes. Do you know what you have done? Do you ever think of the home you have laid waste?

EM'LY: Oh, is there ever night or day, when I don't think of it! Has there ever been a single minute, waking or sleeping, when it hasn't been before me! Oh, my home, oh, uncle.

[EM'LY *reaches out to touch* ROSA DARTLE'*s skirt.*]

ROSA DARTLE: [*controlling the heaving of her breast*] The miserable vanity of these earth-worms! Your home! Do you imagine that I care about your home? Your home! You were bought and sold from your home.

EM'LY: Oh, not that! Say anything of me; but don't visit my disgrace and shame on them.

ROSA DARTLE: [*draws her skirt away from* EM'LY*'s hand*] I speak of his home - where I live. I speak of grief in a house where you wouldn't have been admitted as a kitchen-girl.

EM'LY: No! no! he used all his power to deceive me, and I believed him. I trusted him, I loved him!

[ROSA DARTLE *springs up from her seat. She strikes out at* EM'LY *but only beats the air.*]

ROSA DARTLE: You love him? You? And tell that to me? with your shameful lips? Why don't they whip these creatures? If I could order it to be done, I would have this girl whipped to death.

[ROSA DARTLE *slowly, very slowly, breaks into a laugh, and points at* EM'LY *as if she were a sight of shame for gods and men.*]

ROSA DARTLE: [*with a laugh*] She love! And that he ever cared for her. Ha. The liars these people are! I came here, you pure fountain of love, to see - what you were like. I was curious. I am satisfied. Also to tell you, that you had best seek that home of yours and hide your head among those excellent people whom your money will console. I thought you a broken toy, a tarnished spangle. But, finding you true gold, a very lady, and an ill-used innocent, with a heart full of love - I have something more to say. Attend to it; for what I say I'll do. Do you hear me? What I say, I mean to do! [she pauses until her rage subsides] Hide yourself, somewhere out of reach. In some obscure life - or, better still, in some obscure death.

[EM'LY *is crying softly.* ROSA DARTLE *stops to listen.*]

ROSA DARTLE: If you are still here tomorrow, I'll have your story and your character known to everyone. And I will be assisted by a gentleman who not long ago wished to marry you.

EM'LY: What, what shall I do!

ROSA DARTLE: What shall you do? James Steerforth, in his tenderness, would have made you his servant's wife. Think on that. Feel grateful to his servant who would have taken you as a gift from Mr. Steerforth. Marry that good man. If this will not do, die! There are doorways and dust-heaps for a death, and despair such as yours - find one!

[EM'LY *lies prostrate on the floor.*]

BLACKOUT

Em'ly is no match for Rosa Dartle's stored up feelings of wrath, love, and lust. In Em'ly's confusion and guilt, she can only suffer and huddle in a corner. Em'ly is still innocent in spite of her experience. She reaches out to a stranger; she touches Rosa's skirt to ask for help. Em'ly's despair is so great that she stops breathing and faints. Rosa's anger is like no other that we have seen. At times she can hardly speak, her breathing is so fierce. But when she does, she spits out certain words that cut like a knife.

* * *

ROSA DARTLE'S LAMENT ON THE DEATH OF STEERFORTH

From the novel *DAVID COPPERFIELD.*

CHARACTERS: DAVID COPPERFIELD: once thought of Steerforth as a Greek god. He now knows Steerforth's faults but, in view of his past friendship, David feels he must break the news of Steerforth's death to Mrs.

Steerforth.

MRS. STEERFORTH: an arrogant woman who spoiled her most beloved son.

ROSA DARTLE: stands by Mrs. Steerforth's side as she has always done.

SETTING: Mrs. Steerforth, now an invalid, occupies her son's bedroom as her own. It is exactly as James Steerforth left it: his trophies and photographs have not been moved.

SUMMARY:

David, in mourning for his young wife, Dora, has come to tell Mrs. Steerforth that her son, James, died at sea in a terrible storm. David has been shown up to Mrs. Steerforth's bedroom because she can no longer come downstairs. At her chair, as usual, is Rosa Dartle. Seeing David, Rosa knows immediately that he is the bearer of terrible news and the scar on her upper lip turns bright red and white.

MRS. STEERFORTH: I am sorry to observe you are in mourning.

DAVID: I am unhappily a widower.

MRS. STEERFORTH: You are very young to know so great a loss. I am grieved to hear it. I hope Time will be good to you.

DAVID: I hope Time will be good to all of us. Dear Mrs. Steerforth, we must all trust to that, in our heaviest misfortunes.

MRS. STEERFORTH: [*alarmed*] Yes, yes…?

DAVID: [*his voice trembling*] James…James Steerforth…

MRS. STEERFORTH: [*to herself*] James…James [with a forced calm] My son is ill.

DAVID: Very ill.

MRS. STEERFORTH: You have seen him?

DAVID: I have.

MRS. STEERFORTH: Are you reconciled?

[DAVID *is unable to say Yes or No. He looks to* ROSA *and says with his lips 'dead'!*]

[*In despair and horror,* ROSA *throws her hands up in the air, then covers her face.* MRS. STEERFORTH *will not let herself know what has passed between* DAVID *and* ROSA. MRS. STEERFORTH, *handsome still and looking so like* STEERFORTH, *is rigid.*]

DAVID: Mrs. Steerforth, I beg you to be calm and prepare yourself for what I have to tell you.

[MRS. STEERFORTH *sits like a stone figure.*]

DAVID: [*falteringly*] When I was last here, Miss Dartle told me he was sailing. The night before last was a dreadful storm. If he were at sea that night, and near a dangerous coast, as it is said he was; and if the vessel that was seen should really be the ship which –

MRS. STEERFORTH: Rosa! Come to me!

[ROSA *comes to* MRS. STEERFORTH'*s side and breaks out into a frightful laugh.*]

ROSA: Now, is your pride appeased, you madwoman? Now has he made atonement to you - with his life! Do you hear? - His life!

[MRS. STEERFORTH, *sits stiff in her chair. A dull moan escapes from her body. She looks at* ROSA *with a wide stare.*]

ROSA: [*beating her breast*] Look at me! Moan, groan, look at me!

Look here! [*she grabs at her scar*] at your dead child's handi-work!

[MRS. STEERFORTH'*s moans are inarticulate and stifled.   Her mouth is rigid and her face is frozen in pain.*]

ROSA: Do you remember when he did this? Do you remember when he did this, and disfigured me for life? Look at me, marked until I die.

DAVID: Miss Dartle, for Heaven's sake -

ROSA: [*turning on David*] I will speak! Be silent, you! Look at me, I say, proud mother of a proud, false son! Moan for your cor-ruption of him.

[ROSA *trembles as though her passion were killing her by inches.*]

ROSA: You, who from his cradle reared him to be what he was, and stunted what he should have been! Are you rewarded, now, for your years of trouble?

DAVID: Oh, Miss Dartle, shame! Too cruel!

ROSA: I tell you, I will speak to her. No power on earth should stop me. Have I been silent all these years, and shall I not speak now? [turning on Mrs. Steerforth] I loved him better than you ever loved him! If I had been his wife - I should have been, who knows it better than I? [striking her scar relent-lessly] Look at it! He repented of it! And I attracted him. He loved me. Yes, he did. When he grew weary of her, his little conquest... by then, I was a mere disfigured piece of furniture between you, with no feelings, no remembrances. Moan for what you made him; not for your love. I loved him better than you ever did!

DAVID: Miss Dartle, can you possibly not feel what you are doing to her...?

ROSA: Who feels for me?

DAVID: Possibly his faults… -

ROSA: [*bursting into tears*] Faults! Who dares malign him? He had
a soul worth millions of the friends to whom he stooped!

DAVID: No one can have loved him better than I, but you must
have compassion for his mother…

ROSA: [*tearing her hair*] It's false. I loved him!

[MRS. STEERFORTH *once again gives a dull moan and sinks to the
floor.* ROSA DARTLE *suddenly kneels down and begins to loosen* MRS.
STEERFORTH'*s dress.*]

ROSA: [*at* DAVID] A curse upon you! It was an evil hour that you
ever came here! A curse upon you! Go away!

[DAVID *goes to the door. He turns to see* ROSA *holding the impassive
mother in her arms, weeping over her, kissing her, rocking her like
a child.*]

BLACKOUT

Perhaps the center of Rosa's madness and of her need to speak is her scar.
Feel it on your lips. Don't take too long to imagine it. It need not be
labored. Only when Mrs. Steerforth needs attention does Rosa forget
the scar. Rosa's voice is altered. She screams, talks, croons: she is a
woman maddened with grief. Em'ly and Martha suffer their sins almost
to madness. So, too, does Rosa Dartle's unrequited love for Steerforth
drive her to the point of insanity.

* * *

URIAH HEEP – A BIT AHEAD OF HIS MOMENT

From the novel *DAVID COPPERFIELD*

CHARACTERS: DAVID COPPERFIELD: on a visit to Mr. Wickfield.

MR. WICKFIELD: almost at the end of his moral rope.

URIAH HEEP: as sinful and shameful as ever.

SETTING: The home of Mr. Wickfield.

SUMMARY:

Dinner is over. Agnes and Mrs. Heep have gone to their rooms. The three men are left alone. Uriah Heep is flushed and feeling triumphant after his talk with David about his love for Agnes Wickfield. Before David can intercede to keep Mr. Wickfield from drinking, Uriah has managed to entice Mr. Wickfield to drink his third glass of wine.

URIAH: [*to* MR. WICKFIELD] We seldom see our present visitor, and I should propose to give him welcome in another glass or two of wine, if you have no objections. Mr. Copperfield, your health and happiness!

[MR. WICKFIELD *drinks*]

URIAH: Come, fellow-partner, if I may take the liberty - suppose you give us something or another appropriate to a toast.

MR. WICKFIELD: [*to* DAVID] To your Aunt, Miss Betsey.

[MR. WICKFIELD *drinks. He is ashamed of himself for drinking and ashamed of his need to conciliate* URIAH.]

URIAH: [*humbly exultant*] Come, fellow-partner! I'll give another toast, to the divinest of her sex.

[MR. WICKFIELD *is holding his empty glass. He sets the glass down, puts his hand to his forehead, and shrinks back in his chair.*]

URIAH: I'm an humble individual to give you her health, but I admire - adore her.

[MR. WICKFIELD *holds his head with both hands as though in terrible pain.*]

URIAH: [*off his guard*] Agnes, Agnes Wickfield is the divinest of her sex. May I speak out, among friends? To be her father is a proud distinction, but to be her husband -

[MR. WICKFIELD *utters a cry and rises from the table.*]

URIAH: [*turning a deadly color*] What's the matter? You are not gone mad, after all, Mr. Wickfield? If I say I've an ambition to make your Agnes my Agnes, I have as good a right to it as another man. I have a better right to it than any other man!

[MR. WICKFIELD *is mad for the moment. He tears out his hair. He beats his head.*]

DAVID: [*throws his arms around him to contain him*] You must calm yourself. Out of love for Agnes, you must not abandon yourself to this wildness.

[MR. WICKFIELD *slowly stops thrashing and quiets down.*]

MR. WICKFIELD: I know. I know! But look at him!

[*He points to* URIAH, *who is pale and glowering in a corner.* URIAH, *very much off in his calculations, has been taken by surprise.*]

MR. WICKFIELD: Look at my torturer. I have step by step abandoned name and reputation, peace and quiet, house and home.

URIAH: [*hurriedly ready to compromise*] I have kept your name and reputation for you, and your peace and quiet, and your house and home too. Don't be foolish, Mr. Wickfield. If I have gone a little beyond what you were prepared for, I can go back, I suppose? There's no harm done.

MR. WICKFIELD: See what he is - oh, see what he is!

URIAH: [*pointing a long finger at David*] You had better stop him, Copperfield. He'll say something presently - mind you! - he'll be sorry to have said afterwards, and you'll be sorry to have heard!

MR. WICKFIELD: I'll say anything! Why should I not be in all the world's power if I am in yours?

URIAH: Mind! I tell you! [to David] If you don't stop his mouth, you're not his friend! [to Mr. Wickfield] Why shouldn't you be in all the world's power, Mr. Wickfield? Because you have got a daughter. You and me know what we know, don't we? Let sleeping dogs lie. Can't you see I am as humble as I can be? I tell you, if I've gone too far, I'm sorry.

MR. WICKFIELD: [*wringing his hands, speaks to* DAVID] What I have come to! I was on my way downward. I have infected everything I touched. I have brought misery on what I dearly love.

[*He drops into a chair and sobs weakly.* URIAH *comes out of the corner.*]

MR. WICKFIELD: [*he points to* URIAH] He has always been at my elbow, whispering to me. He is in my house, in my business...

URIAH: [*defiant and fawning*] You haven't need to say so much, nor half so much, nor anything at all. You wouldn't have took it up so, if it hadn't been for the wine. You'll think better of it tomorrow, sir. If I have said too much, or more than I meant, what of it? I haven't stood by it!

[AGNES *enters the dining room.*]

AGNES: Papa, you are not feeling well. Come with me!

[MR. WICKFIELD, *leaning on his daughter, leaves the room with her.*]

URIAH: Copperfield, we'll make it all smooth. I'm useful to him, you know; and he understands his interest when he isn't in liquor! What an agreeable man he is, when all is said, Master Copperfield! I will apologize, to be sure. When a person's humble, you know, what's an apology? [*putting his hand on DAVID's shoulder*] I plucked a pear just now, before it was ripe. But it'll ripen yet! [with a writhe and a jerk] It only wants attending to. I can wait!

BLACKOUT

Uriah constantly reminds Mr. Wickfield of the dangers that are ahead for him, "You have not gone mad, after all" "Remember what we know" "When he isn't drinking" etc. His tone of voice is a warning. Mr. Wickfield is so tightly wound that he hardly breathes. His torso is narrowed as if he is shrinking from the world.

For breaking down suddenly, try swallowing air or a gasp: that should bring on the crying. If by then the scene doesn't bring it on, try the technique for crying: Breathe and utter the vowel 'Uh.' The thought of weeping and the several 'uh' sounds will bring on crying. Do not let the 'uh' come from the throat area. Place the 'uh' in the front half of the mouth.

David, for the most part, looks on in horror. Uriah is still in charge, humble though he pretends to be.

* * *

RALPH NICKLEBY'S BITTERNESS

From the novel *NICHOLAS NICKLEBY*

CHARACTERS: **RALPH NICKLEBY:** a usurer for whom money is everything.

SETTING: Ralph Nickleby's home.

SUMMARY:

After leaving the crazed Gride moaning over the loss of his important papers, Ralph arrives at his home. A letter is on the table. He lets it lie there for some time, as if he has not the courage to open it. At length he reads it and turns deadly pale. Note: Ralph is referring to the probable marriage of Nicholas (the nephew whom he hates.) to Madeline Bray.

RALPH NICKLEBY: The worst has happened. The company has failed. I see - the rumor was abroad in the City last night, and reached the ears of those merchants. Well, well!

[*He paces violently up and down the room and stops again*].

RALPH NICKLEBY: [*continues*] Ten thousand pounds! And only lying there for a day - for one day! How many anxious years, how many pinching days before I scraped together that ten thousand pounds! How many proud ladies have fawned and smiled at me, and how many spendthrift fools gave lip-service to my face and cursed me in their hearts. Men like me make our money by treachery, by cringing, and stooping. But for my money, they would spurn me aside...

[RALPH *paces, trying to release himself from his bitter regrets. Sitting, his thoughts return.*]

RALPH NICKLEBY: [*continues*] And now, my nephew's triumph in telling me of it. If he had brought it about, I couldn't hate him more. Let me get back at him, however slow - let me defeat him in this marriage, so dear to his heart; let me do this; and it shall be the first link in such a chain, which I will wind about him... and I can bear any loss.

BLACKOUT

Ralph has controlled his emotions throughout the thwarted wedding day, the sudden death of Mr. Bray, the triumph of Nicholas in carrying off Madeline Bray, and the trip to Gride's house where he finds that the will making Madeline a rich woman has been stolen and Gride half crazy over its loss. Try breathing, count to five silently without actually saying the sentences, and bring all this into your mind to start the bitterness. Ralph is caving in to events.

* * *

RALPH NICKLEBY'S LAST THOUGHTS

From the novel *NICHOLAS NICKLEBY*

CHARACTERS:	**RALPH NICKLEBY:** a bitter man's last bitter thoughts.
	VOICE AT THE DOOR: neutral and sympathetic.
SETTING:	Ralph Nickleby's home.

SUMMARY:

Ralph has come from a meeting with the Cheeryble brothers [who are as good and generous as Ralph is not and never has been.] He has heard shocking news: that the deceased Smike was his son and that Smike was brought to the Dotheboys School by one of Ralph's disgruntled employees. Note: "the man detained" refers to Ralph's former employee.

In Dickens words, we read about the walk Ralph took to get to his home after that meeting.

"The night was dark, and a cold wind blew, driving the clouds, furiously and fast, before it. There was one black, gloomy mass that seemed to follow him: not hurrying in the wild chase with the others, but lingering sullenly behind, and gliding darkly and stealthily on. He often looked back at this, and, more than once, stopped to let it pass over; but, somehow, when he went forward again, it was still behind him, coming mournfully and slowly up, like a shadowy funeral train."

Ralph is shivering from head to foot. He has made a kind of pact with himself that he will not think of what has happened until he gets home. He is at home now.

RALPH NICKLEBY: [*sits and speaks his thoughts*] My own child — my own child! I don't doubt the story; I felt it was true; as if I had been privy to it all along. My own child! Dead. Dying beside Nicholas — loving him, and looking upon him as something like an angel. That was the worst! [*he rises and paces restlessly*]

RALPH NICKLEBY: [*continues*] They have all turned from me and deserted me in my very first need. Even money could not buy them now.

[RALPH *tears at his handkerchief.*]

RALPH NICKLEBY: Everything must come out, and everyone must know all. Ten thousand dollars gone at one blow, my plot with Gride shattered, my schemes discovered. I am in danger and grovelling in the dust. [*sits twisted in his chair*] If I had known my child to be alive; if no deceit had ever been practiced, and he had grown up beneath my eye; [he pauses] I might have been an indifferent, harsh father — like enough. But I might have been otherwise, and my son might have been a comfort to me, and we two could have been happy together.

[*he reaches for his handkerchief and muffles his tears*] The death of the child, I did think him dead! And my wife's flight... there was a time when I was not so rough, so hard. Did I first hate Nicholas because he reminded me of her lover.

[RALPH *gnashes his teeth and beats the air.*]

RALPH: That he should have rescued my miserable child; shown him love and tenderness which, from the wretched moment of his birth, he had never known; that he should have taught him to hate his own parent - that Nicholas should triumph in all this...I...I...it is agony, agony! [*cries aloud*] I am ruined. The night has come! I refuse their mercy and their compassion. Is there no devil to help me?

[*Out of the corner of his eye,* RALPH *sees a trunk at one end of the room with a rope lying on top of it.* RALPH *stares at it for some time. He goes to the trunk and starts to move it into the center of the room. He picks up the rope. He is interrupted by a loud knocking at the door.* RALPH *hesitates.*]

RALPH: Who is it?

THE VOICE: I want Mr. Nickleby.

RALPH: [*his voice husky and choked*] What with him?

THE VOICE: That's not Mr Nickleby's voice, surely?

RALPH: Yes, yes, what do you want?

THE VOICE: The Cheerybles want to know if there is anything they can do for you. Do you want that man detained?

RALPH: Yes! Detain him till tomorrow! Let them bring him here — and my nephew – he can come, too, and be sure that I'll be

ready to receive them.

THE VOICE: At what hour?

RALPH: [*fiercely*] At any hour. In the afternoon, tell them. At any hour — at any minute — all times will be alike to me.

[RALPH *listens to the retreating footsteps. He hears the sound of a deep bell.*]

RALPH: [*crying out*] This cursed world comes nearer to its end. I refuse their prayers. Throw me on a dunghill, and let me rot there to infect the air!

[RALPH *looks wildly around. Still holding the rope, he shakes his hands above his head and crumples into his chair entangled in the rope.*]

BLACKOUT

Dry Uncle Ralph Nickleby finds that everyone he has bullied is now turned against him. Moreover, he has discovered that the drudge Smike, whom he hardly knows but has used for his selfish purpose, is the son whom he thought dead. His is passion indeed. He is no longer dry. He cries, he bites his handkerchief, he gnashes his teeth. Nickleby is alone now, and alone in the world, and for once and for all time he can cry out loud, partly in self pity, partly because there are no more feelings to be pent up and finally because he knows that the cloud of death is upon him.

* * *

EM'LY IS KIND TO POOR MARTHA

From the novel *DAVID COPPERFIELD*

CHARACTERS: HAM: a sturdy fisherman, Em'ly's betrothed. He is a simple man, decent, ethical, wise.

DAVID COPPERFIELD: comes to the fishing village where his beloved nurse Peggotty lives along with her family. They have known David since he was a little boy.

EM'LY: an orphan adopted by Uncle Peggotty. Em'ly has been known to aspire at times to something better than being a fisherman's wife.

MARTHA: a girl from the village who has 'gone bad' and is shunned by the villagers, except by Em'ly who is her friend.

PEGGOTTY: David's nurse who has come back to live in the village.

SETTING: 1] Outside of Mr. Peggotty's house.
2] Inside the house.

SUMMARY:

Martha has been following Em'ly, trying to keep herself unseen by any village folk. Finally, she catches up with Em'ly to ask her help. David meets Ham outside of Mr. Pegotty's house

DAVID: [*to Ham who is pacing back and forth*] Ham, what are you doing out here?

HAM: Why, you see, Davy, Em'ly, she's talking to some one in there.

DAVID: I should have thought that was a reason for your being in there, too, Ham.

HAM: Well, Davy, in a general way, so it would be. It's a young woman, - a young woman, that Em'ly knowed once, and don't ought to know no more. It's a poor woman, Davy, trod under foot by all the town.

DAVID: Did I see her tonight, Ham, on the sand?

HAM: She was keeping us in sight. And afterwards she was creeping along until she sees Em'ly. And in at the window, she's whispering "Em'ly, Em'ly, have a woman's heart towards me. I was once like you!" Oh, those were solemn words to hear! "Em'ly, Em'ly, for Christ's sake, I was once like you".

[PEGGOTTY *opens the door and motions* HAM *and* DAVID *to come in. The men enter and see* MARTHA *on the floor, her hair hiding her face.* EM'LY *and* PEGGOTTY *have tears in their eyes.*]

EM'LY: [*in a low voice to Ham*] Martha wants to go to London.

HAM: [*in a low voice*] Why to London?

MARTHA: Better there than here. No one knows me there. Everybody knows me here.

HAM: What will she do there?

[MARTHA *lifts her head, looks darkly at* HAM *for a moment and then lays her head down as if she were in an agony of pain.*]

EM'LY: She will try to do well.

MARTHA: I'll try, if you'll help me away. I never can do worse than I have done here. I may do better. Oh! take me out of these streets, where the whole town knows me from a child!

HAM: [*handing Em'ly his purse*] It's yours, Em'ly. I haven't nothing in all the world that ain't yours, my dear.

EM'LY: [*whispering to Martha*] Is it enough?

MARTHA: More than enough.

[MARTHA *kisses* EM'LY'*s hand. She rises and gathers her shawl about her, covering her face. She is weeping as she goes to the door. She stops as though to say something but continues out the door with a low wretched moaning.*]

[EM'LY *sobs.*]

HAM: Don't, Em'ly! Don't, my dear! You oughtn't to cry so, my pretty!

EM'LY: [*weeping*] Oh, Ham! I am not so good a girl as I ought to be! I know I have not the thankful heart, sometimes, I ought to have!

HAM: Yes, yes, you have.

EM'LY: [*sobbing*] No! no! no! I am not as good a girl as I ought to be. Not near! not near! I try your love too much.

HAM: You always make me happy. I am happy in the sight of you. I am happy, all day long, in the thoughts of you.

EM'LY: Ah! that's not enough! That is because you are good; not because I am!

[EM'LY *is sitting on a stool, rocking back and forth.*]

EM'LY: [*continues*] Oh, aunt, try to help me! Ham, dear, try to help me! Mr. David, please…Oh my heart, my heart!

HAM: [*raising Em'ly up*] We'll say a goodnight to you, Peggotty and Davy. Em'ly will be allright, dear Em'ly, won't you?

[EM'LY *stops crying and kisses* HAM *on the cheek. She clings to his arm as he guides her out the door.*]

BLACKOUT

As Em'ly, if you think about the sadness of Martha's predicament, if you breathe and watch Martha closely, you will find it easy and natural to burst into sobs when Martha is gone. That is what I call putting sadness into the breath.

For Peggotty, tears can come into your eyes when a sympathetic character is in trouble. We do it in the movies all the time.

* * *

EM'LY LEAVES A RUN-AWAY NOTE

From the novel *DAVID COPPERFIELD*

CHARACTERS:

MR. PEGGOTTY: a powerful man whose emotional range matches his physical power.

HAM: his nephew, adopted as a son by Mr. Peggotty. He is able to hold his equally strong emotions in check.

DAVID: a deep and loving friend to the Peggottys.

SETTING: Mr. Peggotty's house.

SUMMARY:

Mr. Peggotty is lighting the lamp that he always puts in the window for Em'ly to see when she is coming home. Note: Steerforth has bought a boat from Mr. Peggotty and has named it The Little Em'ly.

[HAM *enters.*]

MR. PEGGOTTY: Where's Em'ly?

[HAM *motions with his head that she is outside.*]

HAM: Davy, will you come out a minute, and see what Em'ly and me has got to show you?

[*Outside,* DAVID *sees that* HAM *is deadly pale.*]

DAVID: Ham! what's the matter?

HAM: Davy!

[HAM *is grief stricken. He weeps.*]

DAVID: Ham! For Heaven's sake, tell me what's the matter!

HAM: My love, Davy - her that I'd have died for, that I would die for - she's gone!

DAVID: Gone!

HAM: Em'ly's run away! Oh, Davy, think how she's run away, when I pray my good and gracious God to kill her, her that is so dear, - sooner than let her come to ruin and disgrace!

[*A pause.*]

HAM: [*continues*] What am I to say, indoors? How am I ever to break it to him, Davy? Here, you read the note.

[HAM *hands* EM'LY's *note to* DAVID.]

DAVID: [*reads*] "When you, who love me so much better than I ever have deserved, see this, I shall be far away."

[MR. PEGGOTTY *has opened the door. He sees* HAM's *face, hears* DAVID *read the first sentence, and he knows. He stumbles back into the room. He utters a great wail and cry. He grabs at his vest as though it were choking him.* HAM *and* DAVID *enter the house.* DAVID *stands, holding the note, not knowing what to do.*]

MR. PEGGOTTY: [*forcing himself to speak*] Read it, slow, please. I don't know as I can understand.

DAVID: [*reads*] "When I leave my dear home - my dear home - oh, my dear home! – in the morning, - it will be never to come back, unless he brings me back a lady. Oh, take comfort in thinking that I am so bad. Tell uncle that I never loved him half so dear as now. Try to think as if I died when I was little and was buried somewhere. I'll pray for all, often, on my knees. If he don't bring me back a lady... My parting love to uncle. My last tears, and my last thanks, for uncle!" [a pause] That is all.

[MR. PEGGOTTY *stands like stone.*]

DAVID: I beg you, come to yourself.

MR. PEGGOTTY: [*without moving*] I thank you, I thank you!

[MR. PEGGOTTY *remains in shock until slowly he awakens.*]

MR. PEGGOTTY:: Who's the man? I want to know his name.

[HAM *glances at* DAVID *and suddenly* DAVID *knows.*]

MR. PEGGOTTY: There's a man suspected. Who is it?

HAM: Davy! Go out a bit, and let me tell him what I must. You don't ought to hear it.

[DAVID *feels the shock again. He sinks into a chair.*]

DAVID: I...I,I..

[DAVID *can't speak.*]

MR. PEGGOTTY: I want to know his name!

HAM: [*faltering*] For some time past, there's been a servant about here, at odd times. There's been a gen'lm'n too. Both of 'em belonged to one another. The servant, was seen along with - our poor girl - last night. He's been in hiding about here. He was thought to have gone, but he was hiding. Don't stay,

Davy, don't! [*a pause*] A strange carriage and hosses was outside town, a'most before the day broke. The servant went to
it, and come from it, and went to it again. When he went to
it again, Em'ly was with him. The other was inside. He's the
man.

[MR. PEGGOTTY's *face and lips are white, and there is blood trick-
ling down from his mouth.*]

MR. PEGGOTTY: For the Lord's love, don't tell me his name's
Steerforth!

HAM: [*his voice breaking*] Davy, it ain't no fault o'yourn - and I am
far from laying of it to you - but his name is Steerforth, and
he's a damned villain!

[MR. PEGGOTTY *is deadly still; no tears, no cries. All at once, he
awakens. He pulls down his coat from its peg.*]

MR. PEGGOTTY: Bear a hand with this! I can't do it. Bear a hand
and help me. Never mind. I can do it.

[*He takes his hat.*]

HAM: What are you doing, Uncle?

MR. PEGGOTTY: I'm going to seek my niece. I'm going to seek
my Em'ly. I'm going, first, to smash in that there boat, and
sink it where I would have drownded him, as I'm a living soul,
if I had had one thought of what was in his mind.

[MR. PEGGOTTY *becomes wild again.*]

MR. PEGGOTTY: As he sat before me, as he sat before me, face to
face, strike me down dead, but I'd have drownded him, and
thought it right! – I'm going to seek my niece.

[*He starts for the door.*]

HAM: Where would you be going?

MR. PEGGOTTY: Anywhere! I'm going to seek my niece through the world. I'm going to find my poor niece in her shame, and bring her back. Don't stop me! I tell you I'm going to seek my niece!

HAM: [*his hands on his uncle's shoulders*] No, Uncle. Not as you are now. We'll seek her in a little while. Not as you are now, Uncle.

[HAM *holds him until* MR. PEGGOTTY *becomes passive. He begins to cry softly.* DAVID *breaks down cries with him.*]

BLACKOUT

In this chapter, both Em'ly's loving letter of goodbye as well as Mr. Peggotty's first horror and final calm are operatic in concept. Sometimes, opening your eyes wide — but you must feel the horror behind the eyes — will lead to further emotions of confusion, tears, and weeping.

* * *

SMIKE PRAYS

From the novel *NICHOLAS NICKLEBY*

CHARACTERS: SMIKE: who was almost a slave at the Dotheboys school until he was befriended by Nicholas.

SETTING: Smike's bedroom.

SUMMARY:

It was a day of serene and tranquil happiness. The Nickleby family and their new friends picnic together. All have taken to Smike; he is truly a part of the festivities. At last the guests leave and all go to bed. Smike is on his knees saying his prayers as Nicholas has taught him. He stretches his folded hands wildly in the air and falls on the bed in a passion of bitter grief. (At this time no one knows that poor misshapen Smike is madly in love with the beautiful Kate Nickleby.)

BLACKOUT

SMIKE PRAYS is almost a dance: it contains his secret passion for Kate Nickleby.

* * *

THE DREADFUL STRANGER

From the novel *BARNABY RUDGE*

CHARACTERS: **MRS. RUDGE:** a good and religious woman.

THE STRANGER: her estranged husband, a murderer.

BARNABY: Mrs. Rudge's retarded son.

GRIP: Barnaby's pet, a raven.

SETTING: Mrs. Rudge's poor dwelling.

SUMMARY:

Mrs. Rudge, has lived in dread of a visit from The Stranger. He is a miserable wretch with bloodshot eyes, unwashed and unshaven. Now he has found her. She is terrified that her son, the retarded Barnaby, will come home and find him there. Note: Hugh is a stable boy in the neighborhood and a friend of Barnaby's.

[THE STRANGER *sits staring into the fire.*]

THE STRANGER: Is this your house?

MRS. RUDGE: It is. Why, in the name of Heaven, do you darken it?

THE STRANGER: [*sullenly*] Give me to eat, or I dare do more than that. The very marrow in my bones is cold, with wet and hunger.

MRS. RUDGE: You were the robber on the Chigwell road.

THE STRANGER: I was.

MRS. RUDGE: And nearly a murderer.

THE STRANGER: I would have. Someone came upon me. It would have gone hard with him, but he got away too fast.

MRS. RUDGE: You thrust your sword at him!

[THE STRANGER *advances toward her.*]

MRS. RUDGE: Do not so much as touch me, or you are lost, body and soul, you are lost!

THE STRANGER: [*menacing her*] Hear me. I live the life of a hunted beast; a ghost upon the earth, a thing from which all creatures shrink, I am past all fear but that of the hell in which I exist from day to day. Give the alarm, cry out, refuse to shelter me. I won't hurt you. But I will not be taken alive. I fall a dead man on this floor. The blood will be on you and yours, in the name of the Evil Spirit that tempts men to their ruin!

[THE STRANGER *takes a gun from his shirt.*]

MRS. RUDGE: [*her hands clenched, her eyes to Heaven*] Remove this man from men, dear God! Give him one minute's penitence, and strike him dead!

THE STRANGER: Heaven has no such purpose. It is deaf. Give

me to eat and drink.

MRS. RUDGE: Will you leave me, if I do? Will you leave me and return no more?

THE STRANGER: [*sitting at the table*] I promise nothing, nothing but this — I will carry out my threat if you betray me.

[MRS. RUDGE *puts cold meat and bread on the table.*]

THE STRANGER: I want brandy and water.

[*She brings it. He eats and drinks like a famished dog.* MRS.RUDGE *keeps her distance but never takes her eyes off him. She watches his every movement. Finished eating,* THE STRANGER *moves his chair towards the fire again.*]

THE STRANGER: You live here at your ease. Do you live alone?

MRS. RUDGE: [*with effort*] I do not.

THE STRANGER: Who lives here besides you?

MRS. RUDGE: One who...it is no matter who. You had better be gone, or he may find you here. Why do you linger?

THE STRANGER: I need to get warm. Are you rich?

MRS. RUDGE: [*faintly*] Very. Very rich. No doubt I am very rich.

THE STRANGER: At least you're not penniless. You have some money.

MRS. RUDGE: I have a little left.

THE STRANGER: Give me your purse. You had it in your hand at the door. Give it to me.

[*She lays the purse on the table.* THE STRANGER *picks the purse up, takes out the money, and starts counting.*]

MRS. RUDGE: [*hearing* BARNABY *approach*] Take what there is!

Take it all! But go before it's too late. I hear steps. Go!

THE STRANGER: What do you mean?

MRS. RUDGE: Don't stop to ask. I won't answer. Much as I dread to touch you, I would drag you to the door if I had the strength. You miserable wretch, leave this place.

THE STRANGER: [*standing aghast*] If there are spies outside, I am safer here. I'll remain here, and not go till the danger is past.

MRS. RUDGE: [*listening*] It's too late! It's my son, my retarded son!

[*There is a heavy knocking at the door. They look at each other.*]

THE STRANGER: [*hoarsely*] Let him come in. I fear him less than the darkness outside. Let him come in!

MRS. RUDGE: I've dreaded this hour all my life. Evil will fall upon my boy, if you face him. To know the truth about you — God in heaven, spare him from that!

[BARNABY *calls to his mother.*]

BARNABY: Mother, hello, mother.

THE STRANGER: The voice! He fought with me in the road.

[THE STRANGER *is uncertain what to do or where to turn. There is more knocking.* THE STRANGER *grabs a knife from the table and hides himself in the closet.* BARNABY *calls from outside.*]

BARNABY: [*gaily*] Why do you keep us out, Grip and me? Are you there, mother?

MRS. RUDGE: [*hardly able to breathe*] Yes, dear boy, I'm coming.

[*She opens the door.* BARNABY *enters, embraces her, kissing her again and again.*]

BARNABY: We have been in the field, mother—leaping ditches.

The wind was blowing, and Grip — when the wind rolls him over in the dust, he tries to bite it — And Grip takes care of me, mother! He watches all the time I sleep.

[BARNABY *goes to the fireplace.* MRS. RUDGE *takes the seat facing the closet.*]

BARNABY: How pale you are to-night!

[THE STRANGER, *holding the closet door open, listens and watches* BARNABY.]

BARNABY: [*changing color*] You are frightened! Mother...do you see...

MRS. RUDGE: See what?

BARNABY: [*grabbing her hands and whispering*] Why do you look like that? Is it in the room? Like my dreams? The ceiling and the walls, r...r...red, all red? Tell me. Is it?

[BARNABY *falls into a shivering fit in his mother's arms.*]

BARNABY: [*recovering with a vacant look*] Is it gone?

MRS. RUDGE: There's nothing here. Nothing, dear Barnaby. Look! Just you and me.

[BARNABY *bursts into a wild laugh.*]

BARNABY: Hugh and I and Grip — we have been lying in the forest, after night came on, ready when the man came by.

MRS. RUDGE: What man?

BARNABY: The robber. We waited for him. I know him, Mother, look!

[BARNABY *twists his handkerchief round his head, pulls his hat down, and wraps his coat about him.*]

BARNABY: Hahaha! We'll have him. You'll see him, mother. We're going to tie him up. Hugh says so. Why do you look behind me?

MRS. RUDGE: Go to bed, dear, and leave me here.

BARNABY: I don't like bed. I like to lie before the fire. Mother, is to-day my birthday?

MRS. RUDGE: To-day? Don't you remember it was but a week or so ago. Summer, autumn, and winter have to pass before it comes again?

BARNABY: I think to-day must be my birthday too. You cry when it is my birthday. You are sad. [BARNABY *lies down before the fire, falling asleep*] Today you are sad.

[THE STRANGER *leaves the closet. He walks to* BARNABY *and looks intently at his face. He looks at* MRS. RUDGE *and shakes his head as if to say 'yes'. He takes the knife out.*]

MRS. RUDGE: [*whispering, grabbing his arm*] Would you kill him in his sleep!

THE STRANGER: [*shrugging her off, lays the knife on the table*] Woman, if you want one of us to kill the other, wake him. [*close to* MRS. RUDGE, *whispering*] Now I know who he is. Be careful how you use me. I may take revenge. Slowly and surely. He knows me well, it seems. Don't forget, I warn you.

[THE STRANGER *withdraws and goes out into the street.* MRS.RUDGE *falls on her knees beside* BARNABY. *She is like a stone until the tears come.*]

BLACKOUT

Actors are afraid of playing a scene like this; afraid they will be melodramatic and look hammy. They are not playing in a melodrama. These scenes are operatic and large because the themes are large. These people believe in Good and Evil in their very souls. The Stranger actually feels himself possessed by Evil Spirits. His behavior comes from within his exhausted body. It is terrible to be in the same room with him. It is terrible for him to inhabit his own body. This is a medieval belief in evil spirits. The woman is godfearing. Even in her fear and dread of the Stranger she wants him to have a moment's repentance before he dies. The more the characters believe in what they say, the more powerful the scene is. If you say the words with complete attention to what you are saying it will bring you into the belief you need. You can internalize the scene through the words; the words on the tongue will bring the emotional belief into your body. The external will seep into the internal.

Playing Barnaby, imagine a separation in your brain, a space that makes it difficult for you as Barnaby to understand something at normal speed. When you talk it is as if you are trying to connect two parts of what you hear. This is by no means scientific. It is a device to produce a puzzled and confused understanding of what the world is saying to you. You may come up with another method. By all means use it.

* * *

MRS. RUDGE FACES THE WRATH OF
HER HUSBAND

From the novel *BARNABY RUDGE*

CHARACTERS: MRS. RUDGE: visits her son, Barnaby, in prison.

PRISONER RUDGE: the father of Barnaby and the husband of Mrs. Rudge.

JAILOR

SETTING: Courtyard of the prison.

SUMMARY:

Leaving Barnaby, who is in prison for his share in the Protestant riots against the Catholics, Mrs. Rudge sees her husband walking round and round the courtyard with his hands manacled and his eyes on the ground.

It took some twenty years and a violent struggle between them but Mr. Haredale finally captured Rudge, his brother Reuben Haredale's murderer. Rudge is brought to Newgate jail not as a rioter but as a felon. When the rioters decide to force open the jails, Rudge gets out, as does Barnaby, his son. But they are found and brought back to jail when Dennis brings the military to where they are hiding.

Dickens describes Rudge's hatred for his son Barnaby:
"... his presence was a torture and reproach; in Barnaby's wild eyes, there were terrible images of that guilty night; with his unearthly aspect, and his half-formed mind, he seemed to the murderer a creature who had sprung into existence from his victim's blood.   He could not bear Barnaby's look, his voice, his touch..."

MRS. RUDGE: [to the JAILOR escorting her out] May I, sir, speak a word with this prisoner?

JAILOR: But be quick. I am locking up for the night.

[MRS. RUDGE stands by the prisoner, but he doesn't notice her. She stretches out her hand and touches him. He starts backward, trembling from head to foot.]

PRISONER RUDGE: How did you get here?

MRS. RUDGE: My son — our son, is in this prison.

PRISONER RUDGE: What is that to me? I know it. He can no more aid me than I can aid him. If you come to talk of him, I don't want to hear it. If you come, woman-like, to load me with reproaches –

MRS. RUDGE: I do not reproach. Husband, you must hear me.

Escape is hopeless — impossible.

PRISONER RUDGE: You tell me so, do you? You!

[*He raises his manacled hands as if to strike her.*]

PRISONER RUDGE: Do you mean to make me easy in this jail? To make the time between now and death pass pleasantly? You are here for my good — yes, for my good, of course.

[*He grinds his teeth and smiles malevolently at* MRS. RUDGE.]

MRS. RUDGE: Not to load you with reproaches but to restore you to peace and hope. Husband, dear husband, if you will but confess your dreadful crime; if you will but implore forgiveness of Heaven and of those whom you have wronged on earth; if you will rely on the Truth, I promise you, that God will comfort and console you. I swear before God I will cherish you as I did of old, and watch you night and day with my truest love and duty and pray with you.

[PRISONER RUDGE *gazes at her as though he were for a moment awed by her manner. But the moment is gone.*]

PRISONER RUDGE: Get away from me. You plot, don't you! You plot to get me to speak and let them know I am the man they say I am. A curse on you and on your boy.

MRS. RUDGE: On him the curse has already fallen.

PRISONER RUDGE: Let it fall heavier. Let it fall on you and everyone else! I hate you and your boy. Now leave me alone!

[MRS. RUDGE *reaches out to him. He menaces her with his chains.*]

PRISONER RUDGE: I say go — I say it for the last time. The gallows has me in its grasp, and it is a black phantom that may urge me to something more. I curse the hour that I was born! I curse the man I slew, I curse the world!

[*He spits at her. In a paroxysm of wrath and terror and fear of death, he drops to his knees and beats the stone ground with his hands and head.*]

BLACKOUT

Breathing it in, you can darken the look in your eyes. Feel the manacles on your wrists and look at Mrs. Rudge with hate. Everything that is given to you in the scene, "smiling malevolently," spitting at Mrs. Rudge, walking with manacled hands, eyes looking down, will influence you to play the scene with violence. If you breathe with no expression at first, you will come to hatred.

* * *

TWO ARE HANGED

From the novel *BARNABY RUDGE*

CHARACTERS:

HUGH: whose mother was hanged when he was six, leaving him alone in the world. He is about to be hanged for taking part in the Protestants' riots against the Catholics.

A JAILOR: who has an assumed solemnity.

DENNIS: a former hangman, now about to be hung as one of the leaders in the Protestant riots.

BARNABY RUDGE: a retarded young man who is supposed to be hanged later.

HEAD JAILOR

SETTING: Prison yard and a platform next to the scaffolding.

SUMMARY:

It is the morning of the hanging of Hugh and Dennis. Barnaby will be taken elsewhere to be hung. The three are brought into the yard to await the time. There is much noise from the crowd gathered in the square to witness the hanging.

HUGH: [*to* BARNABY *who is sitting on a bench*] D'ye hear? They expect us! I heard them gathering when I woke in the night, and turned over on the other side and fell asleep again. We shall see how they welcome Dennis, our rogue hangman, now that his turn is coming.

[HUGH *laughs heartily. The Jailor comes up at this moment*].

JAILOR: Don't carry on like this. This is a solemn occasion and you should respect it.

HUGH: Why? Can I do better than bear it easily? You bear it easily enough. For all your sad look and your solemn air, you think little enough of it!

JAILOR: You are incorrigible.

HUGH: You're right. I am. Don't be a hypocrite! You make merry of this, every month; let me be merry, too. If you want someone frightened, there's one that'll suit you. Try him.

[*He points to* DENNIS, *who trembles so hard that all his joints and limbs seem racked by spasms.*]

[*Two jailors are trying to hold his arms but in his fear* DENNIS *has demonic strength.*]

DENNIS: [*screaming*] They'll hang me by a trick and keep the pardon back. It's a plot against me. I shall lose my life!

[*He falls in a fit and the jailors are able to drag* DENNIS, *with his legs trailing on the ground, closer to the platform near the scaffolding.*]

HUGH: Don't be downcast, Barnaby. Leave that to him that's being dragged.

[BARNABY *has found feathers and other finery to dress himself up.*]

BARNABY: Oh, no, I'm not frightened. I'm quite happy. I wouldn't desire to live now, if they'd let me. Look at me! Am I afraid to die? Will they see me tremble?

[HUGH *gazes for a moment at* BARNABY. *He reaches out to him.* BARNABY *has a strange unearthly expression; his eyes sparkle brightly.*]

[HUGH *and* BARNABY *are distracted by the abject* DENNIS *who is making a last appeal to the officials assembled on the platform.*]

DENNIS: [*grovelling*] Gentlemen, Gentlemen. [he prostates himself on the stone floor] Governor, dear governor -- Gentlemen — have mercy upon a wretched man that has served the Law for so many years, and don't — don't let me die — because of a mistake.

HEAD JAILOR: You know that we could do nothing, even if we would.

DENNIS: [*looking wildly around for sympathy*] All I ask, sir, — all I want and beg, is time, to make it sure. The Government can't know it's me or they never would bring me to this dreadful slaughterhouse. Stop my execution till they can be told that I've been hangman here, nearly thirty years. Will no one go and tell them?

HEAD JAILOR: [*to* DENNIS] You were well known to have been the hangman, when your sentence was considered.

[DENNIS *shuffles towards the* HEAD JAILOR *and holds up his clenched hands.*]

DENNIS: My punishment's worse, it's worse a hundred times, to me than any man. Let them know that, sir. Let them know that. Stop my execution till they know that!

[*His two jailors approach.* DENNIS *utters a piercing cry.*]

DENNIS: Wait! Wait! [*screaming*] Wait! I know the nobleman who is his father…[*he tries to point to* HUGH] I know of his birth — his father is living, he has influence and rank. I know family secrets, give me time to tell them…

[*His voice gives out.* DENNIS *collapses and sinks down, a mere heap of clothes between the two attendants. He is dragged off.]*

[*The* JAILOR *escorts* HUGH *to the platform.*]

HEAD JAILOR: Is there anything you wish to say.

HUGH: [*he looks back at* BARNABY] Do you see that boy sitting on the bench? If I had ten lives to lose, I'd lay them all down to save that boy – who will be lost through my recklessness. I took him from his mother and didn't think what harm would come of it. I ask her pardon; and his. I had faith enough to believe that his one life would be spared. [*he raises his arm like a prophet*] See what he is!— Look at him! I had hoped for mercy for him. And there is none. Now I call down the wrath of God! On that black tree, of which I am the ripened fruit, I invoke the curse of all its victims. And on the head of that man, who, in his conscience, owns me for his son, I leave the wish that he may die a violent death as I do now, and have the night-wind for his only mourner. To this I say, Amen, amen!

[*His arm falls down by his side;* HUGH *becomes the man he was before.*]

HEAD JAILOR: There is nothing more?

[BARNABY *wants to go to* HUGH. *Without looking at* BARNABY, *Hugh motions him not to come near*]

HUGH: There is nothing more.

HEAD JAILOR: Move forward!

BLACKOUT

Dennis's hysteria is disgusting for all to witness. Pull out all the stops when you scream, but do not hurt your vocal chords. This not your one and only performance. Dennis can begin his scene by mumbling, by talking to the governor over and over in his mind, and by shaking. When the jailors come for him, he should begin to flail and scream and fight hard. It is up to the actors, in rehearsal, to figure out how to keep out of Dennis's way. Dennis should not have to curtail his actions. Hugh has a moment of revelation when he looks at brave, vacant Barnaby. He carries that inspiration with him when he makes his last speech. He begins at a talking pace but then speaks quickly and thunderously as he calls on the wrath of God and gives his curse.

* * *

STEERFORTH IS APPLAUDED FOR HIS CRUELTY

From the novel *DAVID COPPERFIELD*

CHARACTERS: MR. MELL: a poor teacher whose mother is in a home for the impoverished.

STEERFORTH: a wealthy student who is a leader among the students and has the run of the school.

TRADDLES: a student with a sense of fair play.

MR. CREAKLE: the corrupt principal of the school.

SETTING: Mr. Mell's classroom

SUMMARY:

In order to simplify the scene for an acting class, let us say that a bunch of noisy boys, up to any and every kind of mischief and making an unbearable racket, is in the hall, grouped around the doorway of Mr. Mell's classroom. Trying to do his tiresome work, Mr. Mells is teased mercilessly by the boys behind his back — and even to his face. They mimic his poverty, his clothing, his gestures. Mr. Mell, his head aching, feels like an animal baited by a thousand dogs. He can stand it no longer.

MR. MELL: [*rising and calling out to the boys*] Silence! It's impossible to bear it. It's maddening. How can you do it to me, boys?

[*The boys in the hallway stop, some suddenly surprised, some half afraid, and some sorry, perhaps.*]

[STEERFORTH *has remained in the room, lounging with his back against the wall and his hands in his pockets. When the noise in the hall quiets down,* STEERFORTH *begins a sharp whistling.*]

MR. MELL: Silence, Mr. Steerforth!

STEERFORTH: [*turning red*] Silence yourself. Whom are you talking to?

MR. MELL: Sit down.

STEERFORTH: Sit down yourself, and mind your business.

[*From outside the room, there is a titter and some applause. The boys see* MR. MELL'*s white face; their laughter dies down.*]

MR. MELL: If you think, Steerforth, that I am not acquainted with the power you have - or that I have not observed you, these last few minutes, urging your juniors on to every sort of outrage against me, you are mistaken.

STEERFORTH: I don't give myself the trouble of thinking at all about you, so I'm not mistaken, as it happens.

MR. MELL: [*his lips trembling*] And when you make use of your position of favoritism here, to insult a gentleman -

STEERFORTH: A what? - where is he?

TRADDLES: [*from the hallway*] Shame, Steerforth! Too bad!

MR. MELL: To insult one who is not fortunate in life, sir, and who never gave you the least offence, you commit a mean and base action. You can sit down or stand up as you please, sir.

STEERFORTH: [*coming forward towards the desk*] I tell you what, Mr. Mell, once for all. When you take the liberty of calling me mean or base, you are an impudent beggar. You are always a beggar, you know; but now you are an impudent beggar.

[*The teacher and the student are almost ready for a fistfight.* MR. CREAKLE *makes his way into the room.*]

MR. CREAKLE: [*shaking the rigid* MR. MELL] Mr. Mell, you have not forgotten yourself, I hope?

MR. MELL: [*much agitated*] No, sir, no. No, sir. No. I have remembered myself. No, Mr. Creakle, I have not forgotten myself, I - I have remembered myself. I - I - could wish you had remembered me a little sooner, Mr. Creakle. It - it – would have been more kind, more just.

MR. CREAKLE: [*to* STEERFORTH] Now, as he don't condescend to tell me, what is this?

STEERFORTH: [*after a silence*] What did he mean by talking about favorites, then?

MR. CREAKLE: [*the veins in his forehead swelling*] Favorites? Who talked about favorites?

STEERFORTH: He did.

MR. CREAKLE: [*turning on* MR. MELL] And what did you mean by that!?

MR. MELL: I meant, Mr. Creakle, as I said; that no pupil had a right to avail himself of his position of favoritism to degrade me.

MR. CREAKLE: To degrade you? Give me leave to ask you, Mr. What's-your-name, whether, when you talk about favorites, you showed proper respect to me? To me, the principal of this establishment, and your employer.

MR. MELL: It was not judicious, I am willing to admit. I should not have done so, if I had been cool.

STEERFORTH: [*taking liberty*] Then he said I was mean, and then he said I was base, and then I called him a beggar. If I had been cool, perhaps I shouldn't have called him a beggar. But I did, and I am ready to take the consequences of it.

MR. CREAKLE: I am surprised, Steerforth - although your candor does you honor, does you honor, certainly - I am surprised, Steerforth, I must say, that you should attach such an epithet to any person employed and paid in my school.

[STEERFORTH *gives a short laugh.*]

MR. CREAKLE: That's not an answer to my remark. I expect more than that from you, Steerforth.

STEERFORTH: Let him deny it.

MR. CREAKLE: Deny that he is a beggar, Steerforth? Why, where does he go a-begging?

STEERFORTH: If he is not a beggar himself, his near relation's one. It's all the same. [*a pause*]

STEERFORTH: [*continues*] Since you expect me, Mr. Creakle, to justify myself, and to say what I mean, - what I have to say is, that his mother lives on charity in a poor-house.

MR. MELL: [*sotto voce*] Yes, I thought so.

MR. CREAKLE: [*with labored politeness*] Now, you hear what this gentleman says, Mr. Mell. Have the goodness, if you please, to set him right before the assembled school.

MR. MELL: [*speaking through a dead silence*] What he has said is true.

MR. CREAKLE: Be so good then as declare publicly, will you, whether it ever came to my knowledge until this moment?

MR. MELL: I believe not directly.

MR. CREAKLE: Why, you know not, don't you mean?

MR. MELL: You never supposed my worldly circumstances to be very good. You know what my position is, and always has been, here.

MR. CREAKLE: [*his veins swelling ever bigger*] You've been in a wrong position altogether, and mistook this for a charity school. Mr. Mell, we'll part, if you please. The sooner the better.

MR. MELL: [*rising*] I take my leave of you, Mr. Creakle, and all of you. James Steerforth, the best wish I can leave you is that you may come to be ashamed of what you have done today.

[MR. MELL *takes his flute and a few books from his desk and leaves the room.*]

MR. CREAKLE: Thank you, Mr. Steerforth for asserting the independence and respectability of our establishment.

[MR. CREAKLE *shakes hands with* STEERFORTH *and leaves.*]

TRADDLES: [*comes into the room*] I don't care what you say, Steerforth. Mell was ill-used.

STEERFORTH: Who has ill-used him, you girl?

TRADDLES: Why, you have.

STEERFORTH: What have I done?

TRADDLES: What have you done? Hurt his feelings, and lost him his job.

STEERFORTH: His feelings? His feelings will soon get the better of it. His feelings are not like yours, Miss Traddles. As to his situation - which was a precious one, wasn't it? - do you suppose I am not going to write home, and take care that he gets some money? Polly?

BLACKOUT

We have already seen the spoiled James Steerforth as a young man, but in this scene we get a taste of Steerforth's practiced cruelty. He is cool and malignant.

* * *

MANIPULATION

TULKINGHORN CONQUERS LADY DEDLOCK

From the novel *BLEAK HOUSE*

CHARACTERS:

MR. TULKINGHORN: a quietly powerful lawyer who collects the secrets of the people he represents.

LADY DEDLOCK: a beautiful woman with a terrible secret.

SETTING:

Mr. Tulkinghorn's room.

SUMMARY:

Lady Dedlock holds her secret very close: that she has had a child [born dead, so she was told] from an affair with Captain Hawdon. Mr. Tulkinghorn has managed to find out these details and holds them against her. Using no names, he tells her story to Lord Dedlock. Lady Dedlock is very fond of her young maid Rosa, and from the story Tulkinghorn tells it seems that Rosa's reputation will be ruined for having been in the employ of Lady Dedlock.

The evening ended, Mr. Tulkinghorn arrives in his room. He is not ready to sleep. He is sedately satisfied by the effect the story has had. It has given him a sense of power. He rubs his veiny wrists as he paces leisurely about his room. He stops suddenly. Lady Dedlock has knocked and entered the room, closing the door behind her. There is a wild disturbance — either fear or anger — in her eyes. Nothing else in her bearing has changed.

MR. TULKINGHORN: Lady Dedlock?

[*She does not speak at first. She slowly sits in a chair.* TULKINGHORN *and* LADY DEDLOCK *are like two portraits facing one another.*]

LADY DEDLOCK: Why have you told my story?

MR. TULKINGHORN: Lady Dedlock, it was necessary for me to inform you that I knew it.

LADY DEDLOCK: How long have you known it?

MR. TULKINGHORN: I have suspected it a long while — fully known it a little while.

LADY DEDLOCK: Months?

MR. TULKINGHORN: [*formal, with composed deference*] Days.

LADY DEDLOCK: Is this true concerning the poor girl?

[MR. TULKINGHORN *indicates that he does not quite understand the question.*]

LADY DEDLOCK: Is it true?   Do her friends know my story also? Is it the town-talk yet?   Is it chalked upon the walls and cried out in the streets?

MR. TULKINGHORN: No, Lady Dedlock.   That was a hypothetical case.   But it would be a real case if they knew — what we know.

LADY DEDLOCK: Then they do not know it yet?

MR. TULKINGHORN: No.

LADY DEDLOCK: Can I save the poor girl from injury before they know it?

MR. TULKINGHORN: Really, Lady Dedlock, I cannot give a satisfactory opinion on that point.

LADY DEDLOCK: [*forcing herself to speak distinctly*] I will make it plainer. I do not dispute your hypothetical case. I have anticipated it. I know the poor girl will be tarnished by having for a moment been, innocently, in my employ. But I have an interest in her no longer belonging to this place. If you can find so much consideration for the woman under your foot as to remember that, she will be very sensible of your mercy.

[MR. TULKINGHORN, *profoundly attentive, throws this off with a shrug of self-depreciation.*]

LADY DEDLOCK: [*continues*] You have prepared me for my exposure, and I thank you for that, too. Is there anything that you require of me? Can I spare my husband in obtaining his release by certifying to the exactness of your discovery? I will write anything, here and now, that you will dictate. I am ready to do it.

MR. TULKINGHORN: I will not trouble you, Lady Dedlock. Pray spare yourself.

LADY DEDLOCK: I have long expected this, as you know. I neither wish to spare myself nor to be spared. You can do nothing worse to me than you have done. Do what remains now.

MR. TULKINGHORN: Lady Dedlock, there is nothing to be done. I will take leave to say a few words when you have finished.

[LADY DEDLOCK *and Mr.* TULKINGHORN *watch each other all the time.*]

LADY DEDLOCK: My jewels are all in their proper places of keeping. They will be found there. So, my dresses. Some ready money I had with me, but no large amount. I did not wear my own dress, in order that I might avoid observation. I want to be henceforward lost. Make this known. I leave no other charge with you.

MR. TULKINGHORN: [*unmoved*] Excuse me, Lady Dedlock, I am not sure that I understand you. You want —

LADY DEDLOCK: To be lost to all here. I leave to-night. I go this hour.

[MR. TULKINGHORN *shakes his head.* LADY DEDLOCK *rises but he shakes his head.*]

LADY DEDLOCK: Not go as I have said?

MR. TULKINGHORN: No, Lady Dedlock.

LADY DEDLOCK: Do you know the relief that my disappearance will be? Have you forgotten the stain and blot upon this place?

MR. TULKINGHORN: No, Lady Dedlock, not by any means.

[LADY DEDLOCK *has her hand on the door knob, ready to leave.*]

MR. TULKINGHORN: Lady Dedlock, have the goodness to stop and hear me, or before you reach the staircase I shall rouse the house. And then I must speak out before every guest and servant, every man and woman.

[*He has conquered her. She falters, trembles, and puts her hand confusedly to her head.*]

MR. TULKINGHORN: Have the goodness to hear me, Lady Dedlock.

[*He motions to the chair from which she has risen. She hesitates, but he motions again, and she sits down.*]

MR. TULKINGHORN: The relations between us are of an unfortunate description, Lady Dedlock; but as they are not of my making, I will not apologize for them. The position I hold in reference to Sir Leicester is well known to you.

LADY DEDLOCK: [*her eyes are on the ground*] I had better have gone. It would have been far better not to have detained me. I have no more to say.

MR. TULKINGHORN: Excuse me, Lady Dedlock, if I add a little more.

LADY DEDLOCK: I wish to hear it at the window, then. I can't breathe where I am.

[*For a moment* TULKINGHORN *fears that she will jump to her death and he will lose his victory.*]

MR. TULKINGHORN: Lady Dedlock, I am not clear what to do or how to act next. I must request you, in the meantime, to keep your secret as you have kept it so long and not to wonder that I keep it too.

[*He pauses, but she makes no reply.*]

MR. TULKINGHORN: [*continues*] Pardon me, Lady Dedlock. This is an important subject. You are honoring me with your attention?

LADY DEDLOCK: I am.

MR. TULKINGHORN: Thank you. I might have known it from what I have seen of your strength of character. The sole consideration in this unhappy case is Sir Leicester.

LADY DEDLOCK: [*in a low voice and looking at the stars*] Then why, do you detain me in his house?

MR. TULKINGHORN: Because he is the consideration. Sir Leicester is a very proud man. The fall of that moon out of the sky would not amaze him more than your fall from your high position as his wife.

[LADY DEDLOCK *breathes quickly and heavily, but she stands with unflinchingly regal posture.*]

LADY DEDLOCK: Not my flight? Think of it again.

MR. TULKINGHORN: [*with finality*] Your flight, Lady Dedlock, would spread the whole truth, and a hundred times the whole truth, far and wide. It would be impossible to save the family credit for a day. It is not to be thought of.

LADY DEDLOCK: Go on!

MR. TULKINGHORN: Therefore, I have much to consider. This is to be hushed up if it can be. How can it be, if Sir Leicester is driven out of his wits or laid upon a death-bed? What could have caused it? Lady Dedlock, the wall-chalking and the street-crying would come on directly, and you are to remember that it would not affect you merely [whom I cannot at all consider in this business] but your husband, Lady Dedlock, your husband. I must take all this into account, and it renders a decision very difficult.

[LADY DEDLOCK *stands looking out at the stars without a word. She looks as if she is frozen by their cold light.*]

MR. TULKINGHORN: [*mechanically doing business*] In the meanwhile I must beg you to keep your own counsel, and I will keep mine.

LADY DEDLOCK: [*still looking at the distant sky*] I am to drag my present life on, holding its pains at your pleasure, day by day?

MR. TULKINGHORN: Yes, I am afraid so, Lady Dedlock.

LADY DEDLOCK: It is necessary, you think, that I should be so tied to the stake?

MR. TULKINGHORN: I am sure that what I recommend is necessary.

LADY DEDLOCK: [*slowly*] I am to remain on this gaudy platform and it is to fall beneath me when you give the signal?

MR. TULKINGHORN: Not without notice, Lady Dedlock. I shall take no step without forewarning you.

LADY DEDLOCK: [*as if memorizing the rules*] We are to meet as usual?

MR. TULKINGHORN: Precisely as usual, if you please.

LADY DEDLOCK: And I am to hide my guilt, as I have done so many years?

MR. TULKINGHORN: As you have done so many years.

LADY DEDLOCK: [*after a pause*] Is there anything more to be said to-night?

MR. TULKINGHORN: [*softly rubbing hands*] Why, I should like to be assured of your acquiescence in my arrangements, Lady Dedlock.

LADY DEDLOCK: You may be assured of it.

MR. TULKINGHORN: Good. And I would wish in conclusion to remind you, as a business precaution, should it be necessary to recall the fact with Sir Leicester, that throughout our interview I have expressly stated my sole consideration to be Sir Leicester's feelings and honor and the family reputation.

LADY DEDLOCK: I can attest your fidelity, sir.

[*She remains absorbed, but at length she moves with her natural and acquired grace towards the door.* MR. TULKINGHORN *opens the door for her and makes his accustomed bow as she passes out. It is not an ordinary look that she gives him. In a very slight movement, she acknowledges his courtesy.*]

PART TWO

[*In her room,* LADY DEDLOCK *paces with agitation her hair streaming wildly from her flung-back face, her hands clasped behind her head, her figure twisted by pain.*]

BLACKOUT

For me, it would be Lady Dedlock's posture that would lead me to her character. The way she carries her head and neck, the way they are placed on her shoulders, [and what this does to her breathing] are all ways of keeping people from getting to close to her. The only time Lady Dedlock displays any passion before others is when she accidentally hears of the past. Then it is for a moment only. Later, when she is alone, her suffering — almost to madness — shows.

There are a few moments when Tulkinghorn is forced to cover up a disappointment. This he does quickly, undiscernable to anyone else. Otherwise, we never see him in anything but the coldest and most strategic control. Tulkinghorn and Lady Dedlock, two equally determined opponents, clash in their quiet way. Although she covers up her weakness very well, Lady Dedlock is vulnerable. She has the most to lose in her encounter with Mr. Tulkinghorn. That she despises Tulkinghorn is evident, but she has too much to consider to let that hatred get in the way of her battle with him.

* * *

TULKINGHORN AND LADY DEDLOCK:
THEIR FINAL CONVERSATION

From the novel *BLEAK HOUSE*

CHARACTERS: **LADY DEDLOCK:** locked in a deadly encounter with Tulkinghorn.

MR. TULKINGHORN: has all the answers to their disagreement.

A BUTLER

SETTING: Lady Dedlock's dining room.

SUMMARY:

Mr. Tulkinghorn has ferreted out the details of her past that Lady Dedlock has tried so hard to keep to herself. Now they both know that he holds a winning hand. In their first encounter, he set the rules for her conduct. She was to do nothing that would attract attention. But Lady Dedlock has dismissed her young maid so that the girl's chance of a good marriage would not be spoiled by their association. By dismissing the maid, Lady Dedlock has defied Mr. Tulkinghorn. Lady Dedlock is sitting down to dinner alone. She is approached by her butler.

BUTLER: Mr. Tulkinghorn sends his respects and could my Lady please to receive him for a word or two after her dinner?

LADY DEDLOCK: I will see him now.

[*The* BUTLER *leaves and* MR. TULKINGHORN *enters.*]

MR. TULKINGHORN: I apologize for intruding while you are at table, Lady Dedlock.

LADY DEDLOCK: [*dispensing with such mockeries*] What do you want?

[MR. TULKINGHORN *sits on a chair a little distance from her and slowly rubs his rusty legs up and down, up and down, up and down.*]

MR. TULKINGHORN: Lady Dedlock, I am rather surprised by the course you have taken.

LADY DEDLOCK: Indeed?

MR. TULKINGHORN: Yes, decidedly. I was not prepared for it. I consider it a departure from our agreement and your promise. It puts us in a new position, Lady Dedlock. I feel myself under the necessity of saying that I don't approve of it.

[*He stops rubbing his legs and looks at her. Imperturbable and unchangeable as he is, there is an indefinable freedom in his manner. This is new, and it does not escape* LADY DEDLOCK's *observation.*]

LADY DEDLOCK: I don't quite understand you.

MR. TULKINGHORN: Oh yes, you do, I think. I think you do. Come, come, Lady Dedlock, we must not fence and parry now. You know you like this girl.

LADY DEDLOCK: Well?

MR. TULKINGHORN: And you know — and I know — that you have not sent her away for the reasons you have assigned, but for the purpose of separating her from any exposure you may experience.

LADY DEDLOCK: Well?

MR. TULKINGHORN: [*crossing his legs and nursing his knee*] Well, Lady Dedlock, I object to that. I consider that a dangerous proceeding. I know it to be unnecessary and calculated to awaken speculation, doubt, rumor in the house. Besides, it is a violation of our agreement. You were to be exactly what you were before. Whereas, it must be evident to yourself, as it is to me, that you have been this evening very different from what you were before, Lady Dedlock, transparently so!

LADY DEDLOCK: If, in my knowledge of my secret...

MR. TULKINGHORN: [*interrupting her*] Now, Lady Dedlock, this is a matter of business. It is no longer your secret. It is my secret, in trust for Sir Leicester and the family. If it were your secret, Lady Dedlock, we should not be here holding this conversation.

LADY DEDLOCK: That is very true. If in my knowledge of the secret I do what I can to spare an innocent girl from the taint of my impending shame, I act upon a resolution I have taken. Nothing in the world, and no one in the world, could shake it or could move me.

[*She speaks with deliberation and distinctness and with no more outward passion than* MR. TULKINGHORN. TULKINGHORN *is methodical in discussing the business. He no longer is concerned with* LADY DEDLOCK's *sensibility.*]

MR. TULKINGHORN: Really? Then you see, Lady Dedlock, you are not to be trusted. You have put the case in a perfectly plain way. As to sparing the girl, of what importance or value is she? Lady Dedlock, here is a family name, the Dedlocks, compromised.

[LADY DEDLOCK *lifts her eyes and looks at* MR. TULKINGHORN *sternly.* LADY DEDLOCK *has eaten no dinner, but has poured water into a glass with a steady hand. She rises from the table, takes a lounging-chair, and reclines in it, shading her face. There is nothing in her manner to express weakness or excite compassion. She is thoughtful, gloomy, concentrated.*]

MR. TULKINGHORN: [*sotto voce*] This woman is a study.

[*They are silent. Finally* MR. TULKINGHORN *is forced to speak.*]

MR. TULKINGHORN: Lady Dedlock, the most disagreeable part of this business remains, but it is business. Our agreement is broken. A lady of your sense and strength of character will be prepared for my now declaring it void and taking my own course.

LADY DEDLOCK: I am quite prepared.

MR. TULKINGHORN: That is all I have to trouble you with, Lady Dedlock.

[*He starts to leave the room.*]

LADY DEDLOCK: This is the notice I was to receive? I want to understand you.

MR. TULKINGHORN: Not exactly the notice you were to receive. But virtually the same.

LADY DEDLOCK: You intend to give me no other notice?

MR. TULKINGHORN: You are right. No.

LADY DEDLOCK: Do you contemplate undeceiving Sir Leicester to-night?

MR. TULKINGHORN: [*with a slight smile*] No, not to-night.

LADY DEDLOCK: To-morrow?

MR. TULKINGHORN: I had better decline answering that question, Lady Dedlock. If I were to say I don't know when, exactly, you would not believe me, and it would answer no purpose. It may be to-morrow. I would rather say no more. You are prepared. I wish you good night.

LADY DEDLOCK: Do you intend to remain in the house any time? I heard you were writing in the library. Are you going to return there?

MR. TULKINGHORN: Only for my hat. I am going home.

[*In a slight and curious movement*, LADY DEDLOCK *bows her eyes rather than her head*. MR. TULKINGHORN *withdraws*.]

BLACKOUT

The change of tone in both Lady Dedlock and Mr. Tulkinghorn is very subtle. Lady Dedlock does not lose her essential elegance, but she is fighting hard now. Dropping some of his show of good manners, Mr. Tulkinghorn allows himself to interrupt her, to speak with her at times as if she were a male client who needs to understand more clearly what has happened. Instead of the ironic courtesy he had formerly used, his voice has changed to a metallic tone.

* * *

JONAS THINKS HE HAS OUTSMARTED MONTAGUE

From the novel *MARTIN CHUZZLEWIT*

CHARACTERS: JONAS CHUZZLEWIT: sullen and paranoid, Jonas thinks he can handle Montague.

TIGG MONTAGUE: [formerly known as Montague Tigg], a born con man.

JOBLING: a con man

SETTING: Montague's handsome quarters.

SUMMARY:

It is in the nature of Jonas's mean mind that he is overawed by fine clothes and fine furniture while wishing revenge on the man who has such. He has already been set up by a crony of Montagues.

DR. JOBLING: You two gentlemen have business to discuss, I know, and your time is precious. So is mine; I have patients waiting for me in the next room. Good-bye. But allow me, Mr. Montague, before I go, to say this of my friend who sits beside you — this gentleman has done more, sir, to reconcile me to human nature, than any man alive or dead. Good-bye!

MONTAGUE: [*drawing his chair close to* JONAS] I have learned from our friend that you have been thinking—

JONAS: Oh! By god then he'd no right to say so. I didn't tell him my thoughts. If he took it into his head that I was coming here for such or such a purpose, why, that's his look-out. I don't stand committed by that. If I come here to ask a question or two, I don't bind myself to anything. Let's understand that, you know.

MONTAGUE: [*clapping him on the shoulder*] My dear fellow! I applaud your frankness. If men like you and I speak openly at first, all possible misunderstanding is avoided. We investment companies are all birds of prey. The only question is, whether in serving our own turn, we can serve you.

[JONAS *changes his position in the chair, taking on for a more boastful attitude.*]

MONTAGUE: We are not children, Mr. Chuzzlewit; we are grown men, I hope.

[JONAS *agrees and, after a short silence, spreads out his legs; he sticks one arm akimbo to show how perfectly at home he is.*]

JONAS: The truth is…

MONTAGUE: [*with a grin*] Don't say, the truth. It's so like humbug.

JONAS: [*charmed*] The long and the short of it is…

MONTAGUE: Better. Much better!

JONAS: That I didn't consider myself very well used by one or two of the old companies. They carried things much too high for my taste.

[JONAS *pauses for quite some time.*]

MONTAGUE: [*most pleasantly*] Take a glass of wine.

JONAS: [*with a cunning shake of his head*] No, no, none of that, thankya. No wine over business. All very well for you, but it wouldn't do for me.

MONTAGUE: [*leering at him*] What an old hand you are, Mr. Chuzzlewit!

JONAS: [*shakes his head and mutters*] You're right there. Not such an old hand, either, but that I've been and got married. She's young but one never knows what may happen to these women, so I'm thinking of insuring her life. It's only fair, you know, that a man should secure some consolation in case of meeting with such a loss.

MONTAGUE: [*murmuring*] If anything can console him under such heart-breaking circumstances.

JONAS: Exactly. If anything can. Now, supposing I did it here, I should do it cheap, I know, and easy, without bothering her about it; which I'd much rather not do, for it's just in a woman's way to take it into her head, if you talk to her about such things, that she's going to die directly.

MONTAGUE: So it is. You're quite right. Sweet, silly, fluttering little simpletons!

JONAS: Well, on that account, I wouldn't mind patronising this Company. But I want to know what sort of security there is for the Company's going on. That's the...

MONTAGUE: [*holding up his jewelled hand*] Not the truth? Don't use that Sunday School expression, please!

JONAS: The long and the short of it. The long and the short of it is, what's the security?

MONTAGUE: [*referring to papers on the table*] The paid-up capital, my dear sir, on the table, is, at this present moment—

JONAS: Oh! I understand all about paid-up capitals, you know.

MONTAGUE: [*stopping short*] You do?

JONAS: I should hope so.

MONTAGUE: [*moves closer and speaks in* JONAS's *ear*] I know you do. I know you do. Look at me!

[JONAS's *rarely looks straight at anybody. But he does this time.*]

MONTAGUE: You know me? You recollect? You've seen me before?

JONAS: Why, I thought I remembered your face when I first came in, but I couldn't call to mind where I had seen it. No. I don't remember, even now.

MONTAGUE: Was it in Pecksniff's parlor?

JONAS: In Pecksniff's parlor! You don't mean when…

MONTAGUE: Yes, when there was a very charming and delightful little family party, at which yourself and your respected father attended.

JONAS: Well, never mind him. He's dead, and there's no help for it.

MONTAGUE: Dead, is he! Venerable old gentleman, is he dead! You're very like him.

[JONAS *doesn't receive the compliment with much grace.*]

MONTAGUE: [*now in very high spirits*] Do you find me changed since that time? Speak plainly.

JONAS: [*looking at* MONTAGUE's *jewels*] For sure.

MONTAGUE: Was I at all seedy in those days?

JONAS: Yes, you were.

MONTAGUE: Do you like this room?

JONAS: It must have cost a lot of money.

MONTAGUE: You're right. Why don't you [*he whispers and nudges* JONAS] why don't you take premiums, instead of paying 'em? That's what a man like you should do. Join us!

[JONAS *stares at him in amazement.*]

MONTAGUE: Join us. You shall come in cheap.

[JONAS *looks at him harder and harder.*]

MONTAGUE: [*in* JONAS's *ear*] I can tell you how the ordinary man in the street will bring us their money, force it upon us, trust us as if we were the Mint; yet know no more about us than you do of that street-sweeper at the corner. Ha,ha!

[JONAS *gradually breaks into a smile.*]

MONTAGUE: [*gives him a pleasant thrust in the chest*] Yah! you're too deep for us, you dog, or I wouldn't have told you. Dine with me to-morrow!

JONAS: I will.

MONTAGUE: Done! Wait a bit. Take these papers with you and look 'em over.

[*He snatches some papers from the table*]

JONAS: [*greedily*] Yes. Well!

MONTAGUE: [*his laugh shaking him from head to foot*] A man can well afford to be as bold as brass, my good fellow, when he gets gold in exchange! You'll dine with me to-morrow?

JONAS: At what time?

MONTAGUE: Seven. Here's my card. Take the documents. I see you'll join us!

JONAS: I don't know about that. There's a good deal to be looked into first.

MONTAGUE: [*slapping* JONAS *on the back*] You shall look into anything and everything you please. But you'll join us, I am convinced. You were made for it. Bully for you!

BLACKOUT

Dickens has given accurate directions regarding Jonas' body language. His breath is measured; his eyes and facial features are on the alert. At some point he relaxes, his breathing becomes easier, and his usual look of greed and disdain returns.

Montague plays his part with relish. Not only does he want to snare Jonas, he enjoys toying with him. He takes long leisurely breaths. He plays with Jonas as one does with a string to tease a cat.

* * *

MONTAGUE CONS JONAS AT A DINNER PARTY

From the novel *MARTIN CHUZZLEWIT*

CHARACTERS:

JONAS: ready to be gulled.

MONTAGUE: a suave and clever cheat.

DR. JOBLING: a con man.

MR. WOLF: a con man.

MR. PIP: a con man.

SERVANT

SETTING: Montague's dining room.

SUMMARY:

Jonas is invited to an elaborate dinner where he will be gulled into joining a fake business firm that will supposedly make him a great deal of
money. Montague has done a good job convincing Jonas that joining the
investment group will assure his rise in society. Before entering and
meeting the other "gentlemen," Jonas, who is greedy and wants respect,
anticipates the benefits that will come once he joins the venture.

JONAS: [*thinking aloud*] To make a swinging profit, have a lot of
fellows to order about, and get into good society ain't such a
bad look-out.

MONTAGUE: [*greeting* JONAS] My dear friend, I am delighted to
see you. Jobling, you know, I believe?

[JOBLING *steps out of the circle of friends to shake hands.*]

DR. JOBLING: I think so. I trust I have the honor. I hope so. My
dear sir, I see you well. Quite well? That's well!

MONTAGUE: Mr Wolf, Mr Chuzzlewit. Mr Pip, Mr. Chuzzlewit.

MR. WOLF: Exceedingly happy to have the honor.

PIP: Happy to make your acquaintance, Mr. Chuzzlewit.

[*The* DOCTOR *draws* JONAS *a little apart.*]

DR. JOBLING: [*whispering*] Men of the world, my dear sir — men
of the world. Mr. Wolf — literary character — you needn't
mention it - remarkably clever, weekly paper — Mr. Pip —
theatrical man — oh, a capital man!

MR. WOLF: [*resuming his conversation*] Well! And what did Nobley say to that?

PIP: Why, he didn't know what to say. He was mute as a poker. But you know what a good fellow Nobley is!

MR. WOLF: The best in the world! Not a doubt. But you were going to tell us...?

PIP: Oh, yes! So I was. At first he was dumb. But after a minute he said: "Well, Pip, is she or isnt she bandy?" And I said: "To be sure she is, I know." He roared with laughter: "Well said, Pip. Count me in among your fashionable visitors whenever I'm in town, Pip." And so I do, to this day.

[*The* SERVANT *appears.*]

SERVANT: Dinner is served.

[*The guests eat and drink heartily.*]

MONTAGUE: A glass of wine?

JONAS: [*having had several*] Oh! As much of that as you like! It's too good to refuse.

MR. WOLF: Well said, Mr. Chuzzlewit!

PIP: Good for you.

DR. JOBLING: [*hardly stopping eating*] Positively, you know, that's — hahaha! That's epi-grammatic!

MONTAGUE: [*to* JONAS] You're tolerably comfortable, I hope?

JONAS: Oh! You needn't trouble your head about me, Famous!

MONTAGUE: I thought it best not to have a party. You agree?

JONAS: Why, what do you call this? You don't mean to say you do this every day, do you?

MONTAGUE: [*shrugging*] My dear fellow, every day of my life, when I dine at home. This is my common style. It was of no use having anything uncommon for you. You'd have seen through it. You shall take us in the rough!

JONAS: [*glancing around the table*] And pretty smooth, too! This don't cost a trifle.

MONTAGUE: Why, to be candid with you, it does not. But I like this sort of thing. It's the way I spend my money.

JONAS: [*thrusting his tongue into his cheek*] Is it?

MONTAGUE: When you join us, you won't get rid of your share of the profits in the same way?

JONAS: Quite different.

MONTAGUE: Well, and you're right. You needn't. But you don't mind dining expensively at another man's expense, I hope?

JONAS: Not a bit.

MONTAGUE: Then I hope you'll often dine with me?

JONAS: Ah! I don't mind. On the contrary.

MONTAGUE: And I'll never attempt to talk business to you over wine, I take my oath. Oh deep, deep, deep of you to have been so careful the other day! I must tell 'em that. They're the very men to enjoy it. Pip, I've a splendid little trait to tell you of my friend Chuzzlewit who is the deepest dog I know. I give you my sacred word of honor he is the deepest dog I know, Pip!

PIP: By damn and by god, I was sure of it already.

[*The others applaud loudly.*]

DR. JOBLING: [*whispering to* JONAS] Men of the world, my dear sir.

Thorough men of the world! To a professional person like myself it's quite refreshing — it's philosophically improving. It's character, character!

JONAS: [*drinking freely and muttering*] All this at his expense. Let him spend his money. Ain't no extravagance of mine. I ain't no blundering gull to be cheated. Rolled up like a hedgehog I am with my sharpest points towards them, yes, by god!

[*At last, the men, drunk and unsteady, stand up and prepare to leave.*]

MR. WOLF: Montague, this chap is one of us. I hope to further our acquaintance.

PIP: I will have the pleasure of introducing you to the society of friends in which you are qualified to shine.

DR. JOBLING: [*clapping* JONAS *on the shoulder*] Be one of us!

JONAS: [*standing, quite drunk*] I am infinitely obliged to you. There is nothing I would like better. [aside] So long as you stand treat.

[*The men leave.* MONTAGUE *watches* JONAS. JONAS, *very drunk, falls back into his chair, his head tumbled onto the table.*]

BLACKOUT

The friends of Montague show their vulgarity when they eat and drink the good wine and fine food that Montague has provided. When they talk about Nobley, they do a pretty good job acting like men of the world. Knowing that his bird has been bagged, Montague watches over all with cool amusement. Jonas is an easy drunk and ready to consume anything placed before him. He has lost his cunning.

JONAS SQUIRMS IN MONTAGUE'S NET

From the novel *MARTIN CHUZZLEWIT*

CHARACTERS: **JONAS:** selfish and greedy he will stop at nothing.

MONTAGUE: a man who knows how to handle the easily deceived.

SETTING: Montague's board room.

SUMMARY:

Montague has discovered that Jonas killed his father. Jonas tries to flee the country to get away from Montague. Despite Jonas' disguise, Montague has spotted him before he can board the ship.

JONAS: Who said I meant to fly? How do you know that?

MONTAGUE: Who said? Come, come. A foreign boat, my friend, an early hour, a figure wrapped up for disguise! Who said? If you didn't mean to jilt me, why were you there? If you didn't mean to jilt me, why did you come back?

JONAS: I came back to avoid disturbance.

MONTAGUE: You were wise.

[JONAS *stands silent, avoiding* MONTAGUE*'s eyes.*]

MONTAGUE: Now, Chuzzlewit, notwithstanding what has passed, I will be plain with you. Are you attending to me? I only see your back.

JONAS: I hear you. Go on!

MONTAGUE: I say that notwithstanding what has passed, I will be plain with you.

JONAS: You said that before. And I told you once I heard you. Go on.

MONTAGUE: You are a little chafed, but I can make allowance for that. Myself, I am in the very best of tempers. Now, let us see how circumstances stand. A day or two ago, I mentioned to you, my dear fellow, that I thought I had discovered...

JONAS: [*looking fiercely around and at the door*] Will you hold your tongue?

MONTAGUE: Well, well! Quite correct. To repeat, I make, or think I make, a certain discovery which I mention to you in your ear, in confidence. I may desire to turn this little incident to my needs, which do not lie in using it against you.

JONAS: What do you call using it against me?

MONTAGUE: [*with a laugh*] Oh! We'll not enter into that.

JONAS: Using it to make a beggar of me. Is that the use you mean?

MONTAGUES: No. I want you to act as a decoy in the Pecksniff case I told you about. You don't mind that, I know. You care nothing for the man (you care nothing for any man; you are too sharp; so am I, I hope) Ha,ha ha! Now, I am not a moral man, you know. I am not the least affected by anything you may have done; by any little indiscretion you may have committed; but I wish to profit by the secret if I can; Everybody profits by the indiscretion of his neighbor; and the people with the best reputations profit the most.

JONAS: [*speaking slowly*] Lying is of no use now. I did think of getting away this morning, and making better terms with you from a distance.

MONTAGUE: To be sure! To be sure! Nothing more natural.

JONAS: [*with a sneer*] Your great discovery may be true, and may be false. Whichever it is, I dare say I'm no worse than any other man.

MONTAGUE: Not a bit. We're all alike — or nearly so.

JONAS: I want to know this. Is the...the... is it your own?

MONTAGUE: My own?

JONAS: Is it known to anybody else, the secret! Don't waver about that.

MONTAGUE: [*with no hesitation*] No, to no one! What would a secret be worth, do you think, unless I kept it?

[JONAS, *for the first time, looks at* MONTAGUE.]

JONAS: [*with a laugh*] Come! Make things easy for me, and I'm yours. I don't know that I may not be better off here, after all, than if I had gone away this morning. But here I am, and here I'll stay now. Take your oath!

MONTAGUE: On my oath.

JONAS: Shall I go to Pecksniff? When? Say when!

MONTAGUE: Immediately! He cannot be enticed too soon.

JONAS: [*laughing wildly*] By god! There's some fun in catching that old hypocrite. I hate him. Shall I go to-night?

MONTAGUE: [*ecstatically*] This is like business! We understand each other now! Tonight, my good fellow, by all means.

JONAS: Come with me. We must go down there in splendor, and carry documents, for he's a deep file to deal with, and must be drawn on with an artful hand, or he won't follow. I know him. Will you come tonight?

[MONTAGUE *does not relish this proposal.*]

JONAS: We can make our plans on the road. We must not go directly to him. I may not even want to introduce you, but I must have you on the spot. I know the man, I tell you.

MONTAGUE: My friend, I can trust you alone.

JONAS: Trust me! By god, you may trust me now, far enough. I'll try to go away no more — no more! [speaking soberly] I can't get on without you. Will you come?

MONTAGUE: I will, if that's your opinion.

[*They shake hands upon it.* JONAS, *in feverish haste, helps* MONTAGUE *on with his coat. They leave.*]

BLACKOUT

Jonas has a harsh, tough boy tone which we hear at the beginning of the scene. It is the same tone that he uses to good effect with people he's not frightened of. But he is frightened, frightened both of Montague and of the fact that Montague knows his secret – that he fed his elderly father pills to help him die. Jonas knows Montague is too smart for him. Montague is never at a loss in dealing with Jonas.

* * *

PECKSNIFF IS EAGER TO BE GULLED

From the novel *MARTIN CHUZZLEWIT*

CHARACTERS: **MR. PECKSNIFF:** a hypocrite.

JONAS CHUZZLEWIT: his son-in-law who hates him.

SETTING: Jonas drops in on Pecksniff at home.

SUMMARY:

Mr. Pecksniff considers himself to be a man of the world, although close to a saintly one. We see how easily he lends himself to Montague's manipulation. The scene opens as Pecksniff clasps Jonas in his arms.

MR. PECKSNIFF: [*seemingly perturbed*] Jonas. My child! She is well! There is nothing the matter?

JONAS: You're at it again, are you? Even with me? Quit it!

MR. PECKSNIFF: Tell me she is well then. Tell me she is well, my boy!

JONAS: [*disengaging himself*] She's well enough. There's nothing the matter with her.

MR. PECKSNIFF: [*sitting and rubbing his hair*] How is my other child; my eldest; my Cherrywerrychigo?

JONAS: She's the same as usual. She sticks pretty close to the vinegar-bottle. You know she's got a sweetheart?

MR. PECKSNIFF: I have heard of it from headquarters; from my child herself. It has ever been the study of my life to qualify my girls for the domestic hearth; and it is a sphere which Cherry will adorn.

JONAS: She'll need to adorn some sphere or other, for she ain't very ornamental in general.

[JONAS *rocks in his chair, looks at* PECKSNIFF *with cunning. His eyes twinkle with shrewd meaning.*]

MR. PECKSNIFF: What is it you are going to say?

JONAS: By god! Pecksniff, if I knew how you meant to leave your money, I could put you in the way of doubling it in no time. It wouldn't be bad to keep a chance like this snug in the family. But you're such a deep one!

MR. PECKSNIFF: [*much affected*] Jonas! My heart is in my hand. By far the greater part of the inconsiderable savings I have accumulated is already given, with confidence, to a person whom I need not name. [*he squeezes* JONAS' *hand fervently*] [*aside*] God bless you, be careful of it when you get it!

JONAS: Well, I am on my way, now, to see Montague.

MR. PECKSNIFF: Ah, I insist on accompanying you. I can leave a card for Mr. Montague on the way.

PART TWO

CHARACTERS: MR. PECKSNIFF: a bird ready for picking.

JONAS: has done his job; he has brought Pecksniff to Montague.

MONTAGUE: delighted to get at Pecksniff and his money.

SETTING: Mr. Montague's dwelling.

SUMMARY:

Montague has very nicely had Pecksniff brought around, and now will work on him.

MR. PECKSNIFF: [*to* MONTAGUE] I could have wished to have had the honor of introducing you to Mr. Martin Chuzzlewit. He would have been proud indeed to have shaken your hand.

MONTAGUE: Is the gentleman here now?

MR. PECKSNIFF: He is.

MONTAGUE: You said nothing about that, Chuzzlewit.

JONAS: I didn't suppose you'd care to hear of it. You wouldn't care to know him, I can promise you.

MR. PECKSNIFF: Jonas! My dear Jonas! Really!

JONAS: Oh! It's all very well for you to speak up for him. You've nailed him. You'll get a fortune by him.

MONTAGUE: Oho! Is the wind in that quarter? Ha, ha, ha!

[*They all laugh — especially* MR. PECKSNIFF.]

MR. PECKSNIFF: [*clapping* JONAS *playfully on the shoulder*] No, no! You must not believe all that my young relative says, Mr. Montague. You must not attach importance to his flights of fancy.

MONTAGUE: Upon my life, Mr. Pecksniff, I attach the greatest importance to his observation. I trust and hope it's true. There is nothing like building our fortune on the weaknesses of mankind.

MR. PECKSNIFF: Oh, for shame!

[*They all laugh again — especially* MR. PECKSNIFF.]

MONTAGUE: I give you my honor that we do it.

MR. PECKSNIFF: Oh, that I am sure you don't! How can you, you know?

[*Again they all laugh; again* MR. PECKSNIFF *laughs heartily.*]

MONTAGUE: As long as there are gulls upon the wing it must succeed.

MR. PECKSNIFF: [*mildly*] Oh, I know you are joking. I know you are joking ...because, uh...ha,ha, you say so.

BLACKOUT

Montague and Pecksniff are flirting with each other in this little game of getting Pecksniff's money. Montague acts as though he and Pecksniff are truly men of the world. Except when he has to play his part, for the most part Jonas looks on with disgust.

The rhythms of the scene should be observed. Montague's and Pecksniff's are almost lyrical. Jonas throws in his sour comments as a kind of counterpoint.

* * *

A FUNEREAL WEDDING DAY

From the novel *NICHOLAS NICKLEBY*

CHARACTERS: **ARTHUR GRIDE:** a mean and ugly old man.

RALPH NICKLEBY: a humorless and calculating man who cares only for money.

MR. BRAY: a worthless and sickly man, Madeline Bray's father.

SERVANT

SETTING: The Bray apartment.

SUMMARY:

Arthur Gride is a usurer in debt to a more powerful usurer, Ralph Nickleby. Gride is going to marry a very young girl, Madeline Bray. It will bring gain to each of the men and to Madeline's father. Father Bray will get an annuity from Gride in payment for giving up his daughter. Gride and Nickleby arrive at the house for the wedding, and even they are depressed by the mournful silence of the place.

RALPH NICKLEBY: [*speaking in spite of himself in a subdued voice*]

One would think that there was a funeral going on here, and not a wedding.

GRIDE: [*tittering*] He,he! You are so...so very funny!

RALPH NICKLEBY: [*drily*] I need be for this is rather dull and chilling. Look a little brisker, man, and not so like a hangdog!

GRIDE: Yes, yes, I will. But...but...do you think she's coming just yet, do you?

RALPH NICKLEBY: I suppose she won't come till she is obliged and she has a good half-hour to spare yet. Curb your impatience.

GRIDE: I...I...am not impatient. I wouldn't be hard with her for the world. Let her take her time. In time, her time shall be mine.

RALPH NICKLEBY: [*wryly*] I understand why you are so generous.

[*The father,* BRAY, *comes into the room on tiptoe, and holds up his hand cautiously as if there were a sick person who must not be disturbed.*]

BRAY: Hush! She was very ill last night. I thought she would have broken her heart. She is dressed, and crying bitterly in her room. But she's better, and quite quiet now.

RALPH NICKLEBY: She is ready, is she?

BRAY: Quite ready.

RALPH NICKLEBY: And not likely to delay us by any young-lady weaknesses, fainting, and such like?

BRAY: She may be safely trusted now. I have been talking to her this morning. Here — come over here.

[*Father* BRAY *draws* RALPH NICKLEBY *to the further end of the room, and points towards* GRIDE, *who sits fumbling nervously with the buttons of his coat.* GRIDE's *contemptible expression is farther marred by his anxiety and trepidation.*]

BRAY: Look at that man! This seems a cruel thing, after all.

RALPH NICKLEBY: What seems a cruel thing?

BRAY: This marriage. Don't ask me what. You know as well as I do. Look at him. Does it not seem cruel?

RALPH NICKLEBY: No!

BRAY: [*feeling virtuous and moral*] I say it does. It is a cruel thing, by all that's bad and treacherous!

RALPH NICKLEBY: [*after giving* BRAY *time to express his pity*] You see what a dry, shrivelled, withered old fellow he is. If he were younger, it might be cruel. But, Mr. Bray, he'll die soon, and leave her a rich young widow! Miss Madeline obeys your wishes this time; after his death, she will do as she wants.

BRAY: [*ill at ease and biting his nails*] True, true. I couldn't do anything better for her than advise her to accept these proposals, could I? Now, I ask you, Nickleby, as a man of the world, could I?

RALPH NICKLEBY: Surely not. There are a hundred fathers, well off, substantial men who would gladly give their daughters to that very man over there, ape and mummy as he looks.

BRAY: [*eagerly*] Yes, there are! And I told her so, both last night and today.

RALPH NICKLEBY: You told her the truth; though I must say that if I had a daughter, and my freedom, my pleasure, my very health and life, depended on her taking the husband I had chosen for her, I should hope there would be no further argument to have her consent to my wishes.

BRAY: [*relieved*] I must go upstairs for a few minutes, to finish dressing. When I come down, I'll bring Madeline with me.

[BRAY *starts to leave and then stops.*]

BRAY: Do you know, I had a very strange dream last night, which I have not remembered till this minute. I dreamt that it was this morning, and you and I had been talking as we have been just now; that I went upstairs to dress; and that as I stretched out my hand to take Madeline's, and lead her down, the floor sunk with me, and after falling from a tremendous height as only happens in a dream, I landed in a grave.

RALPH NICKLEBY: And you awoke, and found you were suffering from indigestion? Mr. Bray, you are going to have the opportunity for pleasure and enjoyment and you will have no time to think of what you dream at night.

[*Father* BRAY *goes upstairs.*]

RALPH NICKLEBY: [*to* GRIDE] Mark my words, Gride, you won't have to pay his annuity very long. If he's not booked to make the long voyage before many months are past, I wear an orange for my head!

[GRIDE *cackles with delight.* RALPH *takes a chair and both the Bridegroom and his Best Man sit waiting in a profound silence. Suddenly there is an awful scream, followed by more screaming and a confusion of voices.*]

VOICES: How could it happen? I saw him fall. Out of the chair!

[*Madeline's* SERVANT *runs in.*]

SERVANT: He's dead. He died! He died!

RALPH NICKLEBY: Who died, girl? Who died!

SERVANT: Mr. Bray! [she screams in horror] Mr. Bray!

[*She runs from the room.*]

BLACKOUT

Ralph's disgust with Gride and Bray is something that he must control. These are the people he deals with all the time in order to get what he wants. We see his cool rationality in the way Ralph gets people to do his dirty work. His cold unsmiling manner keeps people afraid of him.

The actor playing Mr. Bray can round his shoulders and sink his chest and that will immediately give him the look and feel of a sickly man.

The woman who plays the servant has to have a piercing scream. That kind of sound can do great damage to the voice. The scream must start forward in the mouth, under the hard palate, away from the throat.

* * *

RALPH CONVINCES SQUEERS TO SEEK OUT PEG SLIDERSKEW

From the novel *NICHOLAS NICKLEBY*

CHARACTERS:

RALPH NICKLEBY: at his best when he is getting someone to carry out his plans.

NEWMAN NOGGS: Ralph's disgruntled employee.

MR. SQUEERS: Squeers is the owner of the Dotheboys school. He is a cruel headmaster and in his greed will stoop to anything. He has, at various times, been useful to Ralph Nickleby. Because Squeers is brighter than the others, Ralph's logic is impeccable in manipulating him.

SETTING: Ralph's office.

SUMMARY:

Ralph has asked Squeers to meet with him in order to find the will that has been stolen from Arthur Gride by Gride's old housekeeper, Peg Sliderskew. Ralph's practice is to use others to do the nasty work of trapping people. His employee, Newman Noggs, knows this about Ralph and hates him for it. Ralph suspects Noggs of spying on him and will, when he can spare a moment from his larger plans, put Noggs in jeopardy. Note: Mr. Snawley has been 'persuaded' by Ralph to lie and present himself as Smike's father so that a court will order Smike to leave Nicholas, who has befriended him. Smike will be forced go back to the Dotheboys school in the charge of Mr. Squeers.

RALPH NICKLEBY: Mr. Squeers.

SQUEERS: Sir.

RALPH NICKLEBY: Let us talk business.

SQUEERS: With all my heart and first let me say...

RALPH NICKLEBY: First let me say, if you please — Noggs! Noggs. Noggs!

NOGGS: Did the master call?

RALPH NICKLEBY: I did. Go to your dinner. And go at once. Do you hear?

NOGGS: [*doggedly*] It ain't time.

RALPH NICKLEBY: I say it is.

NOGGS: You alter it every day. It isn't fair.

RALPH NICKLEBY: You don't keep many cooks, and can easily apologize to them for the trouble. Now go!

[RALPH *watches* NEWMAN NOGGS *leave.*]

RALPH NICKLEBY: I have reason to suspect that fellow. Until I've thought of the least troublesome way of ruining him, I'll keep him at a distance.

SQUEERS: [*with a grin*] It wouldn't take much to ruin him, I should think.

RAPLH NICKLEBY: Perhaps not. Nor to ruin a great many people whom I know. You were going to say—?

SQUEERS: [*getting the hint*] Why...uh... what I was a-going to say is, that this here business regarding that ungrateful and hard-hearted chap, Snawley senior, is very inconvenient for me, besides, making Mrs. Squeers a perfect widow — it's a pleasure to me to act with you, of course.

RALPH NICKLEBY: [*drily*] Of course.

SQUEERS: [*rubbing his knees*] Yes, I say of course, but at the same time, when one has to come, as I do now, better than two hundred and fifty mile to take a afferdavid, it does put a man out a good deal, letting alone the risk.

RALPH NICKLEBY: And where may the risk be, Mr. Squeers?

SQUEERS: [*evasive*] I said, letting alone the risk.

RALPH NICKLEBY: And I said, where was the risk?

SQUEERS: [*pleading*] I wasn't complaining, you know, Mr. Nickleby. Upon my word I never seen such a...

RALPH NICKLEBY: I ask you where is the risk?

SQUEERS: [*rubbing his knees still harder*] Where the risk? Why, it ain't necessary to mention — certain subjects is best avoided. Oh, you know what risk I mean.

RALPH NICKLEBY: How often have I told you, and how often am I to tell you, that you run no risk? What have you sworn, or what are you asked to swear, other than at such and such a time a boy was left with you in the name of Smike; that he was at your school for a given number of years, was lost under such and such circumstances, is now found, and has been identified.

SQUEERS: Yes, that's all true.

RALPH NICKLEBY: Well, then, what risk do you run? Who swears to a lie but Snawley — a man whom I have paid much less than I have you?

SQUEERS: He certainly did it cheap, Snawley did.

RALPH NICKLEBY: He did it cheap! Yes, and he did it well, and carries it off with a hypocritical face, but what do you mean by risk? The certificates are all genuine - Snawley had another son, his first wife is dead, none but her ghost could tell that she didn't write that letter, none but Snawley himself can tell that this is not his son, and that his own son is food for worms! The only perjury is Snawley's, and I fancy he is pretty well used to it. Where's your risk?

SQUEERS: [*fidgeting*] Why, you know, if you come to that, I might say where's yours?

RALPH NICKLEBY: You might say where's mine! I don't appear in the business — neither do you. All Snawley's interest is to stick to the story he has told; and all his risk is, to depart from it. What is your risk in the conspiracy?

SQUEERS: [*looking uneasily around*] Don't call it that — just as a favor, don't.

RALPH NICKLEBY: Call it what you like. This was meant originally to be an annoyance against me. Nicholas Nickleby ran off with one of your students and half cudgelled you to death.

This conspiracy, I call it, was for you to repossess a half-dead drudge, so that you could wreak your vengeance on him for running away. And his knowing that you had him again in your power would be the best punishment you could inflict upon him. Is that so, Mr. Squeers?

SQUEERS: [*feeling overpowered*] Why,...uh... in a measure it was.

RALPH NICKLEBY: What does that mean?

SQUEERS: Why, in a measure means, as it may be, that it wasn't all on my account, because you had some old grudge to satisfy, too.

RALPH NICKLEBY: If I had not had, do you think I should have helped you?

SQUEERS: Why no, I don't suppose you would. I only wanted that point to be all square and straight between us.

RALPH NICKLEBY: How can it ever be otherwise? Except that the account is against me, for I spend money to gratify my hatred, and you pocket it, and gratify your hatred at the same time. You are, at least, as avaricious as you are revengeful. So am I. Which is best off?

[SQUEERS *answers with shrugs and smiles.*]

RALPH NICKLEBY: Then be silent, and thankful that you are so well off.

[RALPH *fixes his eyes steadily upon* SQUEERS *and continues.*]

RALPH NICKLEBY: First of all, Nicholas has thwarted me in a plan that I had arranged for the marriage of a certain young lady. In the confusion following her father's sudden death, he fled away with the young lady. Secondly, by some will or settlement — she was entitled to property which, if the existence of this deed ever became known to her, would make Nicholas when he marries her, a rich and prosperous man, and a most formidable enemy. Thirdly, this deed has been stolen from one who obtained it fraudulently, and now fears to take any steps for its recovery. I know who the thief is.

[MR. SQUEERS *listens with greedy ears.*]

RALPH NICKLEBY: [*leaning forward, placing his hand on* SQUEERS'*s arm*] Now, hear my plan which must — I say, must, — be fulfilled. No advantage can be reaped from this deed, whatever it is, save by the girl herself, or her husband. I want that deed brought here. I will give the man who brings it fifty pounds in gold, and I want to burn it to ashes before his face.

SQUEERS: [*wide-eyed with his mouth open*] Yes; but who's to bring it?

RALPH NICKLEBY: Nobody, perhaps, for much is to be done before I can get my hands on it. But if anybody — you!

SQUEERS: Oh no. No,no. That is impossible. Oh, way too too... Oh, no,no....

RALPH NICKLEBY: It is entirely feasible. Peg Sliderskew is a weak and decrepit old woman who was Arthur Gride's housekeeper for years. She took his papers, not for money but for revenge. She has no accomplice, knows nobody and would welcome a confidante with your charm and knowledge. You could convince her not to be found with these tell-tale documents. It would be a lark for you. You live far away. No one would recognize you, and she is certain to succumb to those charms. Think, Squeers, we will defeat Nicholas Nickleby and keep him a pauper which is all he deserves. [RALPH *pauses*] The fifty pounds might even be increased to seventy five...or even, in the event of a very great success, even to a hundred.

[SQUEERS *crosses his legs, uncrosses them, scratches his head, rubs his eye, examines the palms of his hands, and bites his nails.*]

SQUEERS: Uh…is one hundred pound the…uh…highest that you could go?

RALPH NICKLEBY: Yes.

[SQUEERS *is still restless and indecisive. He tries again.*]

SQUEERS: You couldn't go another fifty?

RALPH NICKLEBY: No.

SQUEERS: [*a quick pause*] Well, I try and do the most I can for a friend. And I'll undertake the job. But how are you to get at the woman? That's what puzzles me.

RALPH NICKLEBY: I may not get at her at all. But I'll try. I have hunted people in this city, before. I know where money will solve darker riddles than this! We may as well part. You had better not come here. Wait till you hear from me.

SQUEERS: [*rising*] Good! But if you shouldn't find her out, you'll pay expenses at the hotel, and something more for loss of time?

RALPH NICKLEBY: Yes, yes! You have nothing more you want to say?

[SQUEERS *shakes his head no.* RALPH *motions* SQUEERS *to the door, bowing with a slight smile.*]

BLACKOUT

If you keep your face from changing expression, if you keep your posture stiff and upright, you will feel a pulling down in your torso and it will affect the look in your eye. You then feel close to the character even though you may be a young person playing the part. When you follow Ralph's dialogue, you won't feel that the acting is all up to you. The writing takes care of the scene. Ralph's one-word-answers help to establish his dry, unswerving purpose.

The stage directions for Squeers define the relationship between the two men. Rubbing his knees and squirming will influence the actor to actually feel fearful and uneasily ambivalent toward Ralph. For Newman Noggs, you might feel that some part of your body is distorted. It's as though Noggs' hatred of Ralph is lodged in that distortion.

* * *

SIR JOHN CHESTER BULLIES HUGH

From the novel *BARNABY RUDGE*

CHARACTERS:	**SIR JOHN CHESTER:** a vain and cynical man.
	HUGH: a rough young man afraid of no one.
	PEAK: a servant.
SETTING:	Sir John's drawing room.

SUMMARY:

Expecting a quiet evening, Sir John is disturbed by his servant who tells him of Hugh's arrival. Hugh works at the Maypole Inn as a stable boy. He is most comfortable living and sleeping with the animals. He is rough and untutored.

SIR JOHN CHESTER: Well. What now? You know I am not at home.

SERVANT: [*as cool as his master*] A man, sir, has brought home the riding-whip you lost the other day. I told him you were out, but he said he was to wait while I brought it in, and wouldn't go till I did.

SIR JOHN CHESTER: He was quite right and you're a blockhead. Tell him to come in, and see that he cleans his shoes first.

[*The* SERVANT *lays the whip on a chair and withdraws.* HUGH *enters.*]

SIR JOHN CHESTER: [*his back still turned, his eyes on his book*] Ah, my centaur, are you there?

HUGH: [striding in] Here I am, and trouble enough I've had to get here. What do you ask me to come for, and keep me out when I do come?

SIR JOHN CHESTER: [*surveying* HUGH] My good fellow, I am delighted to see you. How are you?

HUGH: [*impatiently*] I'm well enough.

SIR JOHN CHESTER: You look a perfect marvel of health. Sit down.

HUGH: I'd rather stand.

SIR JOHN CHESTER: Please yourself, my good fellow.

[SIR JOHN *rises, slowly pulls off his robe and sits down before the mirror. He gets dressed and takes no further notice of* HUGH. HUGH *stands sulking in the same spot, uncertain what to do next.*]

HUGH: [*after a long silence*] Are you going to speak to me?

SIR JOHN CHESTER: My worthy creature, you are a bit out of humor. I'll wait till you're quite yourself again. I'm in no hurry.

[HUGH *is humbled and abashed, irresolute and uncertain. Hard words or violence he can return, but this complacent, contemptuous, self-possessed gentleman makes him feel his inferiority. Little by lit-tle, he moves nearer to* SIR JOHN CHESTER's *chair*].

HUGH: [*attempting reconciliation*] Are you going to speak to me, or am I to go away?

SIR JOHN CHESTER: I have spoken, have I not? I am waiting for you.

HUGH: [*with increased embarrassment*] Look, you privately left your whip with me before you rode away from the Maypole Inn. And didn't you tell me to bring it back whenever I might want to see you on a certain subject? I've come and I've brought a letter.

[HUGH *lays the letter on the table.*]

SIR JOHN CHESTER: [*showing no surprise or pleasure*] Did you obtain this by force, my good fellow?

HUGH: Partly.

SIR JOHN CHESTER: Who was the messenger from whom you took it?

HUGH: A woman. Varden's daughter.

SIR JOHN CHESTER: [*gaily*] Oh indeed! What else did you take from her?

HUGH: What else?

SIR JOHN CHESTER: Yes.

[SIR JOHN *is fixing a very small patch of bandage on a very small pimple near the corner of his mouth.*]

SIR JOHN CHESTER: What else?

HUGH: [*after hesitating*] Well, a kiss.

SIR JOHN CHESTER: [*securing the patch*] And what else?

HUGH: Nothing.

SIR JOHN CHESTER: [*smiling*] I think there was something else. I heard of jewelry — a mere trifle — you may have forgotten it. Do you remember anything of the kind — such as a bracelet, for instance?

HUGH: [*muttering*] Damn. Here it is...

SIR JOHN CHESTER: [*stops him*] You took that for yourself, my excellent friend, and may keep it. I am neither a thief nor a receiver. Don't show it to me. You had better hide it again, and lose no time. Don't let me see where you put it either.

HUGH: [*bluntly despite his awe*] You're not a receiver! What do you call that?

[*He points to the letter.*]

SIR JOHN CHESTER: [*cooly*] I call that quite another thing. I shall prove it presently, as you will see. You are thirsty, I suppose?

HUGH: [*gruffly*] Yes.

SIR JOHN CHESTER Step to that closet and bring me a bottle you will see there, and a glass.

[*As* HUGH *does so,* SIR JOHN *watches him and smiles a different smile.* HUGH *brings the bottle.*]

SIR JOHN CHESTER: [*fills the glass*] Drink.

[HUGH *drinks.* SIR JOHN *pours another, and another.*]

SIR JOHN CHESTER: [*filling the glass again*] How many can you drink?

HUGH: As many as you like to give me. Pour on. Fill high. Give me enough of this and I'll do murder if you ask me!

SIR JOHN CHESTER: [*with composure*] As I don't mean to ask you, and you might possibly do it without being asked if you went on much further, we will stop, my good friend, at the next glass. You were drinking before you came here.

HUGH: [*boisterously*] Always when I can get it.

[HUGH *waves the empty glass above his head and throws himself crudely into a dance pose.*]

HUGH: [*laughing and reckless*] Always. Why not? What's so good to me as this? I drink to the drink!

SIR JOHN. CHESTER: You are an exceedingly cheerful young man. [*puts on his cravat with great deliberation*] Quite a boon companion.

HUGH: [*showing his arm to the elbow*] Do you see this hand and this arm? It was once mere skin and bone, and would have been dust in some poor churchyard by this time, but for the drink.

SIR JOHN CHESTER: You may cover it.

HUGH: I should never have been spirited up to take a kiss from the proud little beauty but for the drink. I thank the drink for it. I'll drink to the drink again. Fill me one more. Come. One more!

[SIR JOHN *puts on his waistcoat with care and takes no heed of* HUGH's *high spirits.*]

SIR JOHN CHESTER: You are such a promising fellow, that I must caution you against having too many impulses from the drink, and getting hung before your time. What's your age?

HUGH: I don't know.

SIR JOHN CHESTER: How can you trust yourself in my hands on so short an acquaintance, with a halter round your neck?

[HUGH *looks at* SIR JOHN *with mingled terror, indignation, and surprise.*]

SIR JOHN CHESTER: [*regarding himself in the mirror complacently*] Robbery on the king's highway, my young friend, is a very dangerous occupation. If you open your heart so readily on the subject, I am afraid your career will be an extremely short one.

HUGH: How's this? What do you talk of? Who was it set me on?

SIR JOHN CHESTER: [*wheeling sharply round*] Who? I didn't hear you. Who was it?

[HUGH *falters, and mutters inaudibly.*]

SIR JOHN CHESTER: [*now affably*] Who was it? I am curious to know. Some rustic beauty perhaps? But be cautious, my good friend. They are not always to be trusted.

[*He turns to the mirror again.*]

[HUGH *wants to answer that he,* SIR JOHN CHESTER *himself, has set him on, but the words stick in his throat.* HUGH's *submission is complete. He dreads* SIR JOHN CHESTER *beyond description. He feels that a touch from such a master-hand as* CHESTER's *could send him to the gallows.* HUGH *stands cowering, regarding him uneasily from time to time.*]

[SIR JOHN *finishes dressing. He takes the letter and reads it leisurely.*]

SIR JOHN CHESTER: A woman's letter, full of tenderness and heart! [*holds it to a candle*] It was directed to my son, and you did quite right to bring it here. I opened it on my own responsibility, and you see what I have done with it. Take this for your trouble. [*gives money to* HUGH] If you should happen to find anything else of this sort, or to pick up any kind of information you may think I would like to have, bring it here, will you, my good fellow? [jokingly with a smile] Fail to do so at your peril! And don't beat all downcast or uneasy. Your neck is as safe in my hands as though a baby's fingers clasped it. Take another glass. You are quieter now.

[HUGH *accepts it from his hand, looks stealthily at* SIR JOHN'*s smiling face, and drinks in silence.*]

SIR JOHN CHESTER: [*in winning good humor*] Don't you — don't you drink to the drink any more?

HUGH: [*sullen and attempting a bow*] To you, I drink to you.

SIR JOHN CHESTER: Thank you. God bless you. By the bye, what is your name, my good soul? Your other name?

HUGH: I have no other name.

SIR JOHN CHESTER: A very strange fellow! Do you mean that you never knew one, or that you don't choose to tell it? Which?

HUGH: [*quickly*] I'd tell it if I could. I can't. I have been always called Hugh; nothing more. I never knew, nor saw, nor thought about a father; and I was a boy of six — that's not very old - when they hung my mother up at Tyburn for a couple of thousand men to stare at. They might have let her live. She was poor enough.

SIR JOHN CHESTER: [*with condescension*] How very sad! I have no doubt she was an exceedingly fine woman.

[HUGH *has nothing more to say.*]

HUGH: Goodnight, sir.

SIR JOHN CHESTER: Good night. Remember, you're safe with me — quite safe. So long as you deserve it, my good fellow, you have a friend in me, on whose silence you may rely. Now do be careful of yourself, and consider what jeopardy you might have stood in. Good night! Bless you!

[HUGH *creeps out of the room submissively and subserviently.* SIR JOHN *left alone, smiles more than ever.*]

BLACKOUT

We see the wild and violent Hugh who is not afraid of anything fall apart under the cold and uncanny manipulation of Chester. Sir John deliberately undresses and dresses before Hugh to show his disdain for him. His changes of tone, from affable to deadly serious, confuse and frighten Hugh. The actor who plays Hugh must find body postures that show his general lack of concern for what anybody thinks of him in the beginning of the scene and then for his change of attitude when Sir John begins to twist him mercilessly.

SCENES FOR THE YOUNG ACTOR

HORTENSE AND ESTHER

From the novel *BLEAK HOUSE*

CHARACTERS:	**ESTHER:** a governess and happy to be living at Bleak House. She does not yet know [nor does anyone else] that she is the illegitimate daughter of Lady Dedlock. **HORTENSE:** has been fired by Lady Dedlock and needs another place to work.
SETTING:	Out of doors at Bleak House

SUMMARY:

Esther sees Lady Dedlock's maid, the Frenchwoman Hortense, coming toward her. After having been let go by Lady Dedlock, Hortense has deliberately taken off her shoes to walk through the wet grass back to the Dedlock mansion. Watching Hortense, observing the tightness in her face and her eager burning eyes, Esther is reminded of the women who particpated in the French reign of terror.

HORTENSE: [*still without her shoes*] Mademoiselle, I have taken great liberty to come here, but you know how to excuse it, being so amiable, Mademoiselle.

ESTHER: You wish to speak to me?

HORTENSE: That is my desire, Mademoiselle. A thousand thanks for the permission. I have your leave to speak. Is it not?

ESTHER: Certainly.

HORTENSE: Mademoiselle, you are so amiable! Listen then, if you please. I have left my Lady. We could not agree. My Lady is so high, so very high. Pardon! Mademoiselle, you are right! It is not for me to come here to complain of my

Lady. But I say she is so high, so very high. I will not say a word more. All the world knows that.

ESTHER: Go on, if you please.

HORTENSE: Assuredly; Mademoiselle, I am thankful for your politeness. Mademoiselle, I have an inexpressible desire to find service with a young lady who is good, accomplished, beautiful. You are good, accomplished, and beautiful as an angel. Ah, could I have the honor of being your domestic!

ESTHER: I am sorry...

HORTENSE: Do not dismiss me so soon, Mademoiselle! Let me hope a moment! Mademoiselle, I know this service is more retired than that which I have quitted. Well! I wish that. And less distingue than that which I have quitted. Well! I wish that. I know my wages fewer here. Eh, what of that? Good. I am content.

ESTHER: I assure you that I keep no maid...

HORTENSE: Ah, Mademoiselle, but why not? Why not, when you can have one so devoted to you! Who would be enchanted to serve you; who would be so true and so faithful every day! Mademoiselle, I wish with all my heart to serve you. Do not speak of money at present. Take me as I am. For nothing! Mademoiselle, I come from the South country where we are quick and where we like and dislike very strong. My Lady was too high for me; I was too high for her. It is done — past — finished! Receive me as your domestic, and I will serve you well. I will do more for you than you figure to yourself now. Chut! Mademoiselle, if you accept my service, you will not repent it. And I will serve you well. You don't know how well!

ESTHER: I am not in a position to have a maid and at this moment

I do not wish to have one.

HORTENSE: Hey, Mademoiselle, I have received my answer! I am sorry of it. But I must go elsewhere and seek what I have not found here. Will you graciously let me kiss your hand? [*she looks at* ESTHER'*s hand closely*] I took an oath, Mademoiselle, and I wanted to stamp it on my mind so that I might keep it faithfully. And I will! Adieu, Mademoiselle! I fear I surprised you, Mademoiselle, on the day of the storm?

[HORTENSE *kisses* ESTHER'*s hand, curtseys, and leaves.*]

BLACKOUT

It is hard to tell what Hortense is up to. She is proud, haughty, short-tempered, unforgiving, with eyes that seem to see sideways. She is dangerous. Although Esther is taken aback at Hortense's kissing her hand, she doesn't show it. Esther is loving and generous to others, but she keeps her poise and constraint in saying no to Hortense.

* * *

DAVID TELLS DORA HE IS A BEGGAR

From the novel *DAVID COPPERFIELD*

CHARACTERS: DAVID: in love with Dora.

                    DORA: in love with David.

                    JULIA MILLS: a friend.

SETTING: The drawing room in Dora's home.

SUMMARY:

One day David's Aunt Betsey appears in David's apartment with all her baggage. Aunt Betsey slowly reveals to David that, due to bad invest-ments for which she is solely responsible, she is ruined. Aunt Betsey is being faithful to her long time friend and business advisor, Mr. Wickfield, who, it seems, has actually made the disastrous investments. But the very real fact remains that she and David are impoverished.

David is engaged to gay, lovely, spirited Dora. Dora is not a girl used to any difficulties in life and has certainly never had to think about the cares of a household. David rushes to Dora to break the unexpected news. The childish, adorable fiancee greets him happily. Thinking only of this new condition in his life and without preparing her to hear his bad news, David tells Dora of his poverty and how it will affect them. Note: Jip is Dora's dog.

DAVID: Dora, my beloved, could you love a beggar?

DORA: A beggar? Someone who walks on a pair of crutches, or a wooden leg? How can you ask me anything so foolish? Love a beggar!

DAVID: Dora, my dearest! I am a beggar!

DORA: [*slapping* DAVID's *hand*] How can you be such a silly thing, as to sit there, telling such stories? I'll make Jip bite you!

DAVID: Dora, I am your ruined David!

DORA: [*shaking her curls*] I declare I'll make Jip bite you, if you are so ridiculous.

[DORA *seeing how serious* DAVID *is, trembles and begins to cry*].

DORA: I am so frightened! Go away, please!

DAVID: [*on his knees*] Dora, I beg you, dearest one, don't cry, don't be frightened. It is because I love you so dearly that I offer you a release from our engagement. I am poor. I am not afraid of poverty but perhaps it would be too hard for you, dearest Dora.

[DORA *clings to* DAVID.]

DAVID: Do you love me still, dear Dora?

DORA: [*nestling close to David*] Oh, yes! Oh, yes, I do. Oh, don't be dreadful! Don't talk about being poor, and working hard! Oh, don't, don't! I don't want to hear about eating a crust of bread! Jip must have his steak every day at noon, or he'll die.

DAVID: Yes, yes, Jip will have his steak. But we will live in a frugal home; my aunt will have a room upstairs. I am not dreadful now, Dora?

DORA: Oh, no, no! But I hope your aunt will keep in her own room a good deal. And I hope she's not a scolding old thing!

DAVID: May I mention something that I have been thinking of?

DORA: [*coaxing*] Oh, please don't be practical! Because it frightens me so!

DAVID: Sweetheart! There is nothing to alarm you in all this. I want you to think of it quite differently. I want it to inspire you, Dora!

DORA: Oh, but that's so shocking! I haven't got any strength at all, have I, Jip? Oh, do kiss Jip, and be agreeable!

DAVID: It's impossible to resist kissing Jip.

DORA: Kiss him on the center of his nose.

[DAVID *does so.*]

DAVID: [*resuming seriousness*] But, Dora, dear, I was going to mention something.

DORA: I beg you not to be disagreeable anymore.

DAVID: Indeed I am not going to be, my darling! But, Dora, my love, if you will sometimes think, - not despondingly, you know; far from that! - but if you will sometimes think - just to encourage yourself - that you are engaged to a poor man - and look about now and then at your papa's housekeeping, and try to acquire a little habit - of keeping accounts, for instance –

[DORA *gives a half sob and a half scream.*]

DAVID: It would be useful to us afterwards. And if you would promise me to read a little - a little Cook Book that I would send you, it would be excellent for both of us. For our path in life, Dora dear, is stony and rugged now. We must be brave. There are obstacles to be met, and we must meet, and crush them!

DORA: [looking ill during this heroic speech] I'm so frightened! Go away, please!

[DORA *is about to faint.* DAVID *is terrified that he has really frightened her.*]

DAVID: Dora, I didn't mean to frighten you! Forgive me. Please, darling, don't give way, look up.

[*Their friend,* JULIA MILLS, *who has supported the couple in their romance, arrives.*]

DORA: [*rushing to her*] David will be a laborer, he will have to push a wheelbarrow up and down a narrow plank, oh Julia, oh David.

JULIA: No tears, Dora. Go to your room and freshen up and we can talk.

DORA: I will, I'll go to my room and dab rose-water on my eyes. Tell David, it will be allright. [kisses David] No more tears.

[DORA *leaves.*]

DAVID: [*to* JULIA] Wouldn't you say it is practical that Dora learn to keep accounts and read a Cook Book?

JULIA MILLS: [*after some consideration*] David, I will be as plain with you as if I were a Mother Superior. No. The suggestion is not appropriate to our Dora. Our dearest Dora is a child of nature. She is a thing of light, and airiness, and joy.

[DAVID *sighs.* DORA *returns, looking her lovely self again.*]

DAVID: I must go, dear, before it gets too late. I now get up at five o'clock to work for Dr. Strong.

DORA: A night watchman! Don't get up at five o'clock, you naughty boy. It's nonsensical!

DAVID: My love, I have work to do.

DORA: But don't do it! Why should you?

DAVID: We must work to live.

DORA: How ridiculous!

DAVID: How shall we live, Dora?

DORA: How? Any how!

[DAVID *melts as* DORA *kisses him.*]

BLACKOUT

This will eventually be a delightful scene, but first you must resolve the character of Dora. Reading what follows, you will find that Dora isn't a nitwit at all. Although she never does find out how to run a household, Dora has an awareness of others as well as intuition and wisdom, both of which she has managed to hide. Is Dora anything but a Victorian concoction? In our time, there are tv and movie starlets who, because of their beauty, have been given permission to be eccentric or wilful as long as they are also adorable. Once you accept Dora, you will find that she is quite witty, and the scene will have its humor.

* * *

DORA IS ILL AND WILL SOON DIE.

From the novel *DAVID COPPERFIELD*

CHARACTERS: **DORA:** David's beloved childlike wife is seriously ill and grows progressively worse.

DAVID: knows how ill Dora is and can do nothing for her.

SETTING: Dora's bedroom.

SUMMARY:

David's child-wife, Dora, has been ill for some time now. At first, David was able to carry Dora downstairs, but now she is too weak to sit for long and must stay in her room. Today, Aunt Betsey has curled Dora's hair, and Dora is pleased that it looks pretty even though the pillow makes it messy.

DORA: Not that I am vain of it, but because you used to say you thought it so beautiful; and because, when I first began to think about you, I used to peep in the glass, and wonder whether you would like to have a lock of it. Oh how foolish you were, Doady, when I gave you one!

DAVID: And when I told you how much in love I was.

DORA: When I can run about again as I used to, Doady, let's go and see those places where we were such a silly couple, shall we? And take some of the old walks?

DAVID: Yes, we will, and have happy days. So you must hurry to get well.

DORA: Oh, I shall! I am so much better, you don't know!

[*A pause*]

DORA: You are very lonely when you go downstairs, now?

DAVID: How can I be otherwise when I see your empty chair?

DORA: My empty chair! And you really miss me, Doady? Even poor, giddy, stupid me?

DAVID: Who is there upon earth that I could miss so much?

DORA: Oh, husband! I am so glad, yet so sorry!

[DORA *laughs and sobs; then she is quiet — and eventually quite happy.*]

DAVID: You will get well again, Dora.

DORA: Ah, Doady! Sometimes I think - you know I always was a silly little thing! – I think that will never be!

DAVID: Don't say so, Dora! Dearest, don't think so!

DORA: I won't, if I can help it, Doady. But I am very happy; though my dear is so lonely by himself.

[DAVID *and* DORA *sit quietly for some time.*]

DORA: Doady, I am going to speak to you, Doady. I am going to say something I've thought of saying, lately. You won't mind?

DAVID: Mind, my darling? Why would I mind?

DORA: Because I don't know what you will think, or what you may have thought sometimes. Perhaps you have often thought the same. [DORA *pauses*] Doady, dear, I'm afraid I was too young.

[DAVID *is stricken by her tone. It almost seems as if she is speaking of herself as past.*]

DORA: I am afraid, dear, I was too young. I don't mean in years only, but in experience, and thoughts, and everything. I was such a silly little creature! I'm afraid it would have been better, if we had only loved each other as a boy and girl, and forgotten it. I have begun to think I was not fit to be a wife.

DAVID: [*holding back tears*] Oh, Dora, love, as fit as I to be a husband!

DORA: I don't know. Perhaps! But if I had been more fit to be married I might have made you more so, too. Besides, you are very clever, and I never was.

DAVID: We have been very happy, my sweet Dora.

DORA: I was very happy, very. But, as years went on, my Doady would have wearied of his child-wife. She would have been less and less a companion for him. He would have been more and more sensible of what was wanting in his home. She couldn't have improved. It is better as it is.

DAVID: Dora, dearest, dearest, don't speak to me so. Every word seems a reproach!

DORA: [*kissing* DAVID] No, not a syllable! Oh, my dear, you never deserved it, and I loved you far too well to say a reproachful word to you in earnest — it was all the merit I had, except being pretty — or you thought me so. Is it lonely, downstairs, Doady?

DAVID: Very! Very!

DORA: Don't cry! Is my chair there?

DAVID: In its place.

DORA: Oh, how you cry! Hush, hush! [she whispers] I said that it was better as it is!

[DORA *holds* DAVID *in her arms.*]

DORA: Oh, Doady, after more years, you never could have loved your child-wife better than you do; and, after more years, she would have tried so hard and disappointed you. It is much better as it is!

[DAVID *cries*. DORA *comforts him*.]

BLACKOUT

Just say the words. Don't feel sorry for yourself. Just say the words.

* * *

JONAS GOES A-COURTING

From the novel *MARTIN CHUZZLEWIT*

CHARACTERS: **CHARITY PECKSNIFF:** the sharp-tongued elder sister of Mercy.

MERCY PECKSNIFF: the more affable and flirtatious of the two sisters.

JONAS CHUZZLEWIT: their rough-edged cousin.

SETTING: Mrs. Todgers' Inn. Charity and Mercy in their sitting room.

SUMMARY:

While their father does his errands in London, the sisters have rooms at an Inn where there are a number of young men who are travelling salesmen. They have made much of Mercy Pecksniff; not so much of her elder sister Charity. Charity has just received an unexpected note. Note: Charity and Mercy are also called Cherry and Merry.

CHARITY: [*reading the note*] A gentleman for me! My gracious!

But I don't know any gentlemen. I think there must be a mistake. Merry, who can it be? Isn't it odd? I have a great mind not to receive him really. So very strange, you know!

MERCY: [*politely, with affection*] It is very strange indeed; I can't conceive what this ridiculous unknown person could mean by it.

CHARITY: [*with some sharpness*] Quite impossible to divine! Though still, at the same time, you needn't be angry, dear.

MERCY: [*singing as she sews*] Thank you. I am quite aware of that, my love.

CHARITY: I am afraid your head is turned.

MERCY: [*gathering her sewing*] Do you know, dear, that I have been afraid of that, myself, all along! So much nonsense is enough to turn a stronger head than mine. What a relief it must be to you, dear, to be so very comfortable in that respect, and not to be worried by those odious men! How do you do it, Cherry?

[MERCY *leaves the room.*]

[JONAS CHUZZLEWIT, *not bothering to be invited in, knocks and enters.*]

JONAS: Cousin! Here I am, you see. You thought I was lost. Well! How do you find yourself?

CHARITY: [*offering her hand*] I am quite well.

JONAS: That's right. And you've got over the fatigues of the journey have you? How's the other one?

CHARITY: My sister is very well, I believe. I havn't heard her complain. Perhaps you would like to see her and ask her yourself?

JONAS: [*sitting beside* CHARITY] No, no cousin! Don't be in a hurry. There's no occasion for that, you know. What a cruel girl you are!

CHARITY: It's impossible for you to know whether I am or not.

JONAS: Well, perhaps it is. Did you think I was lost? You haven't told me that.

CHARITY: I didn't think one way or the other.

JONAS: Didn't you, though? Did the other one?

CHARITY: It's impossible for me to say what my sister may, or may not have thought. She never said anything to me about it.

JONAS: Didn't she laugh about it?

CHARITY: No. She didn't even laugh about it.

JONAS: [*lowering his voice*] She's a terrible one to laugh, ain't she?

CHARITY: She is very lively.

JONAS: Liveliness is a pleasant thing — when it don't lead to spending money, ain't it?

CHARITY: [*demurely disinterested*] Very much so, indeed.

JONAS: [*nudging her with his elbow*] Such liveliness as yours I mean, you know. I should have come to see you before, but I didn't know where you was.

CHARITY: I am amenable to my papa's directions.

JONAS: I wish he had given me his direction. And then I should have found you out before. Why, I shouldn't have found you even now, if I hadn't met him in the street this morning. What a sleek, sly chap he is! Just like a tom-cat, ain't he?

CHARITY: I must trouble you to have the goodness to speak more respectfully of my papa, Mr. Jonas. I can't allow such a tone as that even in jest.

JONAS: By god, you may say what you like of my father, then. I think it's liquid aggravation that circulates through his veins, and not regular blood. How old should you think my father is, cousin?

CHARITY: Old, no doubt, but a fine old gentleman.

JONAS: A fine old gentleman! It's time he was thinking of being drawn out a little finer too. Why, he's eighty!

CHARITY: Is he, indeed?

JONAS: And bygod, now he's gone so far without giving in, I don't see much to prevent his being ninety; no, nor even a hundred. Why, a man with any feeling ought to be ashamed of being eighty, let alone more. Where's his religion, I should like to know, when he goes flying in the face of the Bible like that? Three-score-and-ten's the mark, and no man with a conscience, and a proper sense of what's expected of him, has any business to live longer. But there's enough of my father. I called to ask you to come and take a walk, cousin, and see some of the sights; and to come to our house afterwards, and have a bit of something. Your father will most likely look in in the evening, he says, and bring you home. See, here's his writing. [*he hands* CHARITY *her father's note*] I made him put it down this morning in case you wouldn't believe me. There's nothing like proof, is there? Haha! You'll bring the other one, you know!

[CHARITY *reads the note, then hesitates enough to impart a proper value to her consent.*]

CHARITY: Oh, very well.

[*She leaves the room.* JONAS *is left to poke into whatever there is to poke into.* CHARITY *returns, accompanied by her unwilling sister*].

JONAS: Ah! There you are, are you?

MERCY: Yes, Monster, here I am, and I would much rather be anywhere else, I assure you.

JONAS: You don't mean that. You can't, you know. It isn't possible.

MERCY: [*laughing heartily*] You can have what opinion you like, Monster. I'm content to keep mine; and mine is that you are a very unpleasant, odious, disagreeable person.

JONAS: Oh, you're a sharp gal! She's a regular teazer, ain't she, cousin?

CHARITY: I'm unable to say what the habits of a regular teazer might be; and even if I possessed such information, it would ill become me to admit it existed in the person of my beloved sister whatever her real nature may be.

MERCY: Well, my dear, the only observation I have to make is, that if we don't go out at once, I shall certainly take my hat off and stay at home.

JONAS: Naw, ye don't!

[JONAS *hurries the sisters out of their lodging.*]

BLACKOUT

When the sisters are not fighting outright, they are scornful of each other, which they disguise with sarcasm and sweetness. Charity begins the putdowns, but Mercy holds her own quite successfully.

THE MARRIAGE PROPOSAL

From the novel *MARTIN CHUZZLEWIT*

CHARACTERS:

JONAS CHUZZLEWIT: has important matters in mind.

CHARITY PECKSNIFF: has assumed that she is the favorite of the two sisters as far as Jonas is concerned.

MERCY PECKSNIFF: has adopted a mocking manner towards Jonas.

SETTING:

The Pecksniff parlor.

SUMMARY:

Jonas is pretending to be in a good mood, but he has serious matters to discuss. He knows that it will go hard with him, but he intends to follow through and face the risk.

JONAS: [*peeking in the doorway*] Boo!

CHARITY: [*jumping up and screaming*] Who are you? What do you want? Speak! or I'll call my Pa.

JONAS: Aw! I only wanted to scare you.

[MERCY *enters the room. She sees* JONAS.]

MERCY: Oh my goodness me! You here, Monster. Well, I'm very thankful that you won't trouble me much!

[MERCY *starts to leave.* CHARITY *looks on with disinterest.*]

JONAS: [*takes* MERCY's *arm*] You're as lively as ever, are you? Oh! You're a wicked one!

MERCY: [*pushing him away*] Oh, go along! I'm sure I don't know what I shall ever do, if I have to see much of you.

[*She starts to leave.*]

JONAS: Don't go.

MERCY: You're very anxious I should stay, Monster, aren't you?

JONAS: Yes, I am. Upon my word I am. I want to speak to you.

MERCY: Poo.

[MERCY *leaves the room.* JONAS *runs after her.* CHARITY *hears them scuffling.* JONAS *brings* MERCY *back into the room.*]

CHARITY: Upon my word, Mercy, I wonder at you. There are bounds even to absurdity, my dear.

MERCY: Thank you, my sweet. Much obliged to it for its advice. Oh! do leave me alone, you monster!

[JONAS *pulls* MERCY *and drags* CHARITY, *forcing them to sit down on the sofa on either side of him.*]

JONAS: [*clasping them at their waists*] Now, I have got both arms full, haven't I?

MERCY: [*playful*] One of them will be black and blue to-morrow, if you don't let me go.

JONAS: [*grinning*] Ah! I don't mind your pinching, a bit.

MERCY: Pinch him for me, Cherry. I never did hate anybody so much as I hate this creature.

JONAS: No, no, don't say that. And don't pinch either, because I want to be serious. Cousin Charity!

CHARITY: Well! what?

JONAS: I want to have some sober talk. I want to prevent any mistakes, you know, and to put everything upon a pleasant under-standing. That's desirable and proper, ain't it?

[*Neither of the sisters speak.* JONAS' *throat is dry.*]

JONAS: [*to* CHARITY] She'll not believe what I am going to say, will she, cousin?

[JONAS *timidly squeezes* MISS CHARITY.]

CHARITY: Really, Mr. Jonas, I don't know, until I hear what it is. This is quite impossible!

JONAS: Why, you see, her way always being to make a game of people, I know she'll laugh, or pretend to; I know that, before-hand. But you can tell her I'm in earnest, cousin; can't you? You'll confess you know, won't you? You'll be honorable, I'm sure.

[*The sisters are silent.*]

JONAS: [*increasingly uncomfortable*] You see, Cousin Charity, nobody but you can tell her what pains I took to get into her company when you were both at the boarding-house in the city because nobody's so well aware of it, you know. Nobody else can tell her how hard I tried to get to know you better, in order that I might get to know her without seeming to wish it, can they? I always asked you about her, and said where had she gone, and when would she come, and how lively she was, and all that; didn't I, cousin? I know you'll tell her so, if you haven't told her so already, and...and...I dare say you have, because I'm sure you're honorable, ain't you?

[*The sisters remain silent.*]

JONAS: Even if you kept it to yourself, and haven't told her. It don't much matter, because you'll bear honest witness now; won't you? We've been very good friends from the first;

haven't we? And of course we shall be quite friends in future, and so I don't mind speaking before you a bit. Cousin Mercy, you've heard what I've been saying. She'll confirm it, every word, she must. Will you have me for your husband? Eh?

[JONAS *turning to* MERCY, *releases his hold of* CHARITY.]

[CHARITY, *crying passionately, incoherently, angrily, hurries away to her room.*]

MERCY: [*pushing* JONAS *off and slapping him*] Let me go. Let me go after her.

JONAS: Not till you say Yes. You haven't told me. Will you have me for your husband?

MERCY: No, I won't. I can't bear the sight of you. I have told you so a hundred times. You are a fright. Besides, I always thought you liked my sister best. We all thought so.

JONAS: But that wasn't my fault.

MERCY: Yes it was; you know it was.

JONAS: Any trick is fair in love. She may have thought I liked her best, but you didn't.

MERCY: I did!

JONAS: No, you didn't. You never could have thought I liked her best, when you were by.

MERCY: There's no accounting for tastes...at least... I didn't mean to say that. I don't know what I mean. Let me go to her.

JONAS: Say "Yes," and then I will.

MERCY: If I ever brought myself to say so, it should only be that I might hate and tease you all my life.

JONAS: That's as good as saying it right out! It's a bargain, cousin.

We're a pair, if ever there was one.

[JONAS *manages to kiss* MERCY *who is slapping him. He breaks into laughter and lets* MERCY *get away.*]

BLACKOUT

Both sisters are devastated by what Jonas has done. They are too shocked to let Jonas's proposal of marriage turn into a family fight. Not just yet.

* * *

THE SISTERS FIGHT AFTER JONAS JILTS CHARITY

From the novel *MARTIN CHUZZLEWIT*

CHARACTERS: **MR. PECKSNIFF:** ever the peacemaker.

CHARITY PECKSNIFF: the jilted one.

MERCY PECKSNIFF: the lucky one.

JONAS: gets away with it.

SETTING: An upstairs bedroom.
Pecksniff's parlor.

SUMMARY:

Jonas Chuzzlewit has been courting Charity Pecksniff. It is understood by the family that he is going to propose to Charity. Instead, Jonas jilts Charity in the most shocking way, and proposes to her younger, prettier sister, Mercy. Hearing his daughters in a heated and vehement argument, Pecksniff enters Charity's bedroom.

MR. PECKSNIFF: [*shutting the door and guarding it*] Children! Girls! Daughters! What is this?

CHARITY: The wretch! the false, mean, odious...wretch - before my very face proposed to Mercy!

MR. PECKSNIFF: Who has proposed to Mercy!

CHARITY: He has. That thing, Jonas, down-stairs.

MR. PECKSNIFF: Jonas proposed to Mercy? Indeed!

CHARITY: Have you nothing else to say? Am I to be driven mad, papa? He has proposed to Mercy, not to me.

MR. PECKSNIFF: [*adapting quickly*] Oh, For shame! for shame! Can your sister's triumph move you to this terrible display, my child? Oh, really this is very sad! I am sorry; I am surprised and hurt to see you so. Mercy, my girl, bless you! See to her. Ah, envy, envy, what a passion you are!

[PECKSNIFF *escapes to the parlor to confront Jonas.*]

PART TWO

SETTING: The parlor.

MR. PECKSNIFF: [*embracing him*] Jonas! Jonas! the dearest wish of my heart is now fulfilled!

JONAS: Very well, I'm glad to hear it. That'll do. [removes himself from Pecksniff's embrace] I say, as it ain't the one you said you're so fond of, come up with another thousand, for the dowry, Pecksniff, as we said. Make it five. It's worth that, to keep your treasure to yourself, you know. You get off very cheap that way, and haven't any sacrifice to make.

MR. PECKSNIFF: You are your dear father's son. I put my trust in your good instincts. [*he indicates the wine bottle*] Shall we?

JONAS: Bygod, I could, yes, after what I been through.

BLACKOUT

The actors playing the sisters have to invent a complete dialogue for their argument. Take the trouble to have even more dialogue than is finally needed. Find comments that are particular to each sister's personality. Then go at it for a real screaming fight.

* * *

OLD MARTIN QUESTIONS MERCY

From the novel *MARTIN CHUZZLEWIT*

CHARACTERS: **MERCY:** engaged to be married to Jonas.

OLD MARTIN CHUZZLEWIT: warns Mercy about the consequences of marriage.

JONAS: the impatient lover.

SETTING: A Graveyard.

SUMMARY:

Old Martin has unexpectedly taken an interest in the Pecksniff family. Mr. Pecksniff and his daughters could not be more attentive to their rich cousin. Old Martin comes upon Mercy sunning in the graveyard. Mercy is not used to being asked serious questions.

MARTIN: When are you to be married?

MERCY: Oh! dear Mr. Chuzzlewit, my goodness me! I'm sure I don't know. Not yet awhile, I hope.

[MERCY *giggles as is her wont.*]

MARTIN: [*with unusual kindness*] Come! You are young, good-looking, and I think good-natured! Frivolous you are; but you must have some heart.

MERCY: [*nodding shrewdly*] I have not given it all away, I can tell you.

MARTIN: Have you parted with any of it?

[MERCY *plucks at the grass and says nothing.*]

MARTIN: Have you parted with any of it?

MERCY: My dear Mr. Chuzzlewit! Really you must excuse me! How very odd you are.

MARTIN: If it is odd to desire to know whether you love the young man you are to marry, I am very odd.

MERCY: [*pouting*] He's such a monster, you know.

MARTIN: Then you don't love him? Is that your meaning?

MERCY: Why, my dear Mr. Chuzzlewit, I'm sure I tell him a hundred times a day that I hate him. You must have heard me tell him that.

MARTIN: Often.

MERCY: And so I do.

MARTIN: Being at the same time engaged to marry him.

[MERCY *suspects that* MARTIN *dislikes* JONAS.]

MERCY: [*meaning to be captivating*] Oh yes, my dear Mr. Chuzzlewit, I told him when he asked me — that if I ever did marry him, it should only be that I might hate and tease him all my life.

MARTIN: [*pointing to the graves*] Look about you, and remember that from your bridal hour to the day you are buried here, there will be no appeal against him. Think, and speak, and act, for once, like an accountable person. Are you forced into this match by any one?

MERCY: [*shrugging*] No, I don't know that I am.

MARTIN: Don't know that you are! Are you?

MERCY: No, nobody ever said anything to me about it. If any one had tried to make me have him, I wouldn't have had him at all.

MARTIN: I am told that he was at first supposed to be your sister's admirer.

MERCY: Oh, goodness! My dear Mr. Chuzzlewit, it would be very hard to make him, though he is a monster, accountable for other people's vanity. And poor dear Cherry is the vainest darling!

MERCY: It was her mistake, then?

MERCY: I hope it was, but, all along, the dear child has been so dreadfully jealous, and so cross — it's impossible to please her, and it's of no use trying.

MARTIN: [*softly, hoping for her confidence*] Have you any wish to be released from this engagement?

MERCY: [*pouting, shrugs her shoulders, toys with the grass*] No. I don't know that I have. I am pretty sure I haven't. Quite sure, I might say. I don't mind it.

MARTIN: Has it ever occurred to you, that your married life may perhaps be miserable and full of bitterness?

MERCY: [*tearing the grass by the roots*] What shocking words! Of course, I shall quarrel with him. I should quarrel with any husband. Married people always quarrel, I believe. But as to being miserable, and bitter, and all those dreadful things, you know, why I couldn't be that, unless he always had the best of it; and I mean to have the best of it myself. I always do now. [MERCY *nods her head and giggles*] For I make a perfect slave of him.

MARTIN: [*rising*] Let it go on. I sought to know your mind, my dear, and you have shown it to me. I wish you joy.

[JONAS *is standing at the front gate of the graveyard.* MARTIN *points to the gate which* JONAS *has just entered and chooses to leave by another gate.*]

MERCY: [*to herself*] Oh, you terrible old man! What a perfectly hideous monster to be wandering about churchyards in the broad daylight, frightening people out of their wits!

[JONAS *comes to her side.*]

MERCY: Don't come here, Monster, or I'll go away directly.

JONAS: [*sits beside* MERCY, *sulking*] What's my uncle been a-talking about?

MERCY: About you. He says you're not half good enough for me.

JONAS: Oh, yes, I dare say! We all know that. He means to give you some present worth having, I hope. Did he say anything that looked like it?

MERCY: That he didn't!

JONAS: A stingy old dog he is. Well?

[JONAS *puts his arm around* MERCY'S *waist.*]

MERCY: [*in mock amazement*] Monster! What are you doing, Monster?

JONAS: [*uncomfortably*] Only giving you a squeeze. There's no harm in that, is there?

MERCY: But there is great deal of harm in it, if I don't consider it agreeable. Go along, will you!

[JONAS *withdraws his arm; for a moment he looks at her more like a murderer than a lover. He clears his brow by degrees.*]

JONAS: I say, Mel!

MERCY: What do you say, you vulgar thing, you low savage?

JONAS: When is it to be? I can't afford to go on dawdling about here half my life, and Pecksniff says that my father's being so lately dead, we can be married as quiet as we please, and my being lonely is a good reason to the neighbors for taking a wife home so soon, especially one that he knew. [JONAS *tries another squeeze*] When shall it be?

MERCY: Upon my word!

JONAS: Upon my soul, if you like. What do you say to next week?

MERCY: To next week! If you had said next month, I should have wondered at your impudence.

JONAS: But I didn't say next month, I said next week.

MERCY: [*pushing him off and rising*] Then, Monster, I say no! not next week. It shan't be till I choose, and I may not choose it to be for months. There!

[JONAS *looks up at her and holds his peace.*]

MERCY: No fright of a Monster shall dictate to me or have a voice in the matter. There!

[JONAS *holds his peace.*]

MERCY: If it's next month, that shall be the very earliest; but I won't say when it shall be till to-morrow; and if you don't like that, it shall never be at all. And if you follow me about and won't leave me alone, it shall never be at all. And if you don't do everything I order you to do, it shall never be at all. So don't follow me. There, Monster!

[MERCY *skips away.*]

JONAS: [*looking after her*] By god, my lady! You'll catch it for this, when you are married. It's all very well now — it keeps one on, somehow, and you know it — but I'll pay you off scot and lot by-and-bye. [JONAS *gets up to leave*] I never could abide a mouldy old churchyard.

[MERCY *looks back.*]

JONAS: [*with a sullen smile, nodding to himself*] Ah! Make the most of it while it lasts. Take your own way as long as it's in your power, my lady! I'll pay you back. I'll marry you and know who's master, and who's slave! Monsters have claws, my girl.

BLACKOUT

We have already seen that Jonas can be mean and sullen, but this is the first time we get a sense of the killer in him. He's much more danger-ous than we were led to expect. Jonas has a difficult time keeping his face from revealing what he thinks. We also see how his breathng changes. Mercy, with her fiance in tow, is careless and exasperating. She has no idea of how bad this marriage will be.

* * *

JONAS PROVOKES TOM PINCH

From the novel *MARTIN CHUZZLEWIT*

CHARACTERS: **JONAS CHUZZLEWIT:** cowardly and mean-spirited.

TOM PINCH: intelligent and ethical, an apprentice student to Mr. Pecksniff and as such, the family's scapegoat — butt of their many jokes.

MERCY: affianced to Jonas.

MR. PECKSNIFF: father to Mercy and Charity, a pleasant hypocrite.

CHARITY: his older daughter, cruelly jilted by Jonas who favored Mercy.

SETTING: The Pecksniff parlor.

SUMMARY:

Tom Pinch, using a country road, makes his way back to the Pecksniff home where he has a room. He is accosted by Jonas who, leaning against a gate, refuses to let him pass out of pure meanness. They scuffle. Jonas expects to give this "servant," this "nobody" a few telling blows. Instead, Tom easily bests him and by accident bloodies his ear. Tom helps Jonas up and they both return to the Pecksniff home. Holding the bloody handkerchief to his ear, Jonas enters the room. Tom follows. Mercy is the first to see her wounded lover.

MERCY: [*shrieking*] What has happened to Jonas? Father, come quick.

JONAS: Don't make a noise about it. It's nothing worth mentioning. I didn't know the road; the night's dark; and just as I came up with Mr. Pinch…[JONAS *turns his face - towards Tom - but not his eyes.*]

JONAS: [*continues*] I ran against a tree. It's only skin deep.

MR. PECKSNIFF: [*rising from his chair*] Cold water, Merry, my child! Brown paper! Scissors! A piece of old linen! Charity, my dear, make a bandage. Bless me, Mr. Jonas!

JONAS: Oh, bother your nonsense. Be of some use if you can. If you can't, get out!

[MISS CHARITY, *though called upon to lend her aid, sits upright in one corner, with a smile upon her face. She doesn't move a finger*]

MERCY: [*washing the wound*] Hold still, Monster, I must get it clean.

MR. PECKSNIFF: [*holding* JONAS's *head*] Hush, child, you don't mean that. I see your hand tremble. [*patting* JONAS *on the shoulder*] My good fellow, hold still, there's a scout.

JONAS: I'm not your good fellow and I'm not a scout. Just wrap it up, will you.

MR. PECKSNIFF: Ha, ha, with a blow like this, you are still your old self.

[PECKSNIFF *holds the end of a bandage while* MERCY *wraps it around* JONAS' *head. The wrapping finished,* PECKSNIFF *stands back to survey the handiwork.*]

MR. PERCKSNIFF: Good, good work. A beautiful job. Well, now let us all to bed.

[*The family leaves the parlor.* TOM PINCH *sits mournfully ruminating what had taken place.* CHARITY *comes back into the parlor silently.* TOM *is astonished to see her standing before him with her finger on her lip.*]

CHARITY: [*whispering*] Mr. Pinch, dear Mr. Pinch! Tell me the truth! You did that? There was some quarrel between you, and you struck him? I am sure of it!

[*It is the first time* CHARITY *has ever spoken kindly to him.* TOM *is stupefied with amazement.*]

CHARITY: [*eagerly*] Was it so, or not?

TOM: I was very much provoked.

CHARITY: [*her eyes sparkling*] Then it was?

TOM: Yes. We had a struggle for the path. But I didn't mean to hurt him so much.

CHARITY: Not so much! Don't say that. It was brave of you. I honor you for it. If you should ever quarrel again, don't spare him for the world, but beat him down and set your shoe upon him. Not a word of this to anybody. Dear Mr. Pinch, I am your friend, forever, for breaking the head of Jonas Chuzzlewit.

[CHARITY *seizes* TOM's *hand, presses it to her breast, and kisses it.*]

BLACKOUT

Charity is transcendant, her breath ecstatic.

* * *

THE ONCE YOUNG LOVERS MEET AGAIN

From the novel *LITTLE DORRIT*

CHARACTERS:	FLORA FINCHING NEE CASBY: caught in the throes of youth.
	ARTHUR CLENNAM: a more realistic past lover.
	MR. CASBY: Flora's father.
SETTING:	Flora's home.

SUMMARY:

Arthur has lived and worked in China for some twenty years. In his youth, he left a grim, unforgiving family life. Upon the death of his father in China, Arthur has had to come back to settle business matters. He finds the cruel coldness of his mother and the bleak surroundings of his home unchanged. He is a lonely man, unmoored. Before he left for China, he and Flora, both very young at the time, thought of themselves as lovers. But their romance was broken up by Arthur's mother.

Arthur has dropped in to see Mr. Casby, Flora's father and, of course, he will see Flora. Flora comes into the parlor where Mr. Casby and Arthur are visiting. They see each other for the first time in years. The Flora he remembered as always tall, has grown to be very broad and short of breath, but that is not all. The Flora who had seemed enchanting in all she said and thought is now diffuse and silly. This is too much. The Flora who had been spoiled and artless long ago is determined to be spoiled and artless now. Here is the fatal blow.

FLORA: [*giggling*] I am ashamed to see you. I'm a fright, I know you'll find me changed, I'm an old woman, it's shocking to be found out!

ARTHUR: Not at all. You're just what I expected. Time hasn't stood still with me, as you can well see.

FLORA: Oh! But with a man it's so different and really you look so amazingly well that you have no right to say anything of the kind, while, as to me, you know—oh! [*with a little scream*] I am dreadful!

[*Papa, the Patriarch, sits and glows with vacant serenity.*]

FLORA: [*a non-stop talker, never coming to a full stop*] But if we talk of not having changed, look at Papa, isn't he precisely what he was when you went away. If we go on this way much longer people will begin to suppose that I am Papa's Mama!

ARTHUR: That will be a long time from now.

FLORA: Oh, you insincerest of creatures, you havn't lost your old way of paying compliments, when you used to pretend to be so sentimentally struck you know—at least I don't mean that, I — oh I don't know what I mean!

[FLORA *titters confusedly and gives* ARTHUR *one of her old glances.*]

[*The Patriarch perceives that his part in the piece is to get off the stage. He leaves.*]

ARTHUR: [*reaching for his hat*] I must be on …

FLORA: You mustn't think of going yet, Arthur — I mean Mr. Arthur — or Mr. Clennam — I don't know what I am saying—without a word about the dear old days gone for ever, when I come to think of it I dare say it would be much better not to speak of them and it's highly probable that you have a more important engagement and oh, do let me be the last person in the world to interfere with it though there was a time, but I am running into nonsense again.

[ARTHUR *can't help wondering whether* FLORA *was such a chatter-er back then? He wondered what had fascinated him about her then.*]

FLORA: [*chatting with incredible speed and only a few commas, no periods.*] Indeed I have little doubt, that you are married to some Chinese lady, nothing more likely than that you should propose to a Chinese lady and nothing more natural I am sure than that the Chinese lady should accept you and think herself very well off too.

ARTHUR: [*with a smile*] I am not married to any lady, Flora.

FLORA: [*tittering*] Oh good gracious I hope you never kept yourself a bachelor so long on my account! But of course you never did why should you, please don't answer, I don't know why I'm running on, oh do tell me something about the Chinese ladies do they really wear tails down their back and plaited too or is it only the men, and when they pull their hair so very tight off their foreheads don't they hurt themselves, and why do they stick little bells all over their bridges or don't they really do it?

[FLORA *gives him another of her old glances.*]

FLORA: [*not waiting for a reply*]Then it's all true and they really do! Goodness, Arthur!—Oh, excuse me — old habit – Mr. Clennam far more proper —what a country to live in for so long a time, the little shoes too and the feet screwed back in infancy is quite surprising, what a traveller you are!

[ARTHUR *does not know how to respond to* FLORA'*s old glances.*]

FLORA: Dear dear, only to think of the changes at home, Arthur— oh, cannot overcome it, and seems so natural, such changes Arthur—there, I am doing it again, seems so natural, most improper — who could have ever imagined Mrs. Finching when I can't imagine it myself!

ARTHUR: Is that your married name? Finching?

FLORA: Finching oh yes isn't it a dreadful name, but as Mr F. said when he proposed to me which he did seven times and, after all, he wasn't answerable for it and couldn't help it could he, excellent man, not at all like you but excellent man!

[*For one moment,* FLORA *has at last talked herself out of breath. She recovers as she wipes a tear from her eye.*]

FLORA: No one could dispute, Arthur — Mr Clennam — that it's quite right you should be formally friendly to me under the altered circumstances and indeed you couldn't be anything else, at least I suppose not you ought to know, but I can't help recalling that there was a time when things were very different.

ARTHUR: [*sensing her essential goodness*] My dear Mrs. Finching...

FLORA: Oh not that nasty ugly name, say Flora!

ARTHUR: Flora. I assure you, Flora, I am happy in seeing you once more, and in finding that, like me, you have not forgotten the old foolish dreams, when we saw, in the light of our youth and hope...

FLORA: [*pouting*] You don't seem so. You take it very coolly, but however I know you are disappointed in me, I suppose the Chinese ladies – those Mandarinesses — are the cause or perhaps I am the cause myself, it's just as likely.

ARTHUR: No, no, don't say that.

FLORA: Oh I must you know, what nonsense not to, I know I am not what you expected, I know that very well.

[ARTHUR *is distressed to hear her take on the tone of a lover's quarrel.*]

FLORA: One remark, I wish to make, one explanation I wish to offer, when your Mama came and made a scene of it with my Papa and when I was called down into the little breakfast-room where they were looking at one another seated on two chairs like mad bulls what was I to do?

ARTHUR: It was all so long ago and so long concluded, is it worth while seriously to—

FLORA: I can't Arthur, be denounced as heartless by the whole society of China without setting myself right when I have the opportunity of doing so, and you must be very well aware not that I mean to say you could have written to me or I you watched as I was, but one sign and I should have known that it meant Come to Pekin, barefoot.

ARTHUR: [*gently*] You were not to blame, and I never blamed you. We were both too young, too dependent and helpless, to do anything but accept our separation. Think how long ago.

FLORA: One more remark, I wish to make, one more explanation I wish to offer, for five days I had a cold in the head from crying which I passed entirely in the back drawing-room—there is the back drawing-room still on the first floor and still at the back of the house to confirm my words—when that dreary period had passed a lull succeeded years rolled on and Mr. F. became acquainted with us at a mutual friend's, he was all attention, he called next day, he soon began to call three evenings a week and to send in little things for supper it was not love on Mr. F.'s part, it was adoration, Mr. F. proposed with the full approval of Papa and what could I do?

ARTHUR: Nothing whatever, but what you did. Let an old friend assure you of his full conviction that you did quite right.

FLORA: One last remark, I wish to make, one last explanation I wish to offer, you no longer wear a golden chain you are free I trust you may be happy, here is Papa who is always tiresome and putting in his nose everywhere where he is not wanted.

[*With these words, and a hasty timid gesture,* FLORA *behaved as she did when she was eighteen. As much as* ARTHUR *wanted to laugh at* FLORA's *coy behavior he also felt her sincerity. She simply cherished those memories.*]

MR. CASBY: Arthur, you must stay to dinner.

FLORA: You must.

ARTHUR: [*rising*] I appreciate your goodness... Thank you, dinner would be most welcome but I must leave on an errand. I am most...

[ARTHUR *puts on his hat and backs his way out of the room while* FLORA *is still talking.*]

FLORA: And I revere the memory of the late Mr. F. and I should be at home to-morrow at half-past one. The decrees of Fate are beyond recall...

ARTHUR: Goodnight, goodnight all.

BLACKOUT

Memorizing the words will make it easy for you to be a non-stop talker. There must be no stopping for thought. The only stops are for coy looks or girlish laughter. Arthur is truly a gentleman. He listens as best he can. When Flora's monologue becomes too much for him, he takes a deep breath and continues to listen until he can get away.

INDEX

BEATRICE MANLEY

The first actor in America to play the title role in Brecht's *Mother Courage*, Beatrice Manley has had a distinguished theatrical career. She debuted on Broadway at the age of 20 in Maxwell Anderson's *The Eve os Saint Mark*, and went on to appear in *The Cherry Orchard* with Eva LaGuillienne, *Snafu*, produced by George Abbott, and *Eastward in Eden* with Beatrice Straight. Co-founder of the San Francisco Actor's Workshop, she helped to produce and perform the first West Coast productions of writers like Samuel Beckett and Jean Genet. She has worked with Andrei Serban and Mabou Mines, taught at The California Institute of the Arts, and written five original plays, two librettos, and a screenplay. She has adopted a number of literary works for the solo performances, including Poe's *A Predicament* and Joyce's *Molly Bloom* soliloquy, and published a previous book, *My Breath in Art: Acting From Within*.